INSECURE GULF

T0386742

POWER AND POLITICS IN THE GULF

Christopher Davidson and Dirk Vanderwalle (editors)

After decades of sitting on the sidelines of the international system, the energy-exporting traditional monarchies of the Arab Gulf (Saudi Arabia, the United Arab Emirates, Kuwait, Bahrain, Qatar and Oman) are gradually transforming themselves into regional, and potentially global, economic powerhouses. This series aims to examine this trend while also bringing a consistent focus to the much wider range of other social, political, and economic issues currently facing Arab Gulf societies. Quality research monographs, country case studies, and comprehensive edited volumes have been carefully selected by the series editors in an effort to assemble the most rigorous collection of work on the region.

KRISTIAN COATES ULRICHSEN

Insecure Gulf

*The End of Certainty and the
Transition to the Post-Oil Era*

HURST & COMPANY, LONDON

First published in the United Kingdom in 2011 by
C. Hurst & Co. (Publishers) Ltd.,
41 Great Russell Street, London, WC1B 3PL
© Kristian Coates Ulrichsen, 2011
All rights reserved.
Printed in India

The right of Kristian Coates Ulrichsen to be identified as the
author of this publication is asserted by him in accordance
with the Copyright, Designs and Patents Act, 1988.

A Cataloguing-in-Publication data record for this book is available from the
British Library.

ISBN: 978-1-84904-127-0 *paperback*

This book is printed on paper from registered sustainable and managed
sources.

www.hurstpub.co.uk

To H.S.

CONTENTS

ACKNOWLEDGMENTS

The author would like to extend special gratitude to Michael Dwyer of Hurst and Company and Dr Christopher Davidson for commissioning and supporting the publication of this book on the evolution of Gulf security. Its contents benefited from insights provided by many colleagues, including David Held, Steffen Hertog, Mari Luomi, Jim Krane, Dennis Kumetat, Eva-Maria Nag, Neil Partrick, Mohamed Raouf and Steven Wright. Family, friends and colleagues at LSE Global Governance provided a convivial atmosphere conducive to productive research and writing, and I thank them all, particularly Brenda, Niels and Tomas Ulrichsen.

ABBREVIATIONS

AHDR	Arab Human Development Report
AQAP	Al-Qaeda in the Arabian Peninsula
ASEAN	Association of Southeast Asian Nations
CDM	Clean Development Mechanism
CENTCOM	(United States) Central Command
FATF	Financial Action Task Force
FTA	Free Trade Agreement
GCC	Gulf Cooperation Council
GTL	Gas-to-Liquids
IAEA	International Atomic Energy Agency
ICI	Istanbul Cooperation Initiative
ICT	Information and Communications Technologies
IRENA	International Renewable Energy Agency
ILO	International Labour Organisation
KAUST	King Abdullah University of Science and Technology
LNG	Liquefied Natural Gas
MENA	Middle East North Africa
MIST	Masdar Institute of Science and Technology
NATO	North Atlantic Treaty Organisation
NDAS	National Democratic Action Society (Bahrain)
OPEC	Organisation of the Petroleum Exporting Countries
PDRY	People's Democratic Republic of Yemen
PFLOAG	People's Front for the Liberation of Oman and the Arabian Gulf
PLAN	People's Liberation Army Navy
SABIC	Saudi Basic Industries Corporation
SAMA	Saudi Arabian Monetary Agency

ABBREVIATIONS

TIMSS	Trends in International Mathematics and Science Study
UAE	United Arab Emirates
UNDP	United Nations Development Programme
UNFCCC	United Nations Framework Convention on Climate Change
WTO	World Trade Organisation

INTRODUCTION

Profound changes are underway in the member-states of the Gulf Cooperation Council (GCC).[1] In all six—Bahrain, Kuwait, Oman, Qatar, Saudi Arabia and the United Arab Emirates—the coming years and decades will bring about a gradual end to the oil era. The uneven dwindling of natural resources in the medium- and longer-term will require a fundamental recasting of state-society relations and a reformulation of the pillars of ruling legitimacy in these redistributive oil monarchies. This is already underway in neighbouring Yemen, where the drawdown of natural resources includes water in addition to oil, and has become entangled with issues of political legitimacy and regime authority, as well as the political economy of equitable resource distribution. Thus, the transition toward a post-oil era will differ substantively from the earlier period of transformational social and economic upheavals that accompanied the entry into the oil era in the 1960s and 1970s. The primary differing variable in the shift to a post-oil future is that socio-economic and demographic constraints will limit regimes' capacity to co-opt political support and essentially buy off oppositional movements and groups.

These changes are occurring against the backdrop of the Gulf States' accelerating enmeshment in the processes of globalisation and its cross-border flows of peoples, ideas and norms, and licit and illicit trade. By 'Gulf States,' this book means the six GCC member-states in addition to Iraq, Iran and Yemen, as they constitute the dominant regional security complex and the referent point for regional hegemonic ambitions on both sides of the waterway known alternatively as the 'Persian' or 'Arabian' Gulf (and neutrally as 'the Gulf' in this book). These globalising patterns add a potentially destabilising dimension to the inter-

1

dependencies that have long bound the Gulf States to the international community. Increasingly these new linkages bypass state structures and controls and constitute both an ideational and material threat to their polities. They thus differ sharply from earlier mutual dependencies centred on the export of hydrocarbons that created the distinctive nature of the oil redistributive 'rentier' states and also bound the region to the wider world.[2]

New and emerging challenges posed by non-state flows also represent a feature of the progressive internationalisation of the Gulf. This is altering the international politics and international relations of the GCC in subtle yet important ways, as the Gulf States emerge as pivotal actors in the global rebalancing between west and east. The interlinking of these processes of internationalisation and globalisation provide the parameters for the Gulf States' engagement in a globalising community in which the loci of power are more diffused than ever before. They also introduce significant new dynamics into national and regional security calculations, as comparative political science demonstrates that states in transition are more vulnerable to predatory political violence and challenges to regime legitimacy. The regionalisation and internationalisation of Yemeni-based instability makes clear the interconnected nature of sources of insecurity and the difficulty, if not impossibility, of containing them within national boundaries. For this reason, Yemen is presented as a case-study in the tangled transition as it currently faces the challenges of managing resource depletion and reformulating rent-based networks of patronage and subsidy that will also confront the GCC states in the years and decades to come.

Consequently this book builds upon, but also goes beyond, the existing literature that focuses on Gulf security in hard and primarily 'military' terms. Existing works by scholars such as Anthony Cordesman provide valuable and otherwise hard-to-find data on the military capabilities and major trajectories of all the participants in the Gulf's regional security equation. Nevertheless, the possession of standing armies and sophisticated weaponry is in itself insufficient to guarantee security and stability, as evidenced during the Iraqi invasion of Kuwait in 1990 and the other GCC states' inability to translate their high levels of military expenditure into an effective response to this act of aggression. Nor does the heavy spending on arms and armaments provide the Gulf States with a solution to the challenges—growing steadily more urgent—of economic diversification that will determine the success or otherwise of the transition toward post-oil frameworks of governance.

Other works have integrated the Gulf region within a broadening theoretical approach to security. Expanding upon the structural concept of a 'regional security complex' developed by Barry Buzan and Ole Waever, recent scholarship by F. Gregory Gause and Henner Furtig have addressed the salient characteristics of the Gulf as a tri-polar regional system based around Iran, Iraq and Saudi Arabia.[3] Both focused upon the regional unit and examined the changing distribution of power within it, and with the United States as a highly-involved external player that determined the outcome of the 1991 Gulf war and reshaped the regional distribution of power by destroying the regime of Saddam Hussein in 2003.[4] Meanwhile, Gerd Nonneman deepened and broadened the concept of security by focusing on the changing 'resources-demands balance' as falling per capita oil rents complicated Gulf States' mechanisms for co-opting support through the spread of wealth and introduced new threats and pressures for change on both the domestic and external levels, which he argued were inextricably linked.[5] He subsequently developed the concept of 'omni-balancing' to describe the patterns of Saudi Arabian (and the other GCC monarchies') balancing between threats and resources within and between the domestic, regional and global levels.[6] In his work on the United Arab Emirates, Christopher Davidson also emphasises the centrality of what he labels the 'ruling bargain' in reinforcing and updating legitimacy resources that underpinned the socio-economic transformation of traditional polities.[7]

This present book builds on, and extends, the broadening of security described above. Significantly, it updates Nonneman's investigation of the resources-demands balance, which was written in 2000, toward the end of a prolonged period of low oil prices, and before the advent of the second oil boom (2002–8). It also differs from Gause and Furtig by inserting Yemen firmly into the regional security equation, and describing how the flows of instability between Yemen and Somalia are tying together one regional security complex (the Gulf) with another (the Horn of Africa). This has profound implications for the states of the Arabian Peninsula, caught 'in the middle,' as it were, of these two major sources of regional instability. Its central focus is how the intertwining of the internal and external dimensions of security are altering local and regional security agendas in an era of accelerating global interconnectivity. With the concept of what security 'is' and 'does' in a state of flux globally, a central objective of this book is to interrogate regional perspectives on the notion of security and map the shifting security paradigm in response to the range of new and emerging threats and challenges identified in part two.

An Integrated Approach to Security

This book therefore examines the evolution of 'Gulf security' in the oil-rich monarchies of the Arabian Peninsula in response to this range of existing and emergent threats and challenges. It argues that the rise of primarily non-military sources of potential insecurity is profoundly reshaping the security paradigm in the Gulf States in the medium- and longer-term. This is inextricably bound up with the broader impact of globalisation on the political economy of the Gulf States, which itself is undergoing a systemic transformation toward post-oil redistributive forms of governance. Regional concepts of security need to be re-conceptualised as part of a holistic approach that locates the drivers of change within the rapidly-globalising international environment and interlinks them with socio-political and economic dimensions. It must also acknowledge that security is composed both of material and ideational considerations and is as much a social construct as a survival mechanism in a world of threats and balances.

Two major objectives form the analytical core of the book. The first part of the book provides an overview of the development of Gulf security structures and examines the key components of its changing paradigm. Crucially, it distinguishes between the idea of security as a social construct (constructivism) and security as material threat (realism). It thus examines the motivations and objectives that guide states and societies in constructing local and regional security agendas. This approach emphasises the importance of belief-systems in shaping and reshaping perceptions of security and in deciding which issues become securitised and why. It speaks to a broader theoretical literature in international relations that studies the role of norms as social constructs in determining approaches to questions of power and security.[8] Furthermore, it integrates the Gulf into research on security studies in the developing world, in which states and regimes may pose a threat to portions of their own societies, and where the Western 'idea of security' as restricted to the external sphere does not necessarily apply.[9]

Delineating the role of local agents is particularly important in deciding which issues come to dominate security agendas in the GCC states. This is because the conduct of foreign and security affairs in these oil monarchies is restricted to a tightly-drawn circle of senior members of the ruling family.[10] In common with many other developing countries' experience, 'regime security' in the Gulf States is frequently conflated with 'national security' and this informs regimes' notions of the hitherto-successful strategies of survival needed to achieve this.[11] Consequently, our understanding of the dynamics of policy formulation is enhanced by taking into consideration the factors that inform regimes' perceptions of their internal security matrix. Indeed, Gause has demonstrated how trans-national considerations play an integral role in foreign policy decision-making as regional states act against *perceived* threats to domestic stability that may emanate from external actors.[12]

This, in turn, is important in determining their posture on external issues such as the unfolding post-occupation dynamics in Iraq, the ongoing dispute between Iran and the international community over Teheran's nuclear policies, and the ideational challenge posed by radicalism and trans-national terrorism. Thus the opening section, consisting of the first three chapters, provides the theoretical underpinning for the book's second objective, which is to delineate the relationship between 'traditional' and 'new' challenges to security and how they relate to each other. The Gulf has witnessed three major inter-state wars since 1980 in addition to Islamic revolution in Iran, the rise of trans-national ideational challenges to national and regional legitimacy, and bouts of civil unrest in Saudi Arabia and Bahrain.[13] These territorially-bounded challenges from Iraq and Iran, and issues of nuclear proliferation and trans-national extremism, remain a source of latent and actual instability in the Gulf. Nevertheless a range of new and longer-term challenges to regional security are emerging and have the potential, if left unchecked or inadequately tackled, to strike at the heart of the social contract and redistributive mechanisms that bind state and society in the Arab oil monarchies.

These include issues such as food, water and resource security, demographic pressures stemming from rising populations and the youth bulge, structural economic deficiencies in the GCC states and progressive state failure on its periphery in Yemen, and ecological degradation and the security implications of long-term climate change, all of which pose new challenges to Gulf security. This deepening and broadening of the concept of security builds upon the cognitive shift in thinking about global security that has occurred in an era of accelerating complexity of global interconnections and trans-national flows of people, capital and ideas.[14] The emergence of these new threats and challenges to national, regional and international security and stability has eroded Cold War-era demarcations between the internal and external spheres of policymaking. Together, they necessitate a more nuanced approach predicated as much on meeting the human security of populations as well as the national security of states, and the book concludes by examining the prospects for any such intellectual and practical reformulation of the notion of security in the region.[15]

Underlying both of these objectives is the argument that difficult challenges lie ahead for the Arab oil monarchies of the Gulf. The regimes must reconfigure the welfare states that were constructed during the 1960s and 1970s during a period of comparatively low populations and high wealth per capita. Demographic pressures and the transition to post-redistributive modes of governance also require them to address the systemic structural problems in their socio-political composition. Simultaneously, the impact of globalisation and the Gulf States' political and economic opening up creates new material and ideational linkages intertwining still further the internal and external dimensions of (in)security. Consequently, the concept of security, and the issue of which values it embraces, and for whom, will be integral to the evolving political economies of the GCC as the oil monarchies progressively move toward the post-oil era.

Security as a Social Construct

The notion of the pursuance of strategies of survival described above determines how ruling elites come to define and construct particular issues as threats to their security.[16] The analytical peg on which *Insecure Gulf* rests is a constructivist approach to international relations, namely one that studies the role of beliefs and norms as social constructs shaping approaches to questions of power and security. It emphasises the importance of local agency in exploring the factors that motivate policymakers to reach and implement the decisions they take. Analysing 'how people act' addresses one of the central deficiencies of the broader international relations literature, namely a neglect of the human dimension in contemporary world politics.[17] Constructivist approaches ascribe value to the location and distribution of nodes of power within society as well as the relationships between knowledge, power and interests. The evolution of a position of 'national interest' on any one issue thus represents the outcome of an inter-subjective process that combines ideational and material factors and is fluid, rather than fixed over time.[18]

Distinguishing between security as discourse and security as material threat also enhances the study of 'securitisation.' This refers to the processes by which issues become constructed as threats to security, and by whom and for what reason. If an issue is successfully securitised, and accepted as such by the relevant audience, the principal actor feels empowered to take extraordinary measures to combat it. These exceed the rules-based systems that otherwise regulate the conduct of normal behaviour, and demonstrate the importance of agency in defining and shaping responses to particular issues.[19] At a macro-level, the global 'war on terror' represented a successful example of securitisation. It enabled the United States to bypass international norms and structures after 11 September 2001 to combat the perceived threat from Al-Qaeda-linked terrorism.[20]

A closer examination of the processes of securitisation in the Gulf ties the region into the broader world-group of developing states, and embeds the study of regional security issues within the realm of comparative politics. This forms part of Keith Krause's identification of a 'security problematic' in contemporary world politics in general, and in the post-Cold War period in particular. This arises out of the fact that perceived threats to security can be ideational as well as material, and tied to the survival not of the state but of a particular referent group. In these instances, the idea of security is critical, and the affiliation of the security of the state with the security of its citizens cannot be automatically assumed to be the case. Traditional conceptions of security in stable, developed nations therefore fail to capture the threat that states or regimes may pose to parts of their own societies. For this reason, it is vital to identify the motivations of the group driving the securitisation of particular issues, as well as the direction in which it is aimed.[21]

In this taxonomy, the internal and external dimensions of security become intertwined as regimes seek security against possible contestation from within their own societies as much as against external aggression from neighbouring states. The Gulf States' external security alignments, both bilaterally with the United States and multilaterally through the creation of the Gulf Cooperation Council, meet this requirement by reinforcing regime security against internal dissent as well as foreign threats.[22] This became evident during the uprising in Bahrain in 1994. The Saudi Arabian Interior Minister, Prince Naif bin Abdulaziz Al-Saud, hastily visited Manama to declare that the security of Bahrain was inseparable from the security of Saudi Arabia.[23] By this, Naif meant the security and ideational solidarity of the ruling Al-Saud and Al-Khalifa families. The unspoken assumption that a ruling family would not be allowed to fall prompted the emergency readying of Saudi forces to intervene militarily to maintain order in Bahrain if the situation so developed.[24] Other examples of a 'one-for-all' attitude binding together regional ruling families can be found in the ritual denunciations of Iran's ongoing seizure of three islands belonging to the United Arab Emirates, with the Secretary-General of the GCC even drawing parallels with Israeli behaviour in the occupied Arab territories.[25]

Regime preoccupations with survival remained paramount in their construction of security strategies in the turbulent aftermath of 11 September 2001. Gulf States' responses to the territorially bounded issues of Iraq and Iran and the ideational challenge of trans-national terrorism demonstrated their awareness of the myriad interlocking linkages between the internal and external spheres of security. These connections were magnified by the proliferation of Arab satellite television channels and internet websites in the 1990s and 2000s. Together, they greatly accelerated the spread of trans-national linkages and contributed to the creation of an Arab 'imagined community.'[26] The steady erosion of regimes' control over the flows of information to individuals and groupings within their own borders directly linked considerations of internal security to external events. No longer could sources of external insecurity be isolated, or contained within national boundaries. Accordingly, regimes began to construe these issues more as threats to their political or popular legitimacy than to their material security. This has guided their formulation of policies to meet the challenges they perceived as emanating from Iraq, Iran and trans-national terror.

Structure of the Book

The book is divided into three parts. The first part consists of three chapters that examine the multiple processes that have shaped, and are likely to continue to shape, the evolution of Gulf security structures. Chapter one provides a contextual historical overview of Gulf security that emphasises a pattern of continuity in the region's myriad interactions with external powers and interests. It describes a cosmopolitan Gulf closely integrated into a trans-continental system that will belie any notions of the region as peripheral to world history until the advent of the oil era. Chapter two shifts the focus to the current security agenda in the Arabian Peninsula and the Gulf and the symbiotic interlinking of internal and external security with regime strategies of survival. It explores the motivations of Gulf policymakers in constructing security agendas that shape their responses to issues such as the perceived 'Shiite crescent' in Iraq and Iran, as well as the material and non-material or ideological threats posed by radical extremism and trans-national terrorism, particularly from Yemen and the emerging linkages with Somalia, which increasingly are binding two hitherto-distinct sub-regional security complexes—the Horn of Africa and the Gulf/Arabian Peninsula—together.

Finally in this section, chapter three looks to the future parameters of Gulf security by outlining four broad factors that will determine the contextual framework within which it will evolve. These are the impact of the processes of globalisation and the revolution in information and communications technologies (ICT), the internationalisation of the Gulf and its emergence as a pivotal actor in the global rebalancing between west and east, the uneven rates of depletion of hydrocarbon resources within individual GCC states and the diverging pathways to post-oil political economies that will result, and the continuing weakness of internal consensus within the GCC itself that inhibits any collective positioning on existing and future challenges to regional security. These demonstrate how intertwined will be the future evolution of the Gulf with the political and opening up of the region to trans-national and cross-border flows of people, information and goods.

Attention in the second part of the book shifts to the emergent and longer-term challenges to security and stability in the Gulf. Three chapters analyse the different aspects of these increasingly non-military threats to Gulf polities. The fourth chapter examines the socio-economic difficulties caused by demographic trends and structural imbalances in all of the GCC states and Yemen. It emphasises the growing disparities of wealth that render the continuation of current levels of welfare expenditure and redistributive mechanisms unsustainable in the long-run. The fifth chapter describes how potential resource scarcities and uneven patterns of distribution may fragment state-society relations and undermine regime legitimacy. This introduces potent new dimensions to the security equation, not least basic issues of food and water security, and the chapter analyses the measures being undertaken in the GCC states to mitigate and overcome them. Meanwhile, the sixth chapter turns to the direct and indirect security risk posed by environmental degradation and long-term climate change. It examines the emerging nexus between weak and fragile states, growing resource scarcities, particularly in access to food and water, and its trans-boundary threats to human and state security as a potential driver of conflict within and between states. The chapter assesses the empirical evidence indicating that the socio-economic and demographic stresses (described in chapter four) and unequal patterns of resource distribution (chapter five) act as multipliers that magnify states and societies' vulnerabilities to these types of external shocks. This is a pivotal issue of concern in the Gulf where numerous actual and potential fault-lines may become sharpened if dwindling access to scarce resources emerges as a source of future contestation.

In part three, chapter seven analyses the interlinking of these sources of insecurity by focusing on the multiple causes of progressive state failure in Yemen. The country is experiencing a crisis of governance and legitimacy and a concomitant erosion of state capacity as it faces a complex combination of socio-political, economic and environmental difficulties. The result is a failing political economy on the south-western flank of the Arabian Peninsula that constitutes a direct and growing threat to the security and stability of the GCC. This has profound regional and international implications for the geopolitics of insecurity in West Asia owing to Yemen's proximity to Somalia and the incidence of failed and failing states on both sides of the commercially vital Gulf of Aden. It also establishes a direct link between Gulf security and the endemic insecurity in the Horn of Africa, and introduces new destabilising flows of weapons and fighters in both directions. This increase in cross-border acts of terrorist cooperation during 2009 facilitated the re-establishment of Al-Qaeda in the Arabian Peninsula in Yemen following its tactical and operational rollback in Saudi Arabia between 2004 and 2006.

A concluding chapter considers how a changing concept of security in the Gulf States can play a stabilising role in transitioning their political economies to the post-oil era. It argues that a reorientation toward the human security of individuals, rather than the national security of states, is most likely to strengthen the internal cohesion of the GCC states. This is integral to reconciling regime security with security for all communities in redistributive states facing the erosion of mechanisms for spreading wealth and co-opting support. Measures to increase the support base and pillars of legitimacy of governing structures in the Gulf should form part of a comprehensive strategy to tackle existing inequalities and emerging sources of insecurity. This in turn will lessen the sources of potential tension and violent contestation of political power and increase the likelihood of a consensual and non-violent transition to a post-oil era. Recent initiatives notwithstanding however, it is by no means clear that local viewpoints on 'human security' are aligned with the developing universal norm, and the conclusion argues that the most likely short- to medium-term option is a 'half-way' compromise that satisfies neither those advocates of continued focus on national security nor proponents of a genuinely human security approach.

The book therefore explores how states and societies in the Gulf are anticipating and reacting to this paradigmatic shift in national and regional security dynamics. It maps the trends and patterns that will shape the future evolution of Gulf security as well as the perceptions and belief-systems that motivate policymaking responses. This approach makes it possible to contextualise the changes underway within the broader political economy framework. It also demonstrates the value of an interdisciplinary approach to the broadening of security studies that integrates aspects of international political economy, comparative politics, international relations and globalisation theory into a holistic study of the complex dynamics and processes underway in the region.

PART ONE

1

HISTORY OF GULF SECURITY STRUCTURES, 1903–2003

On 5 May 1903 the British Foreign Secretary, Lord Lansdowne, used a House of Lords debate on 'Great Britain and the Persian Gulf' to make an official statement of Britain's policy in the region. Lansdowne was a former Viceroy of India (1888–1894) and his policy reflected the considerable commercial and strategic value that successive generations of imperial administrators attached to the Gulf. Lansdowne began by stating that 'our policy should be directed in the first place to promote and protect British trade in those waters.' He went on to add that the British Government 'should regard the establishment of a naval base, or of a fortified port, in the Persian Gulf by any other Power as a very grave menace to British interests, and we should certainly resist it with all the means at our disposal.'[1] This represented what one British historian has labelled 'a sort of Monroe Doctrine for the Persian Gulf.'[2]

Seventy-seven years later, President Jimmy Carter proclaimed for the United States a position of predominance in the Gulf in language remarkably similar to Lansdowne's. Carter's State of the Union Address on 23 January 1980 contained a policy proclamation that subsequently became known as the Carter Doctrine. This declared that 'Any attempt by an outside force to gain control of the Persian Gulf region will be regarded as an assault on the vital interests of the United States of America, and such an assault will be repelled by any means necessary, including military force.'[3] It was a response to the Soviet invasion of Afghanistan in December 1979 and resulting anxieties within the Carter

15

administration that it might be the prelude to a Soviet move toward acquiring a foothold in the Gulf or the Indian Ocean.

These two pronouncements visibly illustrate one of the enduring continuities in the historical evolution of Gulf security structures.[4] The projection of external political and military power has been a recurring feature ever since the arrival of the first Portuguese expedition at Hormuz in 1507.[5] Dutch, Ottoman and British incursions all followed the Portuguese before the final withdrawal of British forces from the Gulf in 1971. Gulf security has always been about much more than mere considerations of oil and great power rivalries, and the principal actors are the sheikhdoms and peoples of the region who have constructed a state system that has proven sufficiently durable to survive three decades of conflict since 1980. This durability was not preordained, however, as the decade that followed British withdrawal was a dangerous period for the newly-independent states in the Arabian Peninsula as they struggled to update the external security guarantees that underpinned their domestic survival.[6] Pragmatic accommodation with, and adaptation to, the foreign incursions thus formed an integral part of ruling elites' strategies of survival in the crucial formative periods of state formation and consolidation. This dynamic interplay between internal and external factors played a crucial role in shaping the modern state-systems in the Gulf and will be explored at length in this opening chapter.

A Cosmopolitan Gulf

The Gulf has been a commercial and strategic asset to outside powers for many centuries, and its linkages with the wider world extend back into late-antiquity and the pre-Islamic period. It is pivotally positioned astride the major trade routes between India and Europe and a dense network of transoceanic linkages connect it to the broader Indian Ocean world. During the nineteenth- and early-twentieth centuries, local shipbuilders and sailors constructed and navigated the *dhows* and *booms* that sailed each season from the Gulf to the Indian sub-continent and along the coastline of east Africa. They exchanged cargoes of Arabian ponies, dates and pearls for goods such as rice, timber and cotton as intricate patterns of intra- and inter-regional trade developed.[7] Powerful processes of migration and acculturation augmented these maritime flows and gave them a human dimension.[8] These multifaceted patterns of settlement and exchange formed a web of inter-connections that tied the trade and peoples of the region into broader, overlapping communities of belonging. They also left a distinctive legacy in the form of a cultural sphere of influence that shaped a cos-mopolitan identity and an externally-focused trading mentality throughout the Indian Ocean region.[9]

This cosmopolitan intermixing of peoples and cultures also influ-enced the development of states and societies in the Gulf. Involvement in maritime trade fostered an outward-oriented mentality among the nascent sheikhdoms on the Arabian (and Persian) coastline of the Gulf. Both Kuwait and Dubai developed into regional entrepôts that serviced the trade of the northern and southern Gulf respectively, with Dubai benefiting greatly from the decline of the Persian port of Lingah in the early twentieth century.[10] Kuwait and Bahrain also became world cen-tres of the pearling trade. This activity dominated traditional industry in the Gulf until it collapsed in the 1930s following the introduction of Japanese cultured pearls and the onset of the Great Depression.[11] Local coalitions of ruling and influential merchant families governed their polities through pragmatic political-economic alliances that laid the foundation for the redistributive policies of the oil-era.[12]

Security—both from internal rivals and predatory external threats—was from a very early stage in these polities' development intimately tied to external powers and structures. British measures to quell the rising incidence of what they regarded as acts of maritime piracy dur-ing the early nineteenth century had lasting consequences for the secu-rity architecture that developed in the Gulf. A series of agreements and treaties formally divided the coastline of the Arabian Peninsula into separate political entities and integrated them into an external security system underpinned by British maritime power.[13] Beginning with the signing of a General Treaty in 1820 and a Maritime Truce in 1835 that outlawed piracy and maritime warfare respectively, Britain concluded individual treaties with the rulers of the Trucial States (subsequently the United Arab Emirates) in 1835, Bahrain in 1861, Kuwait in 1899 and again in 1914, and Qatar in 1916.[14] Significantly, the agreements consolidated and enhanced the internal legitimacy and power of the ruling families by enshrining the principle of familial succession and introducing a measure of external protection for their survival.[15]

A cycle of external penetration and local accommodation developed as rulers sought to maximise their own autonomy and prestige within the parameters available to them. The sheikhs of the Arabian Peninsula regularly played on local and regional events and great power rivalries to their advantage.[16] They also benefited from the inability of the Ottoman Empire to project any substantive degree of power or control over its peripheral territories south of Baghdad, or over its borderlands in the Arabian Peninsula.[17] The result was an administrative vacuum that offered local agents considerable scope to effect change in domestic affairs. Sheikh Mubarak Al-Sabah of Kuwait was particularly adept at manipulating British fears of German and Russian encroachment toward the Gulf during his reign (1896–1915) to consolidate his own position both internally and regionally.[18] This notwithstanding, it must be borne in mind that the security system that developed during the period of British hegemony in the Gulf was constructed on fundamentally unequal relationships of power and control, and was based on the motivations and objectives of the imperial power rather than the interests of the regional states themselves.

The Era of 'Pax Britannica'

The British interlude laid the foundations for the evolution of the modern security system in the Gulf. This formative period encompassed the transformation of the traditional Arabian sheikhdoms into proto-state entities, in addition to the creation of increasingly powerful and centralising states in Saudi Arabia, Iraq and Iran. It led to the embedding of the principle of the external security guarantee in the security calculations of the Arabian Peninsula states. However, it also witnessed the origin of a number of boundary disputes both within the Arabian Peninsula and with Iraq and Iran. This complicated intra-Gulf relations throughout the twentieth century, and, in the case of Iraq's claim on Kuwait, a combination of ideational and material threat led to invasion and military conflict in 1990.

British interests in the Gulf arose from considerations of imperial defence and security. This revolved around protecting the land and sea routes to India, the 'jewel in the crown of the British Empire.' Imperial defence planners considered the Gulf a vital strategic flank on the route to India and were also anxious to stem the flow of smuggled weaponry to tribes on the North-West Frontier of India.[19] The same thinking that prompted the Lansdowne proclamation in May 1903 was vividly expressed by an editorial in the *Times of India* claiming that 'British supremacy in India is unquestionably bound up with British supremacy in the Persian Gulf. If we lose control of the Gulf, we shall not rule long in India...'[20] A sub-imperial system based on British India therefore developed over 'a century of commerce and diplomacy.' This was based on the protective treaty relations signed between the (British) Government of India and the sheikhdoms on the Arabian coastline of the Gulf, and the Political Residency system centred at Bushehr, on the Persian coast.[21]

The Residency system regulated the ties between the Government of India and the smaller Gulf sheikhdoms. The Political Resident (whose headquarters moved from Bushehr to Bahrain in 1946) represented the Government of India in the Gulf. He was assisted by Political Agencies in Bahrain, Kuwait, Muscat, Qatar, Dubai and Abu Dhabi, and by local intermediaries drawn mainly from influential merchant families.[22] Sir Percy Cox, Resident from 1904 to 1914, described his responsibilities as exercising 'an undefined but often decisive influence upon the affairs, and more particularly upon the foreign relations, of the Arab Sultanate of Muscat, the Trucial States of the Pirate Coast, Bahrein and Kuweit [sic].'[23] However, interests between the Government of India and the British Government did not always converge. Advocates of a 'forward policy' in India often clashed with the more cautionary Foreign Office in London mindful of the need to balance Gulf policy against broader geo-strategic and diplomatic considerations.[24]

One issue around which officials in London and Delhi did coalesce was the conviction that German moves toward the Gulf before 1914 were undesirable and ought to be resisted. In 1902, the Ottoman Government granted to the German Anatolia Company a railway concession from the Anatolian city of Konya to the Gulf. Officials at the Foreign Office anxiously watched its progression eastward, and after 1910 its imminent extension to the Gulf heightened British awareness of the strategic importance of Mesopotamia and the northern Gulf coastline around Kuwait.[25] British unease at the apparently political motivations that they suspected drove German commercial policy culminated in the Foreign Office refusing a German request in 1914 to lay a cable in the Gulf as part of a direct telegraphic link between Germany and China.[26]

To the north, British-Indian interests in the Ottoman provinces (*vilayets*) of Baghdad and Basra expanded steadily in the half-century prior to 1914. British shipping interests acquired the rights to navigation on the Tigris and Euphrates rivers in 1846. By 1914, British and Indian commercial interests controlled more than two-thirds of the imports and half of the exports that passed through Basra each year.[27] During the First World War, British and Indian troops invaded and gradually occupied the whole of Mesopotamia, capturing Baghdad in March 1917 and ultimately acquiring a League of Nations mandate over the independent state of Iraq that emerged in 1922.[28] The British Empire reached its greatest territorial extent between 1918 and 1922 and in August 1919 it acquired a substantial measure of informal control over Persia with the signing of the controversial Anglo-Persian Agreement. This marked the high watermark of Britain's position in the Gulf, but it was a short-lived agreement that was never implemented and was formally denounced after the Pahlavi coup in 1921.[29]

Divergent political trajectories in Iraq, Iran and Saudi Arabia after the First World War profoundly altered the dynamics of the nascent security system in the Gulf. During the interwar period the rise of modernising states in Iraq and Iran shifted the centre of gravity in the Gulf away from the British-protected sheikhdoms on the Arabian Peninsula and interfered with the web of cross-waterway linkages as new political boundaries and nation-states developed. The gradual centralisation of authority following the creation of the Kingdom of Saudi Arabia in 1932 similarly changed the balance of power on the peninsula itself. The imposition of formal boundaries to delineate national territory frequently caused friction between Saudi Arabia and its smaller neighbours, not least over the long-running Buraimi Dispute with Abu Dhabi and Oman. This lasted from 1949 until 1974 and tensions escalated into skirmishes in 1955 when two squadrons of the Trucial Oman Levies were deployed to expel a Saudi police garrison from the oasis.[30]

Contemporaneous developments in Iraq and Iran posed challenges of a different sort from that presented by Saudi Arabia, which despite the periodic flare-up of boundary tensions did not present an ideational threat to the political survival of the similarly conservative Gulf monarchies. In Iraq, the July 1958 military coup bloodily overthrew the pro-British ruling elite and triggered a thoroughgoing political and social revolution.[31] Meanwhile in Iran the restoration of the Shah in 1953 led him to entertain grandiose ambitions of attaining Iranian hegemony in the Gulf through an increasingly southward-oriented and interventionist policy toward the region.[32] These events fundamentally reshaped the international relations of the Gulf and introduced into the regional mix expansionist actors with designs to reclaim supposedly 'lost territories' in the Gulf.[33] This occurred during a state of flux in the British-protected security system in the Gulf. A combination of economic stringency and financial difficulty, the accelerating pace of decolonisation in the 1960s, and military setbacks in Aden in 1967 prompted a reconsideration of British defence priorities and the decision to withdraw from all commitments east of Suez.[34]

The period of British withdrawal from the Gulf between 1961 and 1971 presented existential dangers to the small Arabian Peninsula sheikhdoms on the cusp of independence. The loss of their erstwhile protector encouraged Iraq and Iran to renew territorial claims on Kuwait and Bahrain respectively. Immediately after Kuwaiti independence in 1961, the Iraqi prime minister, Abd al-Karim Qasim, declared it to be an 'integral part' of Iraq. This necessitated the intervention of 7000 British troops to forestall any putative invasion.[35] Iran maintained a longstanding territorial claim on Bahrain that intensified following the unexpected British announcement in January 1968 of full military withdrawal from the Gulf by the end of 1971.[36] The issue was settled by a United Nations mission that visited Bahrain in April 1970 and conclusively reported that Bahrainis favoured an independent Arab state.[37] In 1968, the rulers of Abu Dhabi and Dubai offered to meet the annual operating costs of British forces in the Gulf in a bid to prevent the withdrawal of their external guarantor of security.[38] This was declined, and the new states' strategic vulnerability to their more powerful neighbours was vividly underscored by the Iranian seizure of the three islands of Abu Musa and the Greater and Lesser Tunbs on the day before British withdrawal (and the formation of the United Arab Emirates) in December 1971.[39]

The ending of British hegemony was a watershed in the evolution of the international relations and security structures of the Gulf. The passage to independence of Kuwait (in 1961), Bahrain, Qatar and the United Arab Emirates (in 1971) laid down the modern inter-state system that exists to this day. During the 1970s, internal policy in these states (and also in Oman and Saudi Arabia) focused on state consolidation and the creation of the internal redistributive mechanisms that channelled oil rents to their citizenry.[40] Hydrocarbon resources formed the basis of the social contract binding state and society and created the mutual economic interdependencies that integrated these oil-producing states into the international economic system.[41] Nevertheless, the decade was also one of profound uncertainty for regional security structures as the six Gulf States confronted material and ideational threats to external stability in this formative period of nation-building.[42]

The Lost Decade

Nearly ten years elapsed between Britain's military withdrawal from the Gulf on 1 December 1971 and the formation of the Gulf Cooperation Council (GCC) on 25 May 1981.[43] Comparative political science has demonstrated that states in transition are more vulnerable to the threat of political violence or ideological sub- and supra-state contestations of authority.[44] This was compounded in the case of the young Gulf States by the removal of their external security umbrella, which coincided with the consolidation of state structures and building up of reservoirs of legitimacy.[45] During the 1970s, these monarchies faced a powerful ideational challenge from the Popular Front for the Liberation of Oman and the Arabian Gulf (PFLOAG) and its Marxist sponsors in the People's Democratic Republic of South Yemen (PDRY). The Islamic revolution in Iran in 1978–79 delivered a different, more powerful and enduring political and psychological shock to the Gulf monarchies and Iraq.[46] The sense of deep unease at regional security developments was reflected in the hasty decision to form the GCC in 1981 in response to the Islamic revolution and the outbreak of the Iran-Iraq war in September 1980.[47]

The Dhofar rebellion presented the most prolonged material and ideological threat to the security and stability of the Arabian Peninsula during the immediate post-1971 period. The long-running conflict in Oman's south-western province broke out in 1965 and was only quelled with substantial British and lesser Iranian military support in 1975. The Dhofari rebels received political and military support from the socialist republic in south Yemen (the PDRY) and arms from the Soviet Union and China. The Omani Armed Forces also received external assistance, in the form of British loan service personnel that remained after 1971 to direct its upper echelons, as well a squadron of the Special Air Service (SAS).[48] The SAS played a key role in turning around Omani military fortunes following their arrival in 1970, but their deployment was kept secret for reasons of political expediency both in Oman and in the United Kingdom.[49] Nevertheless the extent of

British support for Oman enabled PDRY officials to portray the Dhofar rebellion as a 'war of liberation against foreign occupation' from the 'puppets of colonialism in Oman' and its 'client Government.'[50]

The heavy involvement of external actors in the Dhofar rebellion reflected the broader importance that each side attached to the conflict and its regional repercussions. Chinese policies in support of PDRY and PFLOAG were consistent with its rigid ideological and anti-imperialist motivations in the last years of the Mao period, before the transition began to a policy of moderation (and modernisation) under the leadership of Deng Xiaoping, in 1978. The legacy of this support for a revolutionary and anti-regime movement considerably complicated the normalisation of Chinese relations with the Gulf States in the 1980s, and contrasts sharply with the burgeoning geo-economic and energy relationships in the 1990s and 2000s. These were inaugurated, ironically in view of China's role in Dhofar, with an agreement to import crude oil from Oman to China in 1983, but diplomatic relations with China were not established until 1990. Post-Soviet Russian relations with the Gulf States similarly suffered from the legacy of earlier support for radical movements, with then-President Vladimir Putin's visit to Saudi Arabia and Qatar in 2007 belatedly constituting the first high-level exchange of its kind.[51]

Seen from the perspective of the other side, British motivations for such elevated (albeit indirect) levels of military intervention in Oman even after their formal withdrawal from the Gulf provide a barometer for the shifting geo-strategic value of the region. This now revolved around a steady and secure supply of oil to international markets. Oil from the Gulf States constituted 51 per cent of British oil imports in 1972 while Saudi Arabia and the United States enjoyed a similarly symbiotic relationship.[52] Officials in the United Kingdom feared that should the Sultan's regime in Oman collapse under the ideational challenge from the PFLOAG and PDRY it could 'lead to the disintegration of the United Arab Emirates and the establishment of a radical Arab nationalist or Marxist state in this corner of Arabia.' Memories of the British withdrawal from Aden in 1967 were still raw, and Foreign Office officials in London judged this scenario would have 'serious repercussions on our oil supplies' and the stability of the other oil-producing states should Oman become 'a base for subversion throughout the Gulf.'[53]

In addition to the Dhofar rebellion, events in Sharjah in 1973 provided a further instance of the intertwining of domestic insecurity with trans-national security actions in the Gulf. This occurred as the exiled former ruler, Sheikh Saqr bin Sultan Al-Qasimi attempted to return to power using armed Iraqi mercenaries funded by the Iraqi Ba'ath Party. Although the squad succeeded in assassinating Saqr's cousin and successor, Sheikh Khalid bin Mohamed Al-Qasimi, during its assault on the ruler's palace, Saqr was ultimately arrested by members of the Dubai and Abu Dhabi Defence Forces.[54] Nearly four decades later, curiously, the other Al-Qasimi-controlled emirate in the UAE, Ras al-Khaimah, also became the playground of competing trans-national bids for power. In this instance, the succession to its ailing ninety-two-year old ruler, Sheikh Saqr bin Mohamed Al-Qasimi, was unsuccessfully contested by oldest son and former Crown Prince (until 2003) Sheikh Khalid bin Saqr Al-Qasimi. In 2010, Sheikh Khalid launched a global public relations campaign, spearheaded by an American consultancy (California Strategies) against his half-brother and successor as Crown Prince, Sheikh Saud bin Saqr Al-Qasimi. Making full use of new media and social networking sites such as Facebook, Twitter, blogs and a multi-million dollar advertising campaign, California Strategies sought to appeal to its American-based political audience for a change in regime, in large part by portraying the Crown Prince as a security risk and highlighting supposed closeness to Iran and the financing of terrorism.[55]

Returning to the 1970s, the perceived ideological challenge posed by the PDRY and PFLOAG to the Gulf States reflected an influential trend of academic scholarship that predicted the imminent demise of these traditional monarchical systems in the 1950s and 1960s.[56] The process of consolidating and embedding institutional structures and ideational affinity with the newly-independent polities began in the 1970s and is still ongoing.[57] This holds true also for the development of modern polities in Saudi Arabia and Oman, which both escaped formal colonial control and emerged as independent states much earlier than the other four Gulf States.[58] The admixture of rapid modernisation underpinned by the internal redistribution of oil rents led to the evolution of what J.E. Peterson has labelled 'post-traditional' states in the Arabian Peninsula.[59] These measures enabled the Gulf monarchies to accrue and update their reserves of legitimacy and popular acceptance that guided them through the transformational socio-economic changes brought on by the advent of the oil era. Nevertheless they failed to address the core challenges of moving toward a sustainable long-term political economy, and fostered a 'rentier mentality' that has affected successive generations in the Gulf States who increasingly take for granted the continued redistribution of wealth and provision of public goods by the state.[60]

Continuing instability and uncertainty in regional security structures formed the backdrop to this phase of socio-political maturation in the Arabian Peninsula. Although the United States resisted British approaches to replace them as the external guarantor of Gulf security after 1971, American policy treated the region as a critical part of the geopolitical balance of power during the Cold War.[61] US support was extended through the contextual frameworks of the 1957 Eisenhower Doctrine, which permitted countries to request American economic and military assistance to combat the spread of international communism, and the 1969 Nixon Doctrine, which called on key American partners to maintain a regional balance of power favourable to US interests.[62] This translated into the 'Twin Pillars' approach to supporting Saudi Arabia and Iran as conservative, status quo bulwarks in the region. Both countries shared a common interest in combating socialist and radical nationalist influences in the Gulf and maintaining the steady flow of oil export revenues that underpinned the social contract between state and society.[63] They also provided a counterweight to the projection of growing Iraqi influence in the Gulf as its brand of pan-Arabism was considered destabilising to regional security.[64] This manifested itself in recurring boundary skirmishes with Iran between 1969 and 1975, in border disputes with Kuwait, and in allegations that Baghdad was hosting and assisting PFLOAG cells following their operational defeat in Dhofar by 1975.[65]

The Twin Pillars policy ended in ignominy with the Islamic revolution in Iran in 1978–79 and the outbreak of the Iran-Iraq war in September 1980. These two events had a cathartic impact on the Gulf States and reshaped the structure of regional security. Saudi Arabia, Kuwait and Oman all put forward visions for a cooperative regional organisation to face the new set of challenges and uncertainty caused by events in Iran and Iraq. These developments provided the impetus for Bahrain, Kuwait, Oman, Qatar, Saudi Arabia and the United Arab Emirates to launch the Gulf Cooperation Council on 25 May 1981.[66] The new body was neither a political nor a military alliance and lacked an integrative supra-national decision-making institution for the sharing of sovereignty akin to the European Commission.[67] It also suffered from lingering suspicion among the smaller Gulf States, particularly

Qatar but latterly also the United Arab Emirates, at the potential for Saudi hegemony or dominance within the new organisation.[68] Qatari-Saudi relations, in particular, were strained by Qatari allegations of Saudi involvement in two coup attempts against its emir, Sheikh Hamad bin Khalifa al-Thani, in 1996 and 2005 respectively.[69] Lingering intra-regional tension complicated moves toward reaching common policies on regional issues, and continue to do so.[70] Nevertheless, its formation did alter the regional political architecture and created a loose security community among the six Gulf States that now formed the third axis of the triangular balance of power in the region.[71]

A Broken System

The Gulf region has experienced three major wars based on balance of power considerations since 1980. Together the Iran-Iraq war (1980–88), Iraq's invasion and subsequent expulsion from Kuwait (1990–91) and the US-led invasion of Iraq (2003) created multiple human and material insecurities in addition to destabilising cross-border flows of weaponry and illicit materials, including narcotics. The presence of these interlinking challenges to internal and external security meant that the Gulf did not share in the transformation of security that occurred in Eastern Europe or Latin America during the 1990s and 2000s. In these regions, security became linked to issues of political and economic legitimacy as well as the emergence of new concepts of cooperative security associated with a shift away from realist approaches predicated on a zero-sum notion of national security.[72]

No such transformation of security structures or approaches occurred in the Gulf, as the insertion of the United States as the most powerful regional actor after 1990 further destabilised and unbalanced the regional security system. This occurred alongside the erosion of boundaries between domestic and foreign policy as advances in communications and technology and access to information opened up societies in the Gulf, as elsewhere. During the 1990s the convergence of these two trends provided a cogent ideational tool for political and radical opponents of the GCC regimes. It enabled groups such as Al-Qaeda and its regional offshoots to construct a sophisticated counternarrative of American penetration of the Arabian Peninsula and suppression of Muslims in conflicts across the world.[73] The resulting 'blowback' underscored the interlocking linkages between the internal and external dimensions of security and their relationship to perceptions of political legitimacy and authority.

During the Iran-Iraq war, the deep interconnected fissures running through Gulf societies highlighted the Gulf States' vulnerability to the overspill or activation of cross-border flows and networks. The post-revolutionary Iranian regime initially attempted to export its Islamic revolution to neighbouring states with large Shiite populations. During the early 1980s, Iranian agents were implicated in plots to destabilise internal security in Bahrain (1981), Saudi Arabia (1984) and Kuwait (1985).[74] Saudi Arabia and Kuwait provided very significant levels of financial assistance to Iraq, which included an agreement to forward the profits from their shared neutral zone Khafji oilfield, as well as the provision of loans worth up to $50 billion. Moreover, the two countries opened up their seaports to the import of products bound for Iraqi markets, and the export of oil on behalf of the Iraqi government.[75] In this instance, as also with Bahrain, the presence of substantial Shiite communities meant that the Gulf State regimes feared the trans-national overspill from revolutionary Iran, and reluctantly backed Iraq as the regional bulwark against the spread of Iranian-centric pan-Islamism, which in the case of Saudi Arabia also threatened its core legitimacy as the custodian of the two holiest places in Islam.

Elsewhere in the Gulf States, reactions to the fighting differed, as the countries of the Lower Gulf were less directly affected by the actual or potential spread of instability. Qatar's closer economic and commercial ties with Iran led it to adopt a more neutral position while in Oman Sultan Qaboos maintained diplomatic relations with Iran throughout the war and sent a special representative to prepare diplomatic contacts and dialogue between the warring parties in 1987 as a prelude to the cessation of hostilities the following year.[76] The war also complicated the process of state consolidation in the United Arab Emirates as Abu Dhabi, Ajman, Fujairah and Ras al-Khaimah supported Iraq, while Dubai, Sharjah and Umm al-Qaiwain adopted pro-Iranian positions.[77]

Paradoxically, in light of Iran's immediate post-1979 attempts to export its revolution, the period of greatest direct danger to the Gulf States came relatively late in the conflict. In 1987–88, the 'Tanker War' and persistent attacks on commercial shipping in Gulf waters directly jeopardised the export of oil that formed the basis of the social contract underpinning state-society relations in the GCC states. This constituted a grave danger to internal stability in Gulf regimes already hit by the steady fall in oil prices since the mid-1980s, and led to the re-flagging of the Kuwaiti fleet in 1987.[78] It was, nevertheless, noteworthy that the attacks on international shipping failed to close the Gulf to shipping, and that oil exports continued to flow despite the threat to regional maritime security. This earlier continuation of trade may be indicative of Iranian policymakers attempt to fulfil their oft-made pledges to close the Strait of Hormuz to commercial shipping in the event of a new conflict involving Iran breaking out.[79]

Iraq's invasion of Kuwait on 2 August 1990 posed similarly pro-found questions for security and legitimacy in the GCC as its attack on Iran a decade earlier. These states' enormous oil wealth and lavish expenditure (much of it on lucrative arms deals with the West) neither prevented the Iraqi takeover of Kuwait nor contributed more than a token gesture to its liberation in 1991. King Fahd's decision (under strong pressure) to invite more than 700,000 American-led troops to defend Saudi soil represented a humiliating admission of the kingdom's inability to provide one of the most basic elements of its part of the ruling bargain, namely security for its population.[80] The retention thereafter of up to 5,000 American soldiers in Saudi Arabia had momentous consequences for the mobilisation of oppositional groups such as Al-Qaeda. It allowed individuals such as Osama bin Laden to question the legitimacy of the Al-Saud by very publicly calling into question their suitability to act as guardian of the land of the two holy places.[81] They also gave rise to suspicions, extending beyond radical groups to encompass much intellectual and popular opinion, that held that the Americans had ulterior motives for remaining in the Gulf, and that US security interests were not aligned with the best interests of the Gulf States. Even in post-liberation Kuwait, feelings of frustration at US foreign and security policy in the Middle East led to talk of a 'smothering embrace' and feelings of unease that the United States did not maintain a hegemonic role in the Gulf 'out of love for Kuwait...if America defends its interests, then we have every right also to defend our beliefs and our principles.'[82]

The thirty-four-member multinational coalition liberated Kuwait in a rapid and effective military campaign in early 1991. It was, however, the legacy of the decisions taken between August 1990 and February 1991 that exerted a destabilising influence on the subsequent develop-ment of security policy in the Gulf. The United States emerged from the Gulf War as the overwhelming military power in the region, as in the wider world. Successive Presidential administrations under George H.W. Bush and Bill Clinton designed a 'Dual Containment' policy that excluded Iraq and Iran from regional security structures, while deepening their military relations with the GCC states.[83] This was achieved through the signing of separate defence cooperation agreements with Bahrain, Kuwait, Qatar and the United Arab Emirates (with the first two also being accorded Major Non-NATO Ally status in 2002 and 2004 respectively). The GCC states developed into major logistical and command-and-control hubs for the US Fifth Fleet in Manama in 1995, and the forward headquarters of US Central Command (CENTCOM) in Doha in 2002, while substantial stocks of military equipment were prepositioned at airbases and ports in the United Arab Emirates and Kuwait that became the administrative and logistical lifeline for multi-national forces in Iraq after 2003.[84] These added to existing access to facilities agreements with Oman (dating back to 1980) and the wide range of military agreements underpinning Saudi Arabian security since the 1940s.[85]

'Dual Containment' did not address the central challenge of creating a sustainable and durable security architecture in the Gulf. It suffered from the binary opposition between American refusal to accept Iraqi or Iranian involvement in any regional framework, and these regimes' insistence that the withdrawal of external (American) troops was a sine qua non of any agreement. This produced an unbalanced system that lurched toward a third Gulf war in 2003 and continues to destabilise relations between Iran and the international community. More significantly, the permanent presence of US troops and bases in the Arabian Peninsula led to a growing divergence between political and public opinion as the American military footprint deepened throughout the 1990s. This arose partially as a result of the growing influence of Islamism as a social and political force in all GCC states after 1990; it also reflected an increasing questioning of US motives and perceptions of regional threats, especially after the election of President Khatami in 1997 was greeted with cautious optimism in the Gulf States and a move to normalise relations between the GCC and Iran.[86]

The emerging gap between regime and public opinion opened up a space for oppositional voices to register their discontent at the direction of policy. This occurred on several levels and was most visible among Islamists although it encompassed secular and nationalist

strands of opinion as well. Most notably, it provided the background
to Osama bin Laden's notorious declaration of 'Jihad against Jews and
Crusaders' on 23 February 1998. In it, bin Laden claimed that:

…for over seven years the United States has been occupying the lands of Islam
in the holiest of places, the Arabian Peninsula, plundering its riches, dictating
to its rulers, humiliating its peoples, terrorising its neighbours, and turning its
bases in the Peninsula into a spearhead with which to fight the neighbouring
Muslim peoples.[87]

This statement, issued under the name of the World Islamic Front,
represented nothing less than an existential threat to the ideational and
moral legitimacy of the GCC regimes. It was particularly potent in
Saudi Arabia, where the legacy of successive rulers' promotion of pan-
Islamic nationalism, both as a legitimating tool and a means of countering the ideological challenge of pan-Arabism, left the regime
vulnerable to accusations of deviating from Islamic rule.[88] The advent
of the internet and Arab satellite television channels from the mid-
1990s greatly facilitated the spread of these oppositional narratives by
providing new forums for discussion and mobilisation.[89]

During the 1990s, the ideational challenge to regime legitimacy was
compounded by an extended period of historically low oil prices. This
placed an additional strain on the maintenance of the redistributive
mechanisms that lay at the heart of the Gulf States' political economy.
The general decline in the price of oil, which fell to as little as $10 per
barrel in 1998, coincided with political instability in Qatar and violent
and prolonged opposition to the government in Bahrain in the mid-
1990s.[90] In Saudi Arabia it complicated the regime's longstanding
strategy of co-opting support through the spread of wealth in order to
anticipate or head off opposition movements.[91] This made the rise of
Islamist opposition movements so potentially dangerous to the regime
as it occurred in a period of relative economic hardship when the traditional tools for neutralising dissent and buttressing support were
weakened.[92] It also provided a portent for the difficulties that will
likely become apparent in the transition toward a post-oil era should
it overlap with a drawing-down of regimes' capacity to co-opt support
and maintain living standards that are now taken for granted by citizens of the GCC states.

The convergence of these factors—the emergence of Islamist oppositional movements benefiting from the spread of information and
communications technology during economically straightened times—

demonstrated the interconnections binding together the internal and external dimensions of security in the Gulf States. Each of these had roots beyond the capacity of the state to control and all raised the possibility that they could widen or deepen existing fractures within society. Their emergence required the Gulf States to take measures to broaden their bases of legitimacy and pillars of support. This occurred through a process of carefully-controlled liberalisation that began in the late-1990s and continued through the early 2000s.[93] The recognition that reform was necessary to updating regime legitimacy and coping with the rapidly-changing demands of the globalising world was best expressed in an interview given by the Emir of Qatar to the *New Yorker* in 2000:

We have simply got to reform ourselves. We're living in a modern age. People log on to the internet. They watch cable TV. You cannot isolate yourself in today's world. And our reforms are progressing well. In a tribal country like Qatar, however, it could take time for everyone to accept what we've done. But change, more change, is coming.[94]

The contemporaneous moves toward political reform and economic liberalisation suggested that Gulf rulers, at least temporarily in response to specific circumstances, acknowledged the value of strengthening internal cohesion in order to minimise their vulnerability to external threats.

9/11 and After

Seventeen of the nineteen hijackers who carried out the four attacks on New York and Washington DC on 11 September 2001 were nationals of GCC states.[95] This provided a sobering demonstration of these states' vulnerabilities to opposition toward their political and security alliances with the United States. It enabled the Gulf States to frame their own responses to the attacks within the dominant discourse of the 'war on terror' and link the very survival of their regimes to the success of this counter-terrorism approach.[96] This shielded the GCC from the full force of the George W. Bush administration's political and military measures which, elsewhere in the Middle East, altered the parameters of US policymaking in profoundly significant ways. This occurred as the Bush administration channelled its response in the form of a 'global war on terror' that it subsequently redefined in 2006 into the concept of a 'long war.' These labels reflected the administration's construction of the challenge from Al-Qaeda as a threat to western civilisation itself that required military action to combat it.[97] Its success in securitising the meaning of 9/11 (at least temporarily) legitimated the adoption of extraordinary measures that rested on a special interpretation of international law and the norms and rules of the international system.[98]

A corollary to the 'war on terror' was a greater, albeit ultimately temporary, attention to issues of political reform in the Middle East. This reached its apogee in 2005 with President Bush's second inaugural address in January, and Secretary of State Condoleeza Rice's speech at the American University in Cairo in June, in which she claimed that 'For sixty years, my country, the United States, pursued stability at the expense of democracy in this region, here in the Middle East, and we achieved neither.'[99] Significantly for the Gulf States, the processes of political reform in the GCC predated September 11 and provided an important layer of legitimacy that blunted the impact of Rice's Cairo declaration.[100] These reforms began with the accession to power of a new generation of rulers in Qatar in 1995 and Bahrain in 1999. They aimed at updating traditional channels of state-society interaction and introducing a participatory dimension alongside limited measures of political pluralism.[101] The measures included a new constitution and bicameral National Assembly in Bahrain in 2002; the introduction of municipal elections in Qatar in 1999 and a new constitution in 2003; provision for direct elections to the Majlis ash-Shura in Oman in 2000 and universal suffrage in 2003; expansion of the Majlis ash-Shura and the holding of municipal elections in Saudi Arabia in 2005; the enfranchisement of women in Kuwait in 2005; and very limited elections to the Federal National Council of the United Arab Emirates in 2006.[102]

These reforms amounted to an exercise in political decompression designed to renew the legitimacy of ruling elites and co-opt oppositional groups in a carefully managed, top-down process of incremental change.[103] Although no two pathways to reform are identical, as of 2010 none met Marina Ottaway's definition of a 'political paradigm shift' governing relations between state and society, and the location, source and exercise of political power.[104] Instead, government control persisted and, with the partial exception of Kuwait, the balance of political power remained vested in the ruling families and their neo-patrimonial networks.[105] The stalled reforms raise the possibility that dashed expectations of meaningful reform may generate societal disillusionment with, and disengagement from, the political processes initiated by ruling elites. This has already occurred in Bahrain, where discontent with the outcome of their participation in parliamentary elections is evident among both the Shiite Islamist Al Wefaq National Islamic Society and the secular left-wing National Democratic Action Society.[106]

In addition to introducing a strong external impetus to domestic reform processes, September 11 also highlighted the myriad linkages between globalisation and security in an era of new trans-national and increasingly non-state threats. Al-Qaeda exploited globalising flows of finance and people, and utilised new technologies of communication as it prepared and carried out the attacks.[107] Its use of the tools of globalisation highlighted the dark underside of global interconnections and the existence of a profoundly regressive form of globalisation. This formed part of a broader phenomenon whereby trans-national extremist organisations mobilised across states and within societies to compete with progressive global civil society in the new spaces opened up by the processes of globalisation.[108] It also created, and took advantage of, new forms of Islamic 'imagined communities' and a growing awareness of 'Islamic issues' that transcended state boundaries and further eroded the boundaries between the internal and external spheres of policy.[109]

Saudi Arabia's projection of pan-Islamism as a legitimising tool paradoxically exposed it to contestation on the same grounds, particularly as Saudi fighters travelled abroad to join jihads in places as diverse as Afghanistan, Bosnia and Kashmir. This threat magnified after the mid-1990s as the new Arab satellite television channels broadcast daily footage of Muslim suffering elsewhere in the world. Thomas Hegghammer cites one Saudi official who acknowledged that 'We encouraged our young men to fight for Islam in Afghanistan. We encouraged our young men to fight for Islam in Bosnia and Chechnya. We encouraged our young men to fight for Islam in Palestine...'[110] The full extent of Saudi vulnerability to violent blowback will be discussed fully in the next chapter, but it is important to note that many of these trans-national religious warriors subsequently began to operate autonomously from state control. These processes of globalisation facilitated the emergence of new forms of ideational, non-state and cross-border affiliations that bypassed state structures to reach directly to disaffected elements of society.

This opening chapter has described how the dynamic interaction between internal and external events is the central thread in the evolution of security policy and structures in the Gulf. The postcolonial state system that emerged between 1961 and 1971 demonstrated its durability by surviving intact the three major inter-state wars that have taken place in the Gulf since 1980. Furthermore, a genuine attachment to national symbols has begun to appear, and a tangible sense of belonging has grafted the substance of group identity onto the impersonal framework of the state, which itself has become embedded as the referent point for contestation and advancement.[111] Political maturation marked the smooth replacement of longstanding charismatic leaderships in Bahrain, the United Arab Emirates and (to a lesser extent) Saudi Arabia and Kuwait in 1999, 2004, 2005 and 2006 respectively, although opaque cross-cutting 'political-economic families' still constitute powerful linkages and the survival of a degree of personalisation against the onset of institutionalisation.[112]

By and large, however, the growth of institutional structures and the consolidation of the state are real achievements that suggest that ruling elites in the GCC have partially succeeded in updating their bases of legitimacy and strengthening their internal polities. Nevertheless, the impact of globalisation and the emergence of new trans-national threats, as well as the shifting patterns of conflict from inter-state to intra-societal, introduces profound new dimensions to regional security structures.[113] It also redefines the nature of the existing challenges presented by the unfolding post-occupation dynamics in Iraq, ongoing instability in Iran's relations with the international community, and the ideational and material threat from trans-national terrorist and non-state actors. Furthermore, while the two pillars of oil and external security continue to represent important factors in delimiting the geo-strategic and commercial motivations of external interest in the Gulf, they must not obscure the crucial evolution of domestic and intra-regional challenges to stability. It is the interaction of these internal trajectories with the trans-national and global changes brought about by globalisation that will frame the parameters of changing regional security frameworks.

Together, these new and emerging issues—of resource insecurity and gradual hydrocarbon depletion, demographic growth and generational changes, and cross-border threats from climate change and environmental degradation—will impact on internal societal cohesion and require new responses to existing problems of unequal access to, and distribution of, resources. Meanwhile the trans-national nature of climate change, food and water security (particularly the mining of fossil water in underground aquifers) and environmental degradation will inject potent new sources of tension and sites of contestation into the intra- and international relations of the Gulf States.

2

SECURITY AS DISCOURSE

IRAQ, IRAN AND TRANS-NATIONAL EXTREMISM

In this chapter the focus shifts to the three major contemporary challenges to Gulf security in the first decade of the twenty-first century. It emphasises two salient characteristics that dominate the formulation of security policy in the region. The first is the role of indigenous agency in delineating the linkages between internal and external security and in deciding which issues make it onto national and regional agendas. This is especially important when analysing the Arab oil monarchies, in which the conduct of foreign and security policy is restricted to a tightly-drawn circle of senior members of the ruling family.[1] In order properly to contextualise the formulation of security policies we must consider the factors that inform regimes' perceptions of their internal and regional security. This, in turn, plays a critical role in shaping policy toward external issues such as the unfolding post-occupation dynamics in Iraq, the material and ideological challenge of Iran and its ongoing dispute with the international community, and the threat posed by radicalism and trans-national extremism.

The second characteristic that frames regional discourse on security policymaking is a conflation of regime security with national security, in common with many other states in the developing world. Regime survival was paramount in ruling strategies during the transformational period of socio-economic transition into the oil era during the 1950s and 1960s. It successfully enabled the regimes to survive the shift and maintain control over the processes of state formation and

37

consolidation.[2] The very survival of the monarchies contrasted starkly with the violent ending of monarchical rule in Iraq and Iran in 1958 and 1979 respectively. It also confounded the predictions of political and social scientists who predicted the eventual demise of these traditional polities under the onslaught of modernisation.[3] Yet this very durability masks several existing and latent fault-lines that link internal security to regional and international events, and conditions regime responses to these issues.

Iraq and the 'Shiite Crescent' Perception

The US-led invasion and subsequent occupation of Iraq began in March 2003. It provoked a prolonged and violent insurgency that complicated and delayed the drawdown of American combat troops until the first phase of a staged withdrawal that began on 30 June 2009. A vacuum in security and governance rapidly emerged as Iraqi governing structures withered away, and the Coalition Provisional Authority catastrophically mismanaged the initial stages of the occupation. Its litany of errors, capped by two policy decisions to disband the Iraqi army and promulgate a sweeping de-Ba'athification law in 2003, rapidly eroded the credibility of the occupying forces. These conditions allowed a disparate collection of anti-occupation insurgents to flourish both among Iraqi Sunni communities and Shiite organisations such as the followers of Moqtada Al-Sadr.

Following the destruction of the Al-Askariyya Mosque in Samarra in February 2006 the effects of state collapse accelerated into a high-intensity civil war as Iraqi society fragmented into ethnic and sectarian-based communities.[4] This introduced a complex and lethal dynamic into daily life in Iraq as violence devolved down to neighbourhood level. The resulting battle-lines overlapped the broader ethnic and sectarian divides as militia groups splintered into sub-units and fought each other for control of scarce local economic and political resources.[5] Although the figures are a matter of considerable dispute, estimates of the number of civilian deaths in the violence range from an Iraq Body Count figure of 103,819 by December 2009 to a contentious survey published in *The Lancet* that suggested a much higher number of 654,965 excess deaths by June 2006 alone.[6] These measures of human insecurity were supplemented by the displacement of more than four million Iraqis as a result of ethnic and sectarian cleansing. By the middle of 2007, the International Organization of Migration reported that approximately two million Iraqis had fled to neighbouring countries, primarily Syria and Jordan, and a further 2.2 million were internally displaced within Iraq. This represented the largest displacement of peoples since the expulsion of Palestinians from the newly-created state of Israel in 1948.[7]

The multiple conflicts in Iraq impacted the Gulf States in a variety of ways. Their role as the logistical and administrative hubs for the multi-national coalition exposed the regimes to considerable levels of internal dissent against the invasion in 2003.[8] In its most pronounced form, in Saudi Arabia, pre-invasion popular discontent revealed itself in opinion polls showing that 97 per cent of respondents adamantly opposed any cooperation with an American attack on Iraq.[9] Demonstrations against the war occurred in the other Gulf States as well, with those in Bahrain particularly well-attended and prolonged.[10] This placed policymakers in the GCC in the awkward position of having to balance their security ties with the United States with high levels of popular opposition to the invasion. It prompted many to distance themselves publicly from the United States while privately offering some degree of encouragement and support to the effort to oust Saddam Hussein's regime. In March 2007, this security dilemma prompted King Abdullah of Saudi Arabia to denounce the 'illegitimate foreign occupation' in an unprecedented public display of anger at the Kingdom's primary security partner.[11]

Such elevated levels of public discontent at US actions in Iraq formed part of a larger chorus of anger at the Bush administration's Middle East policies more generally. In this environment, the GCC states might have expected significant repercussions due both to their geographical proximity to Iraq and their leadership's military and political alliance with Washington. This notably did not happen, as the GCC states implemented hard security measures that ensured they remained relatively immune to the cross-border overspill of insecurity in the form of sectarian conflict, refugee flows, and terrorist attacks.[12] Instead, the destabilising flows of men and money ran largely in the other direction, from the GCC into Iraq. Between 1,500 and 3,000 Saudi militants joined the Sunni insurgency and constituted a significant proportion (up to 60 per cent of all foreign fighters in Iraq.[13] In Kuwait, members of two terrorist organisations, the *Mujahideen of Kuwait* and the *Peninsula Lions*, also channelled fighters to the insurgency, and took the Kuwaiti security authorities by surprise.[14] Meanwhile, groups in Saudi Arabia and the smaller GCC states provided large amounts of funding to the insurgent groups and terrorist organisations operating inside Iraq.[15]

With the direct threat from Iraq successfully contained, domestic and international discourse focused instead on analyses of the geopolitical and strategic implications for the balance of regional power.[16] This revolved around the perceived and actual expansion of Iranian influence following the removal of its main counterweight in the Gulf, and its consequences for the Shiite populations in the GCC.[17] As early as February 2003, the Saudi Arabian foreign minister, Prince Saud Al-Faisal, warned President Bush that he would be 'solving one problem and creating five more' if Saddam Hussein was removed by force. Subsequently, in 2005, he opined that the United States was 'handing the whole country over to Iran without reason.'[18] Officials and analysts in the GCC increasingly came to view the empowerment of Iraq's Shiite majority and the rise in Iranian influence in Iraq as the major, if unintended, consequences of the overthrow of the Ba'athist regime. The result was vocal and sustained suspicion of Iran's cultivation of extensive ties with both state and non-state actors in Iraq, which provided Teheran with a degree of strategic depth and stoked deep unease within the GCC.[19]

It was in this context that the theory of a 'Shiite crescent' running from Iran through Iraq and the oil-rich Eastern Province of Saudi Arabia to Lebanon gained considerable traction in popular and political discourse in the Middle East.[20] This occurred as the orgy of political violence and sub-national communalistic challenges to Iraqi state authority sharpened sectarian tensions in the Gulf and the broader region. The accident of geography that situated the region's largest oil reserves in precisely these areas heightened the perceived stakes among policymakers in the GCC and the United States.[21] Between 2005 and 2007, the intense sectarian conflict in Iraq negatively affected the pace of political reform in the GCC. It reinforced the innate conservatism of the ruling families, who interpreted the unfolding chaos in Iraq as proof that US-backed democratisation policies would shift the locus of power decisively away from regime control.[22]

Theories of a 'Shiite crescent' and suspicion that Shiite actors and political groups represent a threat to GCC polities are ahistorical. They rest on a flawed ascription of pan-Shiite trans-national loyalties and an assumption of monolithic unity within Shiism that does not exist in reality. The narrative of sectarian conflict and minority identities is also overly simplistic, but appealing, to regimes as it downplays the domestic roots of socio-political and economic dissent.[23] Shiites in Kuwait, for example, demonstrated their loyalty to the state and the ruling Al-Sabah family during the Iraqi occupation in 1990–91. Their comparatively more advanced associational infrastructure provided the backbone of an organised resistance movement against the Iraqi occupation forces.[24] In Iraq itself, the Shiite community was a house divided, and many held a more complex and positive attachment to Iraqi nationalism than admitted by proponents of a 'Shiite crescent.' The popularity of Moqtada Al-Sadr and his *Jaish al-Mahdi* testified to the ideational appeal of an Iraqi Shiite nationalism that rejected both the foreign occupation and a pro-Iranian alignment.[25] Meanwhile significant unrest among Shiite communities in Saudi Arabia in 1979 and in Bahrain between 1994 and 1999 was motivated primarily by resentment at uneven patterns of development and internal socio-economic marginalisation, rather than any residual loyalties to Iran or direct and indirect Iranian influence.[26]

The sectarian lens nevertheless constituted a powerful filter through which ruling elites throughout the GCC viewed developments in Iraq. In states with significant Shiite communities, such as Saudi Arabia, Bahrain and Kuwait, the potential overspill of sectarian violence and the perceived threat to internal security was instrumental in shaping regimes' initial engagement with the new Shiite-led government in Baghdad.[27] Led by Saudi Arabia, officials in the GCC deeply distrusted the first government led by Prime Minister Nuri Al-Maliki (2006–10), which they suspected was an Iranian proxy and a source of multiple physical and ideational threats to their own polity.[28] This contributed to a self-fulfilling cycle as the Gulf States' reluctance to increase their political and economic engagement with Iraq enabled Iran to take the lead in reconstruction and development projects.[29] These include the new international airport at Najaf that opened in August 2008, the creation of a free trade zone around Basra, and the signing of multiple cooperation agreements between Iraq and Iran, covering issues as diverse as education, industry, environmental protection, and insurance.[30]

A slew of issues remain unresolved as multi-national forces withdraw from Iraq and regional attention turns toward the post-occupation dynamics of Iraqi reconstruction. The long process of drawing down coalition troops began with the signature of the US-Iraq Status of Forces Agreement in November 2008. This provided a timetable for the progressive withdrawal of all American combat troops by 31 December 2011. For their part, British troops ended combat operations in southern Iraq and withdrew to Kuwait between May and July 2009.[31] However, significant questions remain unanswered about the size and future role of the largely American 'residual force' that will remain in Iraq to train the Iraqi armed forces and assist in counter-terrorism operations beyond 2011.[32] This uncertainty extends to the local and regional implications of Iraq's re-integration into the political and security frameworks in the Gulf and the future orientation of its military forces.[33] Kuwaitis, in particular, remain understandably concerned about Iraqi arms acquisitions, and insist that any weaponry supplied to the Iraqi military should be defensive rather than offensive in nature.[34]

A stronger Iraq with a greater sense of national purpose might allay GCC unease at supposed Iranian influence inside Iraq, but also introduces a new dimension to regional threat perceptions.[35] During 2008 and 2009, Maliki increasingly projected himself as an Iraqi nationalist, and took a series of measures that centralised political and military power in his Prime Minister's Office. Alongside the creation of a shadow network of advisors and Tribal Support Councils that bypassed official government structures, these developments carried ominous overtones of Iraq's dictatorial past.[36] Maliki's attempts to remain as Prime Minister following the inconclusive results of the parliamentary election in March 2010 seemed to confirm fears of a contested and destabilising changeover of political power. This agglomeration of centralised power combined with ongoing instances of sectarianism in the Iraqi political process to complicate the normalisation of relations with its Arab neighbours. As of 2010, Saudi Arabia is yet to reopen its embassy in Baghdad, and the Kingdom demonstrated a marked preference for replacing Maliki with the former interim Prime Minister Ayad Allawi. Meanwhile, the souring of relations in 2009 between Kuwait and Iraq over the payment of reparations for the 1990–91 occupation demonstrated the acute sensitivity involved in re-integrating Iraq into the regional fold.[37]

Iraq continues to be a perceived source of multiple material and trans-national insecurities for the GCC. This has changed over time as the dynamics of the war and occupation give way to a post-conflict phase of reconstruction and regional re-engagement. Although the Gulf States remain wary of any reassertion of Iraqi power, American political and military leverage mean that Baghdad is unlikely to pose a hard military threat to them in the foreseeable future. However, this should not lead to the neglect of public diplomacy and political reconciliation with Iraq, as new threats to regional security and stability continue to emerge. These are rooted in the continuing lack of human development and indices of human insecurity in Iraq, such as the 2.3 million internally displaced persons and the high rates of poverty and unemployment.[38] They will continue to act as agents of instability as long as they remain unresolved. Already, Iraq has become an increasingly lucrative conduit in the global drugs trade.[39] This has stimulated trans-national criminal networks and the growth of an illicit cross-border illicit economy. Since 2003, smugglers and organised criminal gangs have taken advantage of porous border controls to channel illegal opiates, cannabis and synthetic pharmaceuticals from Afghanistan via Iran to Kuwait and Saudi Arabia for onward transit to Europe.[40]

The Ideational and Military Challenge From Iran

The potency of the 'Shiite crescent' discourse underscored the complex web of economic and historical interconnections that criss-cross the Gulf. The legacy of these interactions continues to exert considerable influence on the different ways in which individual GCC states view their relationship toward Iran. In the United States, the poisonous legacy of the 1979 hostage crisis has led successive presidential administrations since Carter to depict Iran as a strategic rival and a military threat to its interests in the Gulf. By contrast, ruling elites and much public discourse in the GCC itself focuses more on the ideational and political threat to their polities that emanate from Teheran.[41] Particularly in the smaller Gulf States, this is based on first-hand experience of Iranian attempts to project a measure of power and influence over the Arabian coastline of the Gulf, as part of its historical struggle with Saudi Arabia and Iraq for regional hegemony.[42] The Gulf States thus view Iran primarily in terms of its political and ideational leverage rather than as a military threat, and this is a crucial distinguishing factor from the American-centred debate over Gulf security.[43]

Iran has presented both a material and an ideational threat to its Arab Gulf neighbours in the past. Under the Shah, it maintained a longstanding claim on Bahrain as its 'fourteenth province.' This was

INSECURE GULF

settled by a plebiscite held under United Nations auspices in 1970 that demonstrated overwhelming Bahraini preference for an fully-sovereign, independent Arab state.[44] Nevertheless, individual Iranian political figures continue to make occasional claims that revive the issue, most recently in July 2007 and February 2009.[45] Iran also has occupied three islands belonging to Sharjah and Ras al-Khaimah (now part of the United Arab Emirates) since 1971. As with the periodic comments on Bahrain, Iranian provocations cause great friction with its Arab Gulf neighbours. This was clearly demonstrated in reactions to Iran's decision in August 2008 to open two new offices for maritime rescue and ship registration on the island of Abu Musa. The GCC states all expressed their support for the United Arab Emirates, and the GCC Secretary-General, Abdulrahman Al-Attiya, went as far as to compare the Iranian conduct with Israeli behaviour in the occupied Palestinian and other Arab territories.[46]

The ideological threat that Iran posed to the conservative Arab Gulf monarchies reached a crescendo in the aftermath of the Islamic revolution. Ayatollah Khomeini's rise to power inspired often-marginalised pan-Shiite movements in the Gulf and meshed with post-revolutionary fervour in Iran that aimed to export its particular brand of political Islam. In 2006, the Saudi activist and prominent articulator of Shiite demands, Fouad Ibrahim, recalled the powerful symbolism that Khomeini's ascendancy had on the Shiite communities in Saudi Arabia, and on an ideational affiliation to pan-Shiism:

The most attractive feature was the leadership of Imam Khomeini. The Imam's charismatic features were truly extraordinary and resonated deeply with all Muslims, particularly the Shiites. Second, the new interpretation of Shiite political thought inspired by the Iranian revolution was highly liberating. Third, the Shiites of the peninsula deeply appreciate the independence of Islamic Iran. They compare the Islamic Republic to the Saudi regime, which is dependent on America for its basic security.[47]

Yet this appeal notwithstanding, it was notable that most Shiite organisations and parties in the GCC continued to regard the nation-state as their primary point of reference when articulating demands for reform. They thereby remained rooted in their domestic context and held a far more nuanced attachment to trans-national loyalties than supposed by suspicious ruling elites.[48] During the 1980s, organisations such as the (Saudi) Islamic Revolution Organisation (*Munazamat al-Thawrah al-Islamiyah*) left the pan-Shiite (and Iraqi-founded) umbrella

Movement of Vanguards Missionaries (*Harakat al-Risaliyin al-Tala'*), in part due to differences of opinion over Khomeini's concept of *vela-yat-e-faqih* (guardianship of the Islamic jurists).[49]

Nevertheless, the perceived ideational threat from Iran strongly influenced GCC official circles, and was fuelled by Teheran's initial attempts to export its Islamic revolution to neighbouring states with substantial Shiite populations. Iranian agents were implicated in plots to destabilise internal security in Bahrain in 1981, Saudi Arabia in 1984, and Kuwait in 1985 and again during the 'Tanker War' of 1987–88).[50] Furthermore, statements of Iranian aspiration for regional hegemony built on GCC rulers' unease at the potential disloyalty of their Shiite communities. This tied the external, physical threat posed by Iran to core questions of internal security and ideational legitimacy in the GCC.[51] Between 2005 and 2007, ruling elites in the Gulf States also securitised the threat of sectarian overspill from Iraq. During this period, much local (and international) discourse on the 'Shiite question' regularly conflated perceptions of Shiite loyalties and Iranian meddling into one amorphous threat.[52] This was especially pronounced in Saudi Arabia and Bahrain, where officials feared the politicisation of their Shiite communities and sought to de-legitimise and deflect their demands for political participation and inclusion. They did this by restricting the political spaces available to Shiite groups and depicting activists as potential fifth columnists owing ultimate allegiance to Iran.[53]

This linkage of the internal and external dimensions of the Iranian threat is compounded by the GCC states' bilateral integration in the US security umbrella. Reliance on external security guarantees represents a continuation of their long-established strategy of survival against regional predators.[54] It is profoundly significant as it places the Gulf States within the broader political and ideological conflict between the United States and Iran. Since 1979, American presidential administrations have consistently refused to acknowledge that Iran can play a constructive role in any regional security system. For their part, Iranian officials have systematically called for the departure of all foreign forces from the Gulf as the *sine qua non* of any such agreement.[55] A visible display of this binary opposition between competing visions of regional security occurred in February 2010 when the Obama administration announced plans to expand its missile defence system in the Gulf. This prompted the Iranian speaker of parliament, Ali Larijani, to retort that

45

'It is strange that the American officials do not notice that the problem in the region is your presence.'[56]

The incompatibility of these mutually exclusive positions exposes the Gulf States to very great risk of any significant escalation of tensions between Iran and the international community. The scale and extent of GCC military ties with the United States renders them acutely vulnerable to blowback from any putative military strikes against Iranian nuclear facilities, whether by American or Israeli forces. This operates on both a physical and an ideational level. It demonstrates the strategic dilemma that lies at the core of the Gulf States' security relationship with the United States, as the American presence is both vital to regime survival yet also the lightning rod for oppositional discontent.[57] Public opinion throughout the GCC firmly opposed US policies in Iraq and Afghanistan, in addition to Washington's close ties with Israel and its inability to exert any leverage over the stalled Middle East Peace Process.[58] This divergence between political and popular opinion forms part of a broader 'regimes-peoples' division within Middle Eastern states that was manifested during Israel's conflicts with Hizbollah in July-August 2006 and Hamas in December-January 2008–9.[59] It presents Iran with a range of ideational fault-lines which Teheran may exploit in an effort to detach individual GCC states from the collective American embrace.

Beginning in earnest in 2008, Iranian officials initiated a war of words directed against ruling elites and decision-makers in the GCC designed to leave them in no doubt of Iran's intention to destabilise their polities in the event of conflict. Iran's deputy foreign minister, Manouchehr Mohammadi, pointedly questioned the legitimacy of the traditional monarchies in the Arabian Peninsula and their ability to quell rising domestic unrest at the American military presence.[60] One month later, in mid-September, the defence minister, Mostafa Mohamed Najjar, explicitly warned GCC officials that 'Our response to any attack would be decisive...We are certain the countries of the region would prevent America from attacking Iran.'[61] These comments coincided with a policy decision in Teheran that assigned responsibility for defending the Gulf in the event of attack to the Iranian Revolutionary Guards Corps. Persistent Iranian claims that its naval forces would close the Straits of Hormuz to commercial shipping in the event of any attack also cut to the heart of the GCC states' dependence on the export of oil.[62]

This decision sharpened the ideological danger posed by Iran to the internal security and domestic legitimacy of the GCC states. It came one day after a former Iranian consul-general to Dubai gave an interview to *Gulf News* claiming that Iran had maintained a network of sleeper cells in the GCC since 1979, which could be activated to destabilise internal security on Teheran's orders. Adel Al-Assadi (who defected in 2001) predicted that 'Teheran has enough manpower to destabilise the GCC countries.' He added that 'the practice of recruiting agents in the Gulf is deeply rooted in the way the intelligence institution is operating and is considered a strong point for Iran.'[63] These allegations were promptly repudiated by Iranian officials, who accused the Western media of spreading disinformation about Iranian intentions. They nevertheless tapped into a widely-held suspicion that Iran does indeed maintain a network of undercover agents that could, and would, engage in underhand tactics if ordered to do so.[64] Moreover, they dovetailed with a pattern of perceived Iranian intrigues in the Gulf States, such as the arrest in April 2010 of six men and one woman in Kuwait allegedly belonging to the Revolutionary Guards, further reinforcing GCC policymakers' anxieties.[65]

All six GCC states worry to varying degrees about Iranian influence over their polities, although opinion is divided over how best to confront the issue. Regional policymakers must balance their concern at the possibility of a new conflict in the Gulf with their unease at potentially having to live under the shadow of a nuclear-capable Iran.[66] This explains the comments given by the Saudi chairman of the Gulf Research Centre in Dubai, Abdulaziz Al-Sager, to the *New York Times* in October 2009. Displaying a remarkable level of insouciance to the potential implications of any attack on Iran designed to halt its nuclear programme, Al-Sager told the newspaper that:

The region can live with a limited retaliation from Iran better than living with a permanent nuclear deterrent. I favour getting the job done now instead of living through the rest of my life with a nuclear hegemony in the region that Iran would like to impose.[67]

Nine months later, in July 2010, the United Arab Emirates' Ambassador to the United States stated in similarly blunt language that the benefits of bombing Iran's nuclear facilities would outweigh the short-term costs of such an operation. Ambassador Youssef Al-Otaiba told an audience in Aspen, Colorado that 'We cannot live with a nuclear Iran. I am willing to absorb what takes place at the expense of the security of the U.A.E.'[68] Although his words were dismissed as not indicative of government policy, they, and Sager's earlier comments, underscore the complexities that shape GCC responses toward Iran and the diversity of opinions that inhibit any formulation of a collective approach.

Ties of trade and shared commercial interests provide a powerful rationale for improving relations between the GCC and Iran. In the case of the re-export trade from Dubai, they constitute a major loophole in the international regime of economic and financial sanctions on Iran.[69] These extensive trading links constitute a major irritant in Abu Dhabi's close political and security relationship with the United States, and they demonstrate the difficulties of formulating a common position even at an intra-emirate level.[70] Oman and Qatar also enjoy close economic relationships with Iran, based around, but not limited to, energy cooperation in the Kish and North Field/South Pars gas fields.[71] Within the GCC, there is a broad divergence between these countries' more positive approach toward Iran and the greater wariness toward engagement found in Kuwait, Bahrain and Saudi Arabia. These latter three contain the largest Shiite communities in the GCC, and consequently view Iran through the prism of their internal security as well as of regional stability.[72]

The visit of Iranian President Mahmoud Ahmedinejad to the annual GCC Summit in Doha in December 2007 visibly exposed the tensions inherent in policy approaches toward Iran. It also marked the first time that an Iranian leader had addressed a GCC Summit. Qatar's decision to invite Ahmedinejad was richly symbolic as it came just days after Bahrain hosted the Manama Dialogue. During that annual gathering of regional security policymakers, the American Secretary of Defence Robert Gates, aggressively stated that 'everywhere you turn, it is the policy of Iran to foment instability and chaos, no matter the strategic value or cost in the blood of innocents,' as he urged the GCC states to work together and with the United States to counter the Iranian threat.[73] Perhaps emblematically, Ahmedinejad's appearance caused more discord than goodwill, particularly as the Qatari leadership did not consult with other GCC leaders before extending the invitation to him. Ahmedinejad then went on to embarrass his hosts by ignoring issues of GCC concern, such as the purpose of Iran's nuclear programme or the UAE islands dispute. Instead, he renewed his ambiguous call for regional security cooperation on the unspoken assumption that this would be very much on Iranian terms.[74]

GCC policy toward Iran is therefore fragmented and susceptible to inflammation both by material and rhetorical pressures. The legacy of Iranian attempts to project its own power over the region it (tellingly) labels the *Persian* Gulf renders policymaking as vulnerable to discursive shifts as it is to broader geopolitical considerations. Even the publicly-expressed desire by Gulf States' officials to avoid a fourth regional conflict must be balanced against the implications of potentially having a nuclear-capable neighbour with a record of seeking regional hegemony. Their reliance on the United States as the external guarantor of security compounds the complexity of the Gulf States' internal legitimacy in the event of any conflict between the United States or Israel and Iran. For this reason, even states such as Kuwait, which hold more hard-line positions toward Teheran, feel compelled to state that they will not allow US troops to use their bases for an attack on Iran while states such as Qatar and Bahrain, which host major US military and logistical centres, walk a diplomatic tightrope as they attempt to balance their external reliance on Washington with their commercial and intra-regional linkages with Teheran.[75] This acute sensitivity imparts a degree of fluidity to the triangular nexus of relations between the Gulf States, Iran, and the United States, and it draws out the systemic instability of contemporary security structures in the Gulf region.

Radical Extremism and the Return of Trans-National Terrorism

Radical extremism presents a different, though no less significant, threat to regime legitimacy and internal security in the GCC. Interlinked with this is the material dangers posed by a reconstituted Al-Qaeda in the Arabian Peninsula. The resurgence of trans-national terrorism during 2009 also underscored the significance for the Arabian Peninsula of the crisis of governance and emergence of growing security gaps in Yemen. The nexus of instability and flows of militants, money and materiel between Yemen and Somalia carry profound implications for regional stability. It links one sub-regional security complex (to use the term developed by Barry Buzan and Ole Wæver) in the Arabian Peninsula to another in the Horn of Africa.[76] It also introduces a dangerous new dynamic to regional security, and requires the GCC to rethink security structures in light of the failure to contain the overspill of instability within Yemen itself.

Although the Gulf States faced earlier radical and violent opposi- tional movements such as the Popular Front for the Liberation of Oman and the Arabian Gulf,[77] none presented the same degree of exis- tential threat to internal legitimacy as did the emergence of Al-Qaeda in the Arabian Peninsula in 2002. Security officials throughout the GCC failed to anticipate the rise of this Sunni rejectionist movement. Neither did they foresee the potential danger that the return of several hundred Arab fighters from Afghanistan might present should they intersect with local militant networks.[78] This was partially attributable to a mistaken perception that any domestic unrest would emanate from Shiite oppositional groups in the GCC;[79] it also demonstrated short-sightedness regarding the linkages between policymaking at the local, the regional and the international levels. Years of both tacit and official Saudi support for global Islamic causes might have been expected to raise awareness of the linkages created by the internation- alisation of these issues. Its absence only magnified the initial shock caused by the opening stages of the domestic insurgency that began in Saudi Arabia in May 2003.[80]

Nevertheless, officials and ruling elites in the GCC rapidly came to acknowledge the gravity of the challenge posed by Al-Qaeda in the Arabian Peninsula. The organisation's declared aim of forcing the with- drawal of Western forces and influence from the peninsula was directed at the core of their political economy. Operations such as the failed attack on the Abqaiq oil-processing facility in Saudi Arabia in February 2006 and the failed suicide assault on the Japanese tanker *M-Star* as it passed through the Strait of Hormuz en route from Qatar to Japan in July 2010 attempted to strike at the social and commercial contract binding GCC regimes to their societies, and to the international system more generally.[81] Moreover, the construction of a radical alternative to governing elites sought to tap and mobilise increasing popular discon- tent at the regimes' pro-Western orientation. An unpublished Saudi poll in 2001 stripped bare the depth of these feelings of alienation as it revealed that 95 per cent of young male respondents between the ages of twenty-five and forty-one sympathised with Osama bin Laden.[82]

The violence continued within Saudi Arabia in 2003 and 2004 and began spilling over into neighbouring GCC states. Instances of terror- ism increased in Kuwait during this period, while in Qatar the bomb- ing of the Doha Players theatre was a shocking and high-profile new development in a country with little prior experience of radical violence.[83] Along with their counterparts in Dubai and other emirates, Qatari officials had been suspected of 'paying off' Al-Qaeda in order to forestall attacks on their soil.[84] Saudi Arabia, Dubai and other Gulf States also played an active, if unwitting, role as hubs for the illicit networks that underpinned the financing of terrorist organisations both within the GCC and in Iraq. Although the final report of the 9/11 Commission found no evidence that the Saudi government as an institution, or senior Saudi officials individually, funded Al Qaeda, both it, and an independent task force set up by the Council of Foreign Relations in 2002, addressed the issues of terrorist financing and Saudi Arabia's alleged financial support for terrorism.[85] Indeed, the Council of Foreign Relations report was particularly critical of Saudi-based support for international terrorist organisations, and concluded bluntly that 'for years, individuals and charities based in Saudi Arabia have been the most important source of funds for Al Qaeda. And for years, Saudi officials have turned a blind eye to this problem.'[86]

Accordingly a range of linkages bind internal security with external stability and connect these in turn to the very pillars of regime legitimacy in the GCC. For these reasons, the securitisation of trans-national terrorism has become a highly sensitive issue, particularly when adopted by the United States and other external actors. A case in point arose in June 2008 when the US Department of the Treasury froze the US-based assets of the (Kuwaiti) Society for the Revival of Islamic Heritage and banned US nationals from dealing with it.[87] This provoked understandable outrage from the Kuwaiti parliament and media, and a statement of condemnation from the Minister for Cabinet Affairs, Faisal Al-Hajji, who declared that 'we will not allow any country to interfere in our work. We have strong relations with friendly countries but we will not allow any country to interfere in our affairs.'[88]

Elsewhere in the GCC, local initiatives to tackle the problems of terrorist financing through tighter banking controls and a crackdown on money laundering, greater regulation of previously unlicensed *hawala* networks, and targeting other illicit financial flows and freezing individual accounts, have had generally mixed results.[89] In February 2010, the UAE hosted a joint plenary meeting of the Financial Action Task Force (FATF) and its Middle East and North Africa subsidiary, at which the Governor of the Central Bank, Sultan bin Nasser Al-Suwaidi, announced the implementation of forty FATF recommendations to combat money laundering, in addition to nine special recommendations on terrorist financing.[90] Elsewhere, a report issued by the US Government and Accountability Office in September 2009 provided a cautiously optimistic assessment of gradual improvement in Saudi Arabian measures to combat the financing of terror. In particular, it highlighted progress in disrupting fundraising activities by extremist groups operating inside the kingdom, while noting that deficiencies remained in combating the flow of funds from Saudi-based individuals and charitable organisations to support extremist countries outside Saudi Arabia.[91] This nuanced assessment of local measures must nevertheless be balanced against the failure of a collective GCC initiative to establish a regional counter-terrorism centre owing to insufficient backing from the individual member-states.[92]

Between 2003 and 2006 a combination of measures contributed to the tactical and operational marginalisation of Al-Qaeda in the Arabian Peninsula. The Saudi Arabian security and police forces recovered from their initial wrong-footing to launch a sophisticated and effective counter-offensive.[93] This went alongside an ideological campaign designed to address the ideational challenge to regime legitimacy. Saudi officials and clerics prioritised 'intellectual security' as a key tool in combating radicalisation, and actively adopted cyber counter-measures to counter 'deviant thoughts.' In October 2008, the Interior Minister, Prince Nayef bin Abdulaziz, strongly criticised the role of Saudi Imams as he accused them of having 'failed miserably in discharging their duties' by failing to confront 'the challenge of the deviant ideology.'[94] A soft approach with an emphasis on a 'war of ideas' therefore represented a bid to knit disaffected elements back into the framework of state-society relations by turning the mobilising power of religious legitimacy against them. This was exemplified by the creation of a network of rehabilitation and counter-radicalisation programmes in Saudi Arabia that sought to address the underlying factors behind radicalisation and re-integrate militants into society.[95]

In addition to these 'softer' security measures, Saudi Arabia and the UAE led the Gulf States in 'hard' military expenditures on a range of sophisticated equipment and lucrative arms deals. Data gathered by the Stockholm International Peace Research Institute (SIPRI) found that a remarkable 33 per cent of all major arms transfers to the Middle East between 2005 and 2009 went to the UAE, which by 2009 was the fourth-largest arms importer in the world.[96] Moreover, in both absolute and relative terms, Saudi Arabian military expenditure far surpassed its regional partners during the 1990s and 2000s, as the following table makes clear.

Country	Active military capability (2009)[97]	Military expenditure as % of GDP (2009)[98]	Value and origin of imported arms deliveries (1993–2008)[99]
Bahrain	6,000 Army 700 Navy 1,500 Air Force 8,200 Total	3.4	$1,500,000,000 United States, Western Europe
Kuwait	11,000 Army 2,000 Navy 2,500 Air Force 15,500 Total	5.4	$10,400,000,000 United States, Western Europe, Russia, China
Oman	25,000 Army 4,200 Navy 5,000 Air Force 8,400 Others 42,600 Total	7.5	$2,400,000,000 Western Europe, United States, Russia, China
Qatar	8,500 Army 1,800 Navy 1,500 Air Force 11,800 Total	N/A	$1,800,000,000 Western Europe
Saudi Arabia	75,000 Army 13,500 Navy 20,000 Air Force 16,000 Air Defence 9,000 Industrial Security Force 100,000 National Guard 233,500 Total	10	$101,500,000,000 United States, Western Europe, Russia, China
UAE	44,000 Army 2,500 Navy 4,500 Air Force 51,000 Total	6.3	$17,400,000,000 United States, Western Europe, Russia
Yemen	60,000 Army 1,700 Navy 3,000 Air Force 2,000 Air Defence 66,700 Total	6.8	$2,200,000,000 Russia, China, Western Europe, Other Europe

Sophisticated missile and delivery systems proved less useful than mobile policing in the unconventional operations against small cells of radicalised militants that characterised the major threat to regional security after 2003. This carried echoes of Saudi Arabia's reliance on the United States, rather than its own record of heavy military expenditure and arms imports, as effective deterrence against a putative Iraqi invasion in 1990–91.

Together these hard and soft security measures greatly diminished the capability (if not necessarily the intent) of terrorist organisations in the GCC. However, they did not entirely succeed in eradicating the threat altogether. Jihadist websites continue to proliferate and spread their messages and facilitate communications between different groups and organisations.[100] Terrorist finances remain a threat, particularly in Dubai, which has emerged as one of the global conduits for organised trans-national criminal and terrorist networks and remains a preferred site of political and targeted assassinations.[101] Moreover, the return of foreign insurgents from Iraq and released militants from Guantanamo Bay has introduced a new dynamic into the regional security environment that local officials acknowledge will remain a latent risk for many years to come.[102] These trends intersected in March 2008 when a recent Kuwaiti returnee from Guantanamo Bay, Abdullah Salim Ali Al-'Amii, carried out a suicide bombing in Mosul that killed thirteen Iraqi soldiers and wounded forty-two more.[103]

The prospective return of veterans from the Iraqi insurgency is one of two factors that raise the prospect of a second destabilising wave of trans-national terrorism afflicting the GCC. The other is the reconstitution of Al-Qaeda in the Arabian Peninsula in Yemen, in January 2009. This confirmed the fears of regional security officials that the apparently successful counter-terrorism campaign in the GCC merely displaced the terrorist threat to the under-governed periphery of the Arabian Peninsula.[104] The emergence of two Saudi returnees from Guantanamo Bay in leadership positions in the new organisation, which itself represented a merger between the Saudi and Yemeni 'wings' of Al-Qaeda, exposed the inherent weaknesses in the regional and international security responses to the challenge of trans-national terrorism. Both Saud Al-Shihri and Muhammad al-Awfi spent five months in Saudi Arabia's rehabilitation and counter-radicalisation centres before being deemed ready for re-integration into society in May 2008.[105] Their subsequent disappearance, and reappearance in Yemen, damaged the credibility of the Saudi programmes and also demonstrated how the existence of security gaps in Yemen blunted the efficacy of GCC counter-terrorism measures.[106]

This contraction of state control and faltering political economy in Yemen further illustrates the complex interconnections between the internal and external dimensions of Gulf security structures. Yemen faces the most imminent transition toward a post-oil era with its oil reserves expected to deplete by about 2017 at present rates of extraction and barring any unexpected new discoveries.[107] The difficulties of this transition will be examined at length in chapter seven of this book. From a counter-terrorism perspective, however, its faltering political economy presents the most intractable challenge to the security and stability of the Arabian Peninsula, and in many ways offers a troubling insight into how the troubled transition away from an oil-dependent economy might play out elsewhere in the future.

Saudi Arabia and the other GCC states face a renewed challenge from terrorist infiltration and weapons smuggling from Yemen, as terrorist organisations regroup and reorganise in the country. The scale of the problem became clear in May 2008 when Yemen's vice-president, Abd al-Rab Mansur Al-Hadi, claimed that 16,000 suspected members of Al-Qaeda had been expelled from Yemen since 2003. This figure included many 'Arab Afghans' who had fled Afghanistan for Saudi Arabia following the overthrow of the Taliban in 2001, and subsequently moved to Yemen to avoid capture by Saudi security forces.[108] Despite these arrests, plots and cells continued to be uncovered in Yemen during 2008, including a Yemeni-led cell linked to Al-Qaeda that was planning to attack oil installation facilities in the Eastern Province of Saudi Arabia.[109] This was reminiscent of Al-Qaeda's failed attack in February 2006 at Abqaiq and highlighted the vulnerability of Saudi Arabia's 1800 kilometre border with Yemen to infiltration.[110]

The coordinated attack on the US embassy compound in the Yemeni capital, Sana'a, on 17 September 2008, which killed ten people, marked the start of the 'second generation' of trans-national terrorism in the Arabian Peninsula. This assault meshed the threats to security from Iraq, Al-Qaeda and the growing lawlessness in Yemen itself. Three of the six suicide bombers had recently returned from Iraq, and following their arrival in Yemen reportedly attended Al-Qaeda training camps in the southern provinces of Hadramawt and Ma'arib.[111] Yemeni security officials already suspected these camps of training an aggressive new generation of extremist leaders and jihadi foot-soldiers.[112] Earlier, in February 2006, twenty-three suspected members of Al-Qaeda, including several linked to the bombing of USS Cole in 2000, had escaped from the Political Security Central Prison in Sana'a.[113] Together with the relocation of extremists from Saudi Arabia and the growing incidence of militant flows linking Yemen to the Islamist insurgents of Al-Shabaab in Somalia, they represent a deadly new threat to internal security in Yemen and regional stability in the Arabian Peninsula.[114]

Following the official reconstitution of Al-Qaeda in the Arabian Peninsula in January 2009, policymakers and security analysts in the West and in the GCC began to pay greater attention to the systemic and interconnected crises in Yemen.[115] Moreover, it acquired regional and international dimensions as the group demonstrated both its intent and its capability to undertake terrorist operations beyond Yemen's borders. An early indication of the growing trans-national dimension to regional instability came in March 2009 when it emerged that a Yemeni suicide bomber who killed four South Korean tourists at the UNESCO World Heritage Site of Shibam had trained in Somalia before returning to Yemen to carry out his attack.[116] Other flows of militants and weaponry between Yemen and Somalia culminated in the Somali defence minister accusing Yemeni fighters of sending two boatloads of weapons to Somalia in December 2009 with the intention of 'fuelling the flames in a country already burning.'[117] The regionalisation of localised conflicts thus introduces the problem of state collapse in Somalia and the multiple drivers of conflict and insecurity in the wider Horn of Africa region firmly into the Arabian Peninsula security equation.[118]

The resurgence of Al-Qaeda in the Arabian Peninsula highlighted the new threat to regional stability from the overspill of violence from Yemen. This was highlighted in its official pronouncements and choice of targets, including a new plot to attack oil installation facilities in Saudi Arabia by a cell consisting of forty-seven Saudis and fifty-one Yemenis that was uncovered in March 2010.[119] It came close to assassinating the Saudi Arabian deputy minister of the interior, Mohammed bin Nayef in August 2009. This audacious plot penetrated the heart of the Saudi security establishment and starkly demonstrated the direct linkages between the security gaps in Yemen and insecurity elsewhere in the peninsula. The would-be assassin, twenty-three-year old Saudi national Abdullah Asiri, featured on a list of eighty-five 'most-wanted' terror suspects issued by Saudi security forces in February 2009. After receiving training in Yemen, he returned to the kingdom and gained access to the Prince, the architect of Saudi Arabia's counter-terrorist strategy, by claiming he wished to personally renounce his links to terrorism.[120]

Such a brazen and high-profile attack on a senior member of the Saudi ruling family was unprecedented in the recent history of transnational terrorism in the Arabian Peninsula. It visibly emphasised the direct linkages between the contraction of state power and legitimacy in Yemen and the security and stability of neighbouring states. The situation then became militarised in November 2009 after fighters belonging to the Houthi separatist group of Zaydi Shiites in northern Yemen crossed the international boundary and attacked a Saudi border position.[121] During the air and ground operations that followed, which constituted their largest mobilisation of force since the 1991 Gulf War, Saudi forces took relatively heavy casualties of eighty-two dead and more than 470 injured. However, they conspicuously failed to end the fighting in spite of repeated assertions that they had dislodged the fighters from Saudi territory.[122] Although Saudi forces declared victory in late January 2010, the prolonged operation and high losses inflicted a damaging blow to the kingdom's military credibility.[123] The fighting also gave credence to a regional discourse that portrayed the campaign in terms of a battle for influence between Saudi Arabia and Iran, as Saudi and Yemeni officials accused Teheran of providing (unsubstantiated) assistance to the Houthi rebels, who have been fighting the central government intermittently since 2004.[124]

The failed bombing of a Northwest Airlines jet *en route* from Amsterdam to Detroit on Christmas Day 2009 catapulted the issue of transnational terrorism originating in Yemen up the international agenda. Although Umar Farouk Abdulmutallab was a Nigerian who may have become radicalised while studying for an undergraduate degree at University College London, he spent four months in Yemen immediately prior to the attack, for which Al-Qaeda in the Arabian Peninsula claimed responsibility.[125] It took American intelligence and security agencies completely by surprise, as they had expected any terrorist attack on the US homeland to originate in Afghanistan or Pakistan rather than Yemen.[126] Al-Qaeda in the Arabian Peninsula's demonstration of both its intent and capability to target the United States internationalised the issue and led to its rapid securitisation as a perceived threat to global security. The London meeting on Yemen that occurred on 27 January 2010 and the follow-up that occurred in Riyadh a month later thus marked the beginning of a new phase of international engagement with Yemen and its regional partners in the GCC.[127]

Nevertheless, the priority on counter-terrorism as the frame of reference for international engagement in Yemen opens up a range of troubling new drivers of conflict. Central to this is the channelling of international support (and legitimacy) to a state that has lost much of its domestic legitimacy and experienced two major challenges to its authority.[128] Separatists in southern Yemen and the Houthi rebels in the north-west actively reject the continuation of the political status quo as represented by President Ali Abdullah Saleh, who has been in power since 1978. This deep-rooted opposition manifested itself in expressions of dismay and anger by Yemeni opposition groups that they had not been invited to the conference, which maintained a rigorously state-centric focus.[129] Measures to combat the spread of Al-Qaeda taken in isolation from the complex interplay of factors that led Yemen to the precipice of failed statehood run the risk of aggravating the centrifugal forces that undermined state control and legitimacy in the first place.

New Dimensions of Gulf Security

Regional awareness of the extent of the systemic crises facing Yemen, as well as their implications, heightened throughout 2009 and into 2010. The regionalisation and internationalisation of Yemen-based instability began to stimulate a strategic reassessment of the range of responses from GCC member-states.[130] This conversation gathered pace with their participation in the London meeting, and the decision to host the follow-up meeting at the GCC headquarters in Riyadh. Simultaneously, the GCC Secretary-General, Abdulrahman Al-Attiya, emphasised that the issues of security, stability and development in Yemen were vital to GCC interests.[131] GCC aid already represented some 60 per cent of total assistance provided to Yemen before 2010, but its effectiveness was diluted by capacity and oversight constraints on both sides. Only 7 per cent of a $4 billion aid package promised at a donor meeting in November 2006 had been forthcoming by the January 2010 London meeting, although this figure was not atypical for aid delivery figures from other regions.[132]

It is in the GCC states' interest that Yemen not collapse into failed statehood. Should this happen, it would present a multifaceted danger to their internal security and external stability, and expose the GCC to the multiple sources of human insecurity emanating from the Horn of Africa-Yemen nexus.[133] The difficulty, if not impossibility, of sealing borders and containing problems in the era of global processes and flows means that a strategy of containment is not a sustainable, long-term policy. Yet this is precisely what individual Gulf States initially attempted to do, with Saudi security officials commissioning an elaborate system of border security installations as part of a broader strategy to contain the overspill of instability from Yemen.[134] It reflected a dominant view among Gulf officials that the region was 'an island of stability in a sea of instability' which needed protecting against the multiple sources of external insecurity, as well as a feeling that the scale and complexity of Yemeni problems were such that keeping them at a distance was preferable to getting too closely involved.[135]

The international spotlight on Yemen signals an opportunity for the Gulf States to take the lead in any new approach to tackling its interconnected problems. This requires the GCC states, both individually and at a collective level, to better conceptualise the systemic nature of the crisis facing Yemen, and formulate nuanced and targeted responses.[136] The primary difficulty facing the Gulf States is one of balancing the need to extend substantive political and economic assistance without linking it to Yemeni admission to the GCC.[137] This remains unrealistic for the foreseeable future for political, economic and historical reasons. Also unfeasible in the short- to medium-term is the issue of opening up GCC labour markets to Yemeni migrant workers. Such a move would run counter to three decades of Gulf States' measures to depoliticise and thoroughly control their labour forces. It would expose GCC labour markets and their societies at large to potentially highly-politicised migrants, and reawaken memories of the 1950s and 1960s when Yemeni, Palestinian and Egyptian workers acted as transmission belts of political opposition to the Gulf monarchies.[138]

What is required is a comprehensive approach that repairs and strengthens fractured state-society relations in Yemen. The deteriorating internal security situation is both a cause and a consequence of the erosion of state credibility. It represents the most significant short- and medium-term challenge to the stability of Arabian Peninsula, and carries grave consequences for the GCC if left unchecked or inadequately tackled. It needs a sustained and long-term engagement at the regional as well as international level. Anything less would be nothing more

than a temporary stopgap that would carry the risk of merely exacerbating the existing tensions and fault-lines within Yemen and its envi-
rons. The overlapping linkages between Yemen and the Horn of Africa
therefore call for a reassessment of policy on the part of the Gulf States
and their partners in the international community, and for policymakers to acknowledge that a strategy of containment through hard security measures is no longer a viable option, if it ever was, and construct
a nuanced and collective policymaking framework that addresses all
Yemen's problems rather than focusing merely on counter-terrorism.

A Paradigm in Transition

Developments in Iraq and Iran, as well as Yemen and elsewhere, will
continue to powerfully delineate the local parameters of Gulf security
structures, although at this point in time Iran and Iraq's historical
legacy of past physical and ideological threat outstrips their hard military power. Nevertheless, the internal unrest in each country retains
the capacity to inject destabilising flows of men, materiel and ideology
into the Arabian Peninsula. Moreover, and particularly in Iran, the
combination of domestic instability and international pressure could
result in the regime lashing out in an attempt to re-legitimise or retali-
ate against any perceived or actual external effort to rein it in. Post-
occupation dynamics in Iraq, too, could challenge regional security
structures if a future Iraqi regime builds up its military capabilities and
re-enters the Gulf domain, as numerous points of tension remain unresolved, notably with Kuwait. In addition, the failed attempt by the
Al-Qaeda-linked Abdullah Azzam Brigades to sink the Japanese tanker
M-Star in the Strait of Hormuz in July 2010 constituted a stark
reminder of the region's vulnerability to acts of terrorism targeting the
smooth functioning of hydrocarbons-based exports. Particularly noteworthy was the realisation that the attack was launched from the Arabian coast of the Gulf (in Oman), as well as the substitution of an
actual attack by a militant organisation for the hitherto rhetorical
threats from the Revolutionary Guards to close the Gulf in the event
of military strikes on Iran.

Nevertheless, the evolving security paradigm will increasingly cover
non-traditional and non-military threats that target the security of
individuals and communities as well as states and regimes. The unravelling of the Yemeni polity reflects the complex interplay of socio-po-

litical and economic difficulties with the imminent depletion of natural resources and regime legitimacy. It demonstrates how each individual problem feeds off the others and acts as a threat multiplier that has assumed inter-regional and international dimensions and constitutes the most urgent security challenge to the stability of the Arabian Peninsula. This will be examined in detail in chapter six, while the second section of this book picks up the theme of these new and emerging challenges and integrates them into the study of the changing security paradigm as the region begins the difficult shift to a post-oil framework of governance.

3

CONTEXTUAL PARAMETERS
AND FUTURE TRENDS

The dynamics of Gulf security are in constant flux, with the region having endured three major inter-state wars in three decades and facing continuing instability on its periphery. This rapidly-changing external environment contrasts with the apparent ossification of internal structures at both the domestic and GCC levels. At the individual country level, the ruling families' grip on power survived the limited political liberalisation projects that began to take shape in the late 1990s and early 2000s. Collectively, the Gulf Cooperation Council has taken measures to deepen its integrative process, but it remains primarily a defensive bulwark against the multiple sources of insecurity on its boundaries.[1] Nevertheless, the parameters of Gulf security are shifting in subtle ways that encompass longer-term and increasingly military threats and challenges. These are intertwined with the impact of globalisation and the transformation of the Gulf States' political economy as they move toward post-rentier forms of governance.

Over the coming years and decades, the evolution of Gulf security dynamics will be shaped by four macro-factors. These are the globalising flows of information, people and money that frequently bypass state structures and erode the distinction between the domestic and foreign policymaking realms. The internationalisation of the Gulf together with its repositioning within the global order by virtue of its energy reserves and financial resources; the continuing dominance of hydrocarbons in shaping inter- and intra-state and societal relations albeit at increasingly divergent paces; and the absence of strong centripetal forces within the

63

GCC itself, which inhibits moves to develop common policies on issues such as Iraq, Iran and Yemen. Underpinning all of these factors is the cognitive shift in thinking about global security in an era of accelerating complexity of global interconnections and the broadening and deepening of security agendas since the 1990s.[2]

These shifts in global discourse frame the challenges facing the states of the Gulf. It is noteworthy, however, that they are not matched by similar thinking within the states themselves. Approaches to national and regional security remain predicated largely on realist approaches to security, and it is notable that the attempt to formulate a collective security policy within the GCC failed to take off in any meaningful way. Although there is some awareness, particularly in Kuwait, of the need to take steps toward reducing dependence on oil and its regime of perverse economic incentives, there is very little consensus on the practical measures and political coalition-building that would be necessary to achieve this.[3] Elsewhere in the region, as for example in Dubai, policymaking is largely formulated on an 'ad hoc' basis that simply does not factor in the long-term implications of any particular policy.[4]

This chapter explores the contextual parameters that will confront policymakers in the Gulf States as they move toward the post-oil era. It sets the scene for the three chapters in part two of the book as they examine in detail these emerging and non-military challenges to security. More specifically, the chapters that follow examine how regimes are anticipating and adapting to shifts in the concept and paradigm of security. A constructivist approach focuses on the decisions made by policymakers and the environment within which they must operate. It locates and identifies the drivers of policy and motivations of decision-makers the agency in analysing how and why issues become securitised or not. This is an important caveat in the study of foreign and security policies in the Gulf States, where issues become personalised and the circle of officialdom is relatively limited. For these reasons, discursive study is a valuable analytical tool in the study of policy formulation in the Gulf States, particularly as the emergence of significant non-state actors and trans-national, supra- and sub-state issues all temper the utility of realist approaches to policy formulation and analysis.

New Approaches to Global Security

Concepts of security have shifted substantially in recent decades. The process began during the Cold War but accelerated sharply following its ending in 1989. It occurred alongside the great intensification of global interconnectedness and the stretching of power and authority across multiple layers of global governance.[5] The confluence of these two trends prompted a major reassessment of the concept of national and global security, and their relationship to each other. During the 1990s and 2000s, 'global issues' such as climate change emerged on the international agenda, alongside existing problems of trans-national terrorism, cross-border criminal networks and flows, and the threat posed by nuclear proliferation and state breakdown.[6] These new, 'non-conventional' threats formed the basis for the 2004 *United Nations High-Level Report on Threats, Challenges and Change* as it broadened the focus of security policy to take them into account. Three years later, in April 2007, the UN Security Council discussed for the first time the international security implications of climate change. It identified a range of potential threats to international peace and security from a climate-stressed world, including border disputes, the movement of 'environmental refugees,' clashes over access to dwindling resources, societal strains, and humanitarian crises occurring from extreme weather events such as Hurricane Katrina that devastated New Orleans in August 2005.[7]

Other approaches to security (and also development) take human development, global governance, or human security as their starting-point. The 1994 United Nations Development Programme (UNDP) *Human Development Report* and the 1995 Commission on Global Governance both made the case for a radical, universal, re-conceptualisation of security. The Human Development Report first elucidated the concept of 'human security,' concerned with the security of individuals and communities rather than that of states, as it noted that the concept of security 'for too long has been interpreted narrowly...It has been related more to nation states than to people.'[8] Meanwhile, the Global Governance report, entitled *Our Common Neighbourhood*, argued that 'The concept of global security must be broadened from the traditional focus on the security of states, to include the security of people and the security of the planet.'[9]

More recently, the series of Arab Human Development Reports issued by the UNDP since 2002 culminated in the publication of the fifth report in 2009, entitled *Challenges to Human Security in the Arab Countries*. This asked why, seven years after the first Arab Human Development Report, 'have obstacles to human development in the region proved so stubborn,' and concluded that 'the answers lie in the fragility of the region's political, social, economic and environmental structures, in its lack of people-centric development policies and in its vulnerability to outside intervention.'[10] The report was released just months after the Arab Women's Organisation themed its biennial conference on women and human security. Participants at the event in November 2008 worked on constructing a human security strategy embracing women as equal participants and contributors.[11] These reflect the growing appeal of the concept of human security as a foundation-stone for constructing a new security paradigm for meeting the interlinked challenges of a globalising polity, although, as the conclusion to this book makes clear, they face considerable obstacles to their implementation in the regional-specific context of the Gulf.

The re-conceptualisation of what security 'is' and 'does' has overseen a broadening and deepening of the global security agenda to encompass new and emerging threats. Increasingly, these are longer-term and non-conventional, and they embed the study of security problems firmly within the broader political and socio-economic context of development. Moreover, the impact of globalising processes has led to the emergence of non-state actors and trans-national, increasingly 'global' issues. Their empowering effects have been both positive and negative, with the rise of trans-national terrorism represented by Al-Qaeda the prime example of the latter. This, and other manifestations of Kaldor's theory of 'regressive globalism,' including illicit flows of money, human trafficking and drugs, represent challenges that transcend national boundaries and bypass state structures.[12]

The rise of non-state and trans-national threats to security presents a paradox to realist assumptions of state primacy in the realm of international relations. States remain the central actors, particularly in the GCC, where the conduct of foreign and security affairs is restricted to tightly-drawn circles of senior members of the ruling families.[13] Yet they now confront an array of non-state actors and processes, following programmes that do not reflect a coherent 'national' vision, including multinational corporations, trans-national networks and diaspora ethnic and religious groups. Hence, in the era of globalisation and transnationalism, states no longer are the sole actors and shapers of policy.[14] This challenges realist frameworks and requires a new conceptual approach that takes into consideration the range of factors that inform decision-makers' perceptions of their own security matrix. Hence, a constructivist approach makes it possible to determine which issues do or do not make it on to security agendas, and why this is so.

The remainder of this chapter documents the global rebalancing of power and the emerging parameters through which Gulf security will evolve over coming decades. This broader conception of the idea of what security entails sets the scene for the second part of this book, in which the focus shifts to an analysis of three major trajectories that will significantly alter the evolution of Gulf security over the course of the twenty-first century. These are the impact of demographic trends and structural imbalances within Gulf economies; resource scarcities and inequalities in patterns of distribution; and the stresses imposed by climate change and environmental degradation. All of these will frame the eventual transition toward a post-oil future and constitute very different types of security threats than hitherto faced.

The Global Rebalancing

The continuing acceleration of global interconnectedness is dramatically transforming the global order and reconfiguring notions of state power and political authority. It involves re-thinking the concept of political community into a distinctive form of 'global politics' that operates beyond the sphere of the individual nation-state.[15] A multi-dimensional and poly-centric system of governance developed to govern the globalising processes. This combined sub- and supra-state agencies alongside existing national and inter-state frameworks of governance.[16] In late-2008, the rapid spread of the global financial crisis from its origins in the sub-prime markets of the United States powerfully demonstrated the linkages that bound Gulf economies inextricably to broader global processes.[17] The crisis also made clear to governments throughout the world, including the GCC, their stake in participating in a global recovery and reshaping the institutional architecture to adapt to the new realities of the twenty-first century. However, the first major test of the 'global politics' in action, at the 2009 United Nations Climate Change Conference in Copenhagen, demonstrated the enduring difficulty of reconciling competing national interests with a common identification with the notion of a 'global commons.'[18]

These broader global linkages are mirrored by the revolution in information and communication technologies. This has created new forms of private, public and increasingly virtual spaces in which to mobilise, organise and channel societal demands, in spite of GCC regimes' efforts to delimit and regulate the kinds of openings possible.[19] For example, political bloggers were active discussants during the parliamentary elections in Bahrain in November 2006, Kuwait in May 2008 and May 2009, and the bitterly-contested Iranian presidential election in June 2009.[20] Meanwhile, online networking sites such as Facebook have been embraced by a younger generation of activists who use them for debate and the coordination of activities, unencumbered by state security restrictions on the gathering and conduct of political or activist meetings. In addition, they serve as sites for meeting members of the opposite gender in places such as Saudi Arabia where this would otherwise be circumscribed.[21] Rapid technological advances in wireless mobile devices equipped with cameras further erode boundaries over the control of the flow of information, and make it virtually impossible for officials to suppress public discussion of sensitive or proscribed issues.

In addition, the GCC states find themselves enmeshed in a transformative rebalancing of the global balance of geo-economic power from west to east. Although this has been underway for several years, the global financial and economic crisis in 2008–9 hastened the shift as Asian economies led the world out of recession and recovered market share at the expense of Western competitors. Indeed, the International Monetary Fund estimates that by 2030 the Asian economy will be larger than the United States and European Union combined, and will increase its regional share of world GDP from under 30 per cent to more than 40 per cent.[22] This will have profound implications for institutions of global governance and the relative weight accorded within them. Already, the Gulf States, led by Saudi Arabia's membership of the G20, have started to exert greater influence in reshaping the post-1945 multilateral institutions, in part by thickening their ties with other emerging nations such as China, Russia and India.[23] Ties of energy and food security play a vital role in this deepening relationship and create new linkages that increasingly are opening up a gap between new economic realignments and the Gulf States' continuing reliance on the Western security umbrella.

Shifting Parameters of Gulf Security

Thus globalisation and geo-economic change have enmeshed the Gulf States within a wider interconnected region with multiple ideational and latent physical threats to security. These range from the Israeli-Palestinian conflict and the fallout from Israel's wars of aggression in the west to the threat of nuclear proliferation and armed sub- and intra-state conflict in Iran and Pakistan to the east.[24] Furthermore, the ease of communication and travel now means that the rise of trans-national terrorism in Afghanistan and Pakistan poses a direct threat to the GCC states through the recruitment of personnel and flows of illicit funding in both directions.[25] In particular, the spread of Arabic-language satellite television stations and internet websites has enhanced popular awareness of these 'Islamic' issues that transcend national boundaries and bypass state structures of control.[26] Saudi Arabia had long functioned as a linchpin for the spread of trans-national loyalties and allegiances couched in the language of Islam. These often were not under state (or state-sponsored) control, and their penetrative reach and expansionist potential widened with the spreading of oil wealth and the revolution in information communications and technology (ICT).[27] The contrast between the openness and visibility of the new flows of communications and peoples with previous efforts to keep these under tight state control is profound, and potentially transformational in its impact on the political economy and security of the region.[28]

This links directly to the second contextual factor that will shape the evolution of Gulf security. This is the internationalisation of the Gulf and its emergence as the centre of gravity in the Middle East by virtue of its energy reserves and financial resources. Together, the GCC states account for about 19 per cent of global crude oil production and 8 per cent of the total output of natural gas. In addition, they hold about 37 per cent of proven oil reserves and 25 per cent of proven natural gas reserves globally, with Saudi Arabia having the world's largest oil reserves and Qatar the world's third-largest natural gas holdings.[29] These reserves give the GCC states enormous influence in intergovernmental organisations such as OPEC, as well as in bilateral deals with partner countries seeking to meet their energy security requirements. Moreover, the Gulf States have acquired the confidence and capability to enter the global policymaking arena as major participants in reshaping existing and emerging frameworks of governance. Qatar has been notably successful in using the export of liquefied natural gas from its immense North Field (the largest non-associated gas field in the world) as leverage in its projection of influence at the regional and international levels.[30] The country has also invested the resulting revenues in a strategy that has significantly enhanced Qatar's global 'branding.'[31] It did this through a number of high-profile acquisitions through the state investment arm, Qatar Holding LLC. These included a substantial acquisition of Barclays Bank shares at the height of the financial crisis in 2008 and an iconic 10 per cent purchase of Porsche in August 2009 as well as the acquisition of the flagship Harrods department store in London in May 2010.[32]

Qatar's greater visibility and confidence on the global stage has been matched by Abu Dhabi, Dubai (until the spectacular implosion of its business model in 2008–9) and, to a lesser extent, Saudi Arabia. The combination of their energy reserves and strategic investments both solidified and expanded the economic and political linkages between the Gulf States and China, India and Russia. These are shifting the international relations of the Gulf in subtle yet significant ways and introducing a plethora of new actors with a strategic interest in regional stability and security. Although the political and security alliance with the United States and other western powers continues to underpin the external security guarantee of the GCC states, the eastward shift in focus is gathering momentum and taking on new dimensions. This holds significant implications for the geo-political and economic orientation of the Gulf States and their position within the changing balance of global power. In addition, it reveals an emerging disconnect between the eastward orientation of economic and commercial linkages and the continuing political and security interdependence with the western powers, most notably the United States.

Indian Prime Minister Manmohan Singh visited the Gulf in November 2008 and announced that India viewed the region as an intrinsic part of its broader neighbourhood. Energy security considerations lay behind this statement, as India imports 75 per cent of its total oil requirements, of which 80 per cent of those come from the Gulf States. The sharp increase in the price of oil in 2008 alarmed Indian policymakers and contributed to a decision to move beyond reliance on imported oil to seek 'equity access to foreign oil and gas reserves and achieve strategic energy security.'[33] This decision, important in itself, also enhanced the importance of maritime security in ensuring stable and uninterrupted access to oil and gas supplies from the Gulf. Other areas of joint security concern for India and its partners in the GCC include the safety and security of the four million Indian workers in the GCC, in addition to a shared interest in dismantling trans-national terrorist networks that have carried out major attacks in both regions in recent years. The myriad linkages binding India and the Gulf in a globalising environment were encapsulated in a speech by Prime Minister Singh to mark the inauguration of the Centre for West Asian Studies at Jamia Millia Islamia University in New Delhi in January 2005:

Ongoing processes in West Asia will have a critical impact on the global strategic environment. Strategic thinkers the world over will weigh the possible impact of the large and growing extra-regional military presence in West Asia, or the possibility of radical religious groups seeking to create and fill a political vacuum in this region. Needless to say, the impact of any negative development on India will transcend the obvious political and security repercussions; it will also greatly affect our economy, with our energy security strategy being the first to come under threat.[34]

Significantly, in a move that marked the re-emergence of Indian influence in the Gulf six decades after the decline of the Raj and following an extended period of frigidity between the 1970s and early 1990s, India also signed defence cooperation agreements with Qatar and Oman, covering maritime security, the sharing of data, and common threat perceptions.[35] More significantly, in view of its leading role in the GCC, this emerging partnership was followed by the signing of the Riyadh Declaration in February 2010, in which India and Saudi Arabia upgraded their bilateral relationship into a Strategic Partnership. This ushered in a 'new era based on economic engagement and emerging opportunities' that covered the security, defence, economic and energy arenas. It built upon King Abdullah bin Abdul Aziz's successful visit to India in 2006 and was motivated in part by a strategic reassessment of Saudi regional ties prompted by the threat to stability emanating from Yemen, Afghanistan and Pakistan.[36] However, Indian diplomats have also expressed their unease at China's rapid emergence as a major actor in the Gulf, and gone so far as to state that 'China's proactive focus on expanding ties with the region presents a growing challenge to India... Geo-economics is increasingly going to determine geopolitics.'[37] Nor have India or China yet formulated a grand strategy with regard to the other, and as their dependence on oil and gas from the Gulf States increases, this may become a flashpoint of future tensions.[38]

These growing interests were also reflected in China's tenth Five-Year Plan (2001–5), which referred specifically to energy security for the first time.[39] China has additionally constructed a major naval base at the Pakistani deep-water port of Gwadur. This opened in 2005 and became fully operational in 2008, and provides China with a transit terminal for crude oil imports from Iran and Africa en route to its Xinjiang region. Its broader significance is that it gives China a strategic base on the Arabian Sea, a mere 400 kilometres from the entrance to the Strait of Hormuz, from which it can protect its vital energy security interests and monitor maritime traffic entering and leaving the Gulf.[40] Its emerging blue-water capabilities took another step forward in March 2010 when two Chinese warships docked in Abu Dhabi's Port Zayed following their completion of a six-month mission combating maritime piracy in the Gulf of Aden. Their visit marked the first-ever Chinese naval visit to the Gulf and visibly reflected China's growing capability to protect its interests overseas. Significantly, the Chinese Ambassador to the United Arab Emirates, Gao Yu Sheng, highlighted China's constructive stake in Gulf stability, as he stated that 'Maintaining security in the Gulf is vital to the area and the world, including China.'[41]

China's interest in the Gulf coincided with a major rethinking in Beijing of the concept of energy security, brought on by anxieties at the country's increasing reliance on imported energy supplies. An integral part of this domestic debate concerns the naval capabilities and force projection necessary to ensure China's maritime security of access to overseas energy supplies. High-ranking officials of the People's Liberation Army Navy (PLAN) have emerged as advocates for an enhanced 'Far Sea Defence' (*yuanhai fangwei*) policy. Thus the PLAN deputy political commissar, Yao Wenhuai, argued in December 2007 that China's dependence on seaborne energy imports required a powerful navy to defend its strategic interests:

Particularly for oil and other key strategic supplies, our dependence on sea transport is very great, and ensuring the security of strategic seaways is extremely important. We must fully recognise the actual requirements of protecting our country's developmental interests at sea, fully recognise the security threats our country faces at sea, and fully recognise the special status and utility of our navy in preparing for military conflict.[42]

Although the outcome of Chinese domestic debates are still to be determined, they nevertheless depict an awareness of China's global responsibilities, although in the immediate-term this is likely to be tempered by Chinese officials' preoccupation with domestic consolidation and stability.[43] It is thus too early to state definitively whether China's and India's new security projection toward the Gulf will substantively alter the regional dynamics, although they are trends that complement their strengthening energy interdependencies and will intensify with time.

Russia, too, started to expand its political and economic linkages with the Gulf in general, and reinforced its ties to fellow gas producer Qatar, and Saudi Arabia, in particular. Then-President Vladimir Putin's visit to Saudi Arabia and Qatar in February 2007 was the first by a Soviet or post-Soviet leader since diplomatic relations were restored following the end of the Cold War. The trip was designed to boost joint investment opportunities and cooperation with fellow energy producing countries.[44] It also constituted part of a wider Russian strategic objective to increase its role in the Middle East and become one of the key actors in any new regional security system that might emerge.[45] On Saudi Arabia's side it reflected an attempt by King Abdullah to strengthen ties with Russia as part of a general diversification to reduce dependence on the United States after September 11, 2001. The relationship assumed regional geopolitical implications in 2009–10 with Saudi-Russian negotiations over the possible purchase of a $4 billion air-defence missile system, in part to induce Moscow not to proceed with the sale of such advanced weaponry to Iran.[46] Russian-Qatari ties also coalesced around cooperation in the Gas Exporting Countries' Forum and bilateral agreements such as one reached in April 2010 to develop Russia's Arctic gas reserves in the Yamal peninsula.[47]

In addition to Russia and China's emergence as economic powers in the Gulf and India's re-entry into the region is Turkey's reorientation toward the Middle East. This carries a historical legacy both in Turkey itself, which moved away from the region and toward Europe under Ataturk and his Kemalist successors, and among its former imperial possessions in the Arabian Peninsula. It is in part a structural realignment of Turkish foreign policy as well as a reaction to repeated rebuffs to its aspirations to join the European Union. Especially since the Justice and Development (AK) Party took office in 2002, the term neo-Ottomanism has been used to describe Turkey's apparent reassertion of regional power in the Middle East. During recent years, Turkey has strengthened its previously-cool relationships in the Middle East and deepened its commercial ties with Saudi Arabia and Iran, in particular.[48] Although oil and gas play a central role, economic links are thickening and diversifying, with the announcement of a fifteen-year agreement between Türk Telekomünikasyon and Saudi Arabia, Syria and Jordan to carry fibre-optic traffic between Europe and the Middle East a prominent recent example.[49]

More significant geopolitically was the tripartite Turkish-Brazilian-Iranian agreement reached in May 2010 concerning the swapping of low-enriched uranium for medically-suitable fuel rods. This attempt by two of the leading emerging powers to take their own initiative and try to resolve the stand-off between Iran and the international (US-led) community received cautious approval from Russia and China but was criticised in the United States (and Israel) for undermining the sanctions-based policy approach.[50] Two weeks later, the Gaza flotilla incident, in which the Israeli Defence Force boarded the *Mavi Marmara* in international waters and killed nine activists attempting to breach the Israeli blockade of Gaza, provided further evidence of the broadening and diversification of Turkish policy toward the Middle East. The six-ship Gaza Freedom Flotilla was organised by a Turkish Islamic charity, and Turkish outrage over the deaths of its citizens accelerated an ongoing strategic reassessment of Turkey's regional interests.

The 2010 Arab Public Opinion Poll conducted shortly after the flotilla incident appeared to confirm the reality of Turkey's 'return' to the Middle East. By a wide margin Prime Minister Recep Tayyip Erdogan was voted the most popular individual in the Middle East, well ahead of second-placed Ahmedinejad and the Secretary General of Hezbollah, Hassan Nasrallah, in third.[51] Yet Turkey's re-emergence in its former colonial hinterland does awaken resentment at its former hegemony in the Arabian Peninsula, which public references to neo-Ottomanism have done little to dispel.[52] Much will depend on whether the structural factors that underpin Turkey's reorientation toward the Middle East remain focused primarily on economic and investment agreements or seek to develop a more muscular security dimension outside of the framework of the NATO-led Istanbul Cooperation Initiative. Any such move would likely provoke feelings of scepticism, bordering on hostility, from popular and political opinion in the GCC, motivated by historical memories of occupation and lingering mutual perceptions of mistrust.[53]

The proliferation of powerful external actors in the Gulf presents both an opportunity and a challenge to the evolution of Gulf security structures. On the one hand, energy interdependencies give these powerful states a considerable stake in maintaining a functioning degree of regional security and stability. The realignment of geo-economic power toward Asia may also provide China, Russia, India and Turkey with a degree of leverage toward the United States that lessens the prospect of future unilateral and destabilising American military interventions in the region. This could prevent a repeat of the catastrophically ill-judged invasion and occupation of Iraq in the context of American and Israeli sabre-rattling toward Iran. The flip side of the coin is that future competition for increasingly scarce energy reserves could result in intra-regional relations being characterised more by confrontation than cooperation. In this pessimistic scenario, the introduction of multiple actors into the Gulf may become destabilising if resource security and escalating energy requirements induce them to become more assertive in their bilateral dealings with the region.

Issues of energy interdependence and security of access to resources thus give external actors an interest in regional security structures. To this end, international reactions to the burgeoning incidence of piracy in the Gulf of Aden that accelerated sharply from 2008 may prove a harbinger of future policy trends. The European Union launched its first-ever naval mission (Operation Atalanta) in November 2008 in response to more than 100 acts of piracy against international shipping, including the seizure of the fully-laden Saudi super-tanker *Sirius Star*.[54] It has a mandate to protect deliveries of food aid by the World Food Programme to Somalia, as well as other vulnerable vessels transiting the Gulf of Aden, within the framework of the European Security and Defence Policy.[55] Significantly, many other countries, including China, India, Russia and Iran, also deployed their own warships to protect energy security interests in the Gulf of Aden. The People's Liberation Army Navy dispatched two destroyers and a supply ship in order to protect the 1200 Chinese ships that pass through the region each year. Similar to the EU, it marked a first, in this instance the debut operational mission undertaken by Chinese naval forces outside of East Asia.[56]

With the Gulf region's share of global oil and natural gas production projected to rise from 28 per cent (including Iraqi and Iranian output) in 2000 to 33 per cent in 2020, and with most of that increase going to Asian markets, its strategic significance will only grow in coming decades. China alone accounted for nearly 40 per cent of the increase in global oil consumption between 2004 and 2007, and is projected to account for another 40 per cent of the increase in world demand for oil through 2030.[57] In 2009, moreover, for the first time it surpassed the United States in its volume of oil exports from Saudi Arabia, as surging Chinese demand intersected with a 50 per cent drop in US requirements during the global economic downturn.[58] This introduces a major new dynamic into the regional security matrix as it raises the stakes for a greater number of external actors and contributes to the realignment of the geopolitics of oil.[59] In addition, although European Union member-states have steadily diversified their sources of supply to reduce their share from Saudi Arabia and the GCC, their two largest suppliers (Russia and Norway) will deplete far sooner, and hence may lead to a renewed focus on supplies from the Gulf States.[60] Although individual countries such as Qatar have carefully negotiated long-term bilateral energy deals that tie their interests to regional stability, the internationalisation of the Gulf does carry certain risks. Chief among them is the potential for the current cooperative regional environment to become more conflicted if, in spite of thickening interdependencies and energy dialogues, access to regional energy resources becomes sharpened in the future. Although the debate about 'peak oil' is controversial and highly uncertain, it is likely that the Gulf oil reserves will be among the last to deplete, and in the medium- to longer-term this will further enhance their global significance to an energy-hungry world.[61]

Oil, and more recently, natural gas, is therefore the third factor that explains the level of international interest in the Gulf and frames the challenges facing its political and economic evolution. Oil rents transformed the political economies of the GCC states, shaped their distinctive state-society relationship, and distorted the economic development of the 'rentier' or redistributive states that emerged.[62] Oil and natural gas reserves are not, however, distributed evenly throughout the Gulf, and pockets of energy poverty have already emerged. This is creating intra-regional dependencies that will only solidify over time. Qatar's role as an exporter of natural gas to meet power generation shortfalls in neighbouring Kuwait and Abu Dhabi, despite their own substantial gas reserves, is one example of this.[63] Another, more far-reaching in its implications, is Bahrain's increasing reliance on its shared Abu Saafa oilfield with Saudi Arabia, without which the kingdom would not be able to maintain the export of oil from its own rapidly-depleting reserves.[64] A corollary is greater Saudi leverage over Bahraini domestic developments, as evidenced during the uprising in Bahrain in 1994, when senior Saudi officials made it very clear that the revolt would not be allowed to succeed.[65] Unsubstantiated allegations in Bahrain also hold that Saudi armoured personnel carriers were dispatched across the causeway to Manama and parked around the Pearl Monument roundabout in a highly visible statement that the Al-Saud would not stand idly by and watch the Al-Khalifa ruling family fall.[66]

Highly unequal energy reserves and rates of depletion therefore loom large in shaping intra-regional ties of dependency and development. At 2006 production rates, and barring unexpected new discoveries, both Bahrain and Oman are projected to exhaust their existing oil reserves by 2025. They both face imminent transition to non-oil economies, as does Yemen, where oil output has been shrinking since 2000 and is projected to run out within years rather than decades.[67] These three countries' situation contrasts sharply with the other Gulf States, which do not face the same imminent challenges of resource depletion. In June 2009, the annual BP *Statistical Review of World Energy* estimated that Kuwait has a reserves-to-production ratio of 99.6 years, the United Arab Emirates 89.7 years, Saudi Arabia 66.5 years, and Qatar 54.1 years.[68] Clear differentials have thus opened up within the GCC itself, and may become future sources of tension and insecurity as they widen in scope and the difference between resource-rich and resource-poor becomes more pronounced and visible.

Oil rents played the central role in constructing and subsequently maintaining the social contract and redistributive mechanisms in the rentier-state systems of the Gulf. The welfare strategies for co-opting support developed in the 1960s and 1970s in times of comparatively small populations and seemingly endless resources.[69] In all of the Gulf States, they were vital to cushioning the impact of the transformational socio-economic changes that compressed decades of modernising and evolutionary change elsewhere into a single generational achievement. The primary differing variable in the shift to the post-oil future is that regimes' capacity to co-opt opposition will likely be limited both by socio-economic and demographic constraints as well as the impact of the globalising flows of people, ideas, and norms.[70] For these reasons, any changes to the domestic political economy of resource distribution pose a direct challenge to the security and stability of states in transition. Comparative political science indicates that redistributive states are especially vulnerable to erosion of the ruling bargain and consequent loss of regime legitimacy if mechanisms for co-opting support and depoliticising society begin to break down.[71] This was articulated by one prominent academic critic of the Al-Khalifa in Bahrain, who stated bluntly that 'The future is very bleak...the system must change or transform itself,' otherwise 'without oil there is no future.'[72] Yemen provides a cautionary example of the difficulties inherent in overcoming the reliance on subsidies, as widespread riots broke out in 2005 following a government decision to raise the price of fuel.[73]

Even in resource-rich states, such as Kuwait, the sensitivity of reforms to the welfare and subsidy system is such that officials are extremely wary of making the progressive changes that would gradually construct a more sustainable political economy.[74] This complicates policymaking in these 'extreme rentiers' owing to the vested interests and perceptions of entitlement by several generations that have grown up with no recollections of the pre-oil era. The new system of rising tariffs on water consumption introduced by the Dubai Electricity and Water Authority in March 2008 illustrates the difficulties involved in reforming the rentier economies, even gradually. This measure constituted a potentially groundbreaking effort to curb wasteful consumption and reflect more closely the true cost of water.[75] Nevertheless, its significance was severely diluted because it did not apply to UAE nationals, the very group with the most unsustainable habits of consumption and the least awareness of the need for, or value of, resource conservation.[76]

The fourth and final contextual factor is the continuing lack of internal consensus within the GCC itself. A fundamental tension between bilateralism and multilateralism undercuts attempts to formulate a coherent collective policy on most issues.[77] Chapter one described the lack of an integrative decision-making institution for the pooling of sovereignty and ongoing intra-regional tensions between the six member-states. These systemic factors complicate the creation of a common voice for the GCC. They were in full evidence in regional reactions to Israel's military onslaught against Gaza in January 2009. Abu Dhabi and Qatar organised rival summits that split the GCC, with Saudi Arabia, Bahrain and Kuwait attending the former and snubbing the Doha meeting.[78] More specifically, the Abu Dhabi summit issued a communiqué in support of the Arab Peace Initiative and backing the Palestinian Authority and its President, Mahmoud Abbas. This gathering of 'moderate' US allies contrasted with the more belligerent tone of the Doha meeting, which featured high-profile speeches by the exiled leader of Hamas, Khaled Meshaal, who called for Israeli aggression to be destroyed, and by the President of Syria, Bashar Al-Assad, who urged Arab nations to cut all ties with Israel.[79]

Developments later in 2009 further magnified the intra-GCC differences and underscored the deep tensions that criss-cross and undermine regional policymaking. In May 2009, the decision to situate the planned GCC Monetary Council in Riyadh rather than Abu Dhabi led the United Arab Emirates dramatically to withdraw from the planned monetary union project. Although Oman had already left the project, in 2006, citing the incompatibility of its economic convergence,[80] comments by the UAE Foreign Minister, Sheikh Abdullah bin Zayed Al-Nahyan, left no doubt that his country's withdrawal was in direct response to the decision: 'the UAE was the first country supposed to host the central bank, and we believe it had the right to do so. It did not happen.'[81] This episode was buttressed by other instances of disharmony as relations quickly soured. These included the interruption of cross-border land trade that stranded thousands of lorry drivers without food or water during the summer of 2009. This occurred when Saudi officials stopped accepting UAE identity cards which, they alleged, wrongly depicted a disputed boundary as belonging to the UAE.[82] Embarrassingly, the incident came shortly after the GCC approved in principle a single visa system as part of an initiative to enhance freedom of movement within the GCC similar to the Schengen agreement in Europe.[83]

These incidents demonstrate how moves to formulate a collective decision-making framework in the GCC remain at the mercy of the personalised nature of rule in the individual member-states. The institutionalisation of GCC structures is tangled up with lingering unease within the smaller member-states at potential Saudi hegemony within the organisation. This lay behind the decision in 2005 to abolish their joint military unit (Peninsula Shield), and remains a potent factor, as evidenced in the UAE withdrawal from the monetary union and an unprecedented naval clash over maritime boundaries between Saudi and Emirati vessels in March 2010.[84] Less than two months later, in early May, another small-scale skirmish saw the Qatari coastguard fire on seven Bahraini boats encroaching on its territorial waters, which itself was a reaction to depleting fishing stocks in Bahraini coastal waters. One Bahraini sailor was injured and soon after Al-Jazeera was banned from operating in Bahrain, although this may also have been an over-reaction to a news story focusing on levels of poverty in the Kingdom.[85]

Such ongoing difficulties are further complicated by a second powerful centrifugal force that militates against strengthening GCC influence, namely the continuing dominance of the Gulf States' lucrative bilateral relationships with their major trading partners.[86] An ongoing preference for bilateralism, both on the part of GCC states and their trading partners in the west, undermines efforts to conclude GCC-wide free trade agreements. This was seen most emblematically in 2004 when Bahrain (followed later by Oman) signed an individual free trade agreement with the United States.[87] The controversial decision caused considerable friction within the GCC in general, and with Saudi Arabia in particular, whose foreign minister, Saud Al-Faisal, commented that it was 'alarming to see some members of the GCC enter into separate bilateral agreements with international powers in both the security and economic spheres, taking precedence over the need to act collectively.'[88]

Nevertheless, the conclusion of these bilateral free trade agreements with the United States tapped into a broader policy decision taken by the George W. Bush administration not to deal collectively with GCC member-states. Rather, US policy remained focused on the bilateral approaches integrating each country firmly into the American security umbrella.[89] One explanation for this policy decision is Washington's unease at the potential power a coherent GCC bloc might exercise over strategic oil reserves.[90] Another view holds that it formed part of a Bush administration strategy to fragment the GCC and wean the smaller states away from Saudi Arabia in retaliation for the Kingdom's failure publicly to endorse the invasion and occupation of Iraq in 2003.[91]

These bilateral trajectories have resulted in collective GCC policy-making, particularly in the field of defence, remaining a chimera. Decisions taken since 1991 have integrated each of the GCC states into the American security umbrella on a bilateral basis, and undercut any residual collective approach to security. More recently, the establishment of the NATO-Gulf Istanbul Cooperation Initiative in 2004 added a further layer to these internal divisions, as Bahrain, Kuwait, Qatar and the United Arab Emirates opted in while Oman and Saudi Arabia opted out of the cooperative security partnership. Moreover, in 2002 and 2004 the Bush administration accorded Bahrain and Kuwait Major Non-NATO Ally status, thereby making available a wide range of military and financial advantages not open to the other GCC states.[92] This fused the two trends described above of bilateralism and the Bush-era policy of disfavouring closer GCC integration and extended it into the defence and security sphere of policymaking.

Emerging and Longer-Term Challenges to Security

Having set out the macro-parameters within which Gulf security structures will evolve, part two of this book narrows the focus to examine the emergence of longer-term challenges to security and stability at the level of states and societies. These constitute a range of non-conventional and non-military threats whose full consequences will unfold over a period of decades rather than years. The three major clusters of emerging threats are the impact of demographic and generational change and the challenge of accommodating these trends, the political economy of resource distribution and their growing scarcity, and the impact of environmental degradation and climate change. Taken together, they have the potential profoundly to impact the political economy of the Gulf States and complicate the transition toward any post-oil era. They will require regimes to reformulate the pillars of their legitimacy as well as the redistributive social contracts. Crucial to this transition will be the strengthening of polities that otherwise are vulnerable to fragmentation if existing and latent fault-lines become sharpened and contested by future external and global shocks, such as climate change.

The underlying argument in these next chapters is that the changing political economies in all six GCC states need to be underpinned by a new and broader approach to the study of national and regional security dynamics. They describe the interaction of these political economies in transition with the complex and rapidly-shifting socio-political environment at its various local, regional and global levels. Emphasising the multidimensionality of the processes under examination provides a clearer picture of the challenges likely to face policymakers as they move towards adopting post-rentier forms of governance. In addition, the chapters explore the implications of these shifts for the balance of power among different groups within society just as much as the regional balance of power between states.

Indeed it is this symbiosis between the internal and the external, the local and the global, that is reshaping the Gulf security agenda in an era of accelerating and globalising change. Yet it remains the case that a substantial gap exists between regional policymakers' awareness of these emerging trends and the difficulties that lie ahead, and the policy responses that have been unveiled thus far. Examining the reasons this is so, in the chapters ahead, sheds light on the nature of the policy choices that confront the Gulf States as they attempt to reformulate the social contract and reposition their economies without provoking radical socio-economic upheaval or risking their internal legitimacy or political authority.

PART TWO

4

DEMOGRAPHIC AND STRUCTURAL IMBALANCES IN GULF ECONOMIES

Part two of this book opens with an examination of the demographic trends and structural economic imbalances in Gulf economies. It considers their implications for the medium- and longer-term stability of these polities, and integrates them into the broadening and deepening of the security agenda. With the monarchies of the Arabian Peninsula having experienced four decades of exceptionally rapid demographic growth that is only now beginning to slow, a youth bulge will continue to work its way through the population structure for decades to come. Although this is consistent with the demographic transition model, in which birth and death rates fall from high to low at different rates in four distinctive stages, it places great strain on existing redistributive welfare mechanisms. Accordingly, generational shifts in the GCC states will be closely intertwined with the processes of demographic change and the success or otherwise of projects of economic diversification away from reliance on capital-intensive hydrocarbon industries. At its core is the reformulation of the social contract and the associated shift that this implies from the perverse incentives created by rent-seeking behaviour toward productive notions of work and reward.

This, in turn, introduces new dynamics into issues of regional security and stability. These are discussed at length in chapters five and six. They include the emergence of resource scarcities coexistent with the continuation of unequal patterns of access to, and distribution of, resources. In recent years, and particularly following the oil and commodity price rises of 2007–8, resource security emerged as an urgent issue in GCC states. Nevertheless, the potential for significant unrest in the future remains if greater contestation of resources sharpens latent and existing fault-lines within and between states. Contemporaneously, the potential for exogenous shocks arising from climate change and environmental degradation, caused by the persistence of unsustainable patterns of settlement in the Gulf States, also increases these states' vulnerability to sources of insecurity. Thus, the three chapters in this part of the book contain multiple, interacting strands that will frame the contextual parameters of the transition toward the post-oil era that will unfold at different paces in the different countries. These indices of human development are intertwined in reshaping the sources of human security (or insecurity) that will accompany this transition.

The social and economic trends described in this chapter have profound implications for internal security and stability in the Gulf States. Officials and policymakers are not unaware of this looming crunch, particularly in Kuwait, where it is interlinked with political frustration with the slow pace of reform, but also in Bahrain and Oman, where resource depletion is more imminent, and Yemen and Saudi Arabia, which confront demographic challenges that do not exist in the more lightly-populated smaller Gulf States. There is nevertheless a substantive gap between recognition of the issues and the political measures or willpower necessary to address them in any meaningful or sustainable way that begins to strip away the vested interests and layers of rent-seekers embedded in Gulf polities.[1] This extends even to flagship projects of economic diversification or knowledge-promotion, as they are motivated primarily by a desire for 'branding' rather than a systematic reformulation of productive capabilities. Consequently, the major issue facing policymakers in the Gulf—how to transition away from unproductive rent-seeking behaviour—remains unresolved as officials eschewed the opportunity offered by the 2002–8 oil price boom to undertake structural economic reforms.[2]

Demographic Trends and the Youth Bulge

The countries of the Arabian Peninsula have some of the highest rates of population growth in the world. This has been partially caused by the rapid decline in death rates and lagging declines in birth rates per head of population, and partially by massive levels of in-migration to service the oil-producing rentier states that emerged since the 1970s.

These trends resulted in the population of the Arabian Peninsula increasing from 8 million in 1950 to 58 million in 2007, with a projected rise to 124 million in 2050.[3] A further breakdown of this figure reveals even more remarkable trends, most notably the near-doubling of the Qatari population from 800,000 in 2006 to 1.5 million by the end of 2007, and an unexpected announcement of a 41 per cent jump in the population of Bahrain in the same year.[4] Even without taking into account future surges in in-migration, the Population Reference Bureau estimates that between 2009 and 2050, populations will grow by 61 per cent in Bahrain, 64 per cent in Qatar, 71 per cent in Oman, 74 per cent in Saudi Arabia, 76 per cent in Kuwait, 79 per cent in the United Arab Emirates, and 128 per cent in Yemen.[5]

These figures place growing pressures on states in the Arabian Peninsula, as in the wider Arab world, to provide educational and job-creation opportunities for the large numbers of young people coming of age. As of 2008, 70 per cent of the citizen population in the GCC were below the age of thirty, of which 30 per cent were aged fourteen or under. This means that a youth bulge will continue to work its way through the demographic pyramid for at least another two generations, even if birth rates fall to a low level.[6] Yet birth rates remain high in the region's two most populous countries (Saudi Arabia and Yemen), at twenty-nine and thirty-eight births per 1000 of total population. This compares to figures of thirteen in Qatar, fifteen in Bahrain and eighteen in Kuwait, which themselves are similar to the United Kingdom (thirteen) and the United States (fourteen).[7] Meanwhile, as recently as the early 1990s, Oman had the second-highest fertility rate in the world, after Niger, and while an aggressive campaign to promote birth spacing reduced the birth rate from its previous figure of over forty, it remains high, at twenty-five per 1000 in 2009.[8]

The combination of rapid population growth with inadequate employment opportunities represents a major long-term challenge to internal cohesion in the GCC. This dilemma is not unique to the region; it is one shared by the wider Arab and developing world as a whole, as economies struggle to generate sufficient jobs to absorb even the rates of natural increase without exacerbating the already-high levels of existing unemployment.[9] Nevertheless, its impact in the GCC states is compounded by stratified labour markets and rentier mentalities that have created imbalanced and dual labour market systems that are unique in the contemporary world.[10] Signs of socio-economic strain have already emerged in all the GCC states and Yemen. They may be expected to have a particularly destabilising effect on successive generations of citizens under the age of forty, who take for granted the redistribution of wealth and provision of public goods, and lack any point of comparison with the hardships experienced by their elders.[11]

Rising disparities of income and wealth provide a visible indicator of the growing inequalities within GCC societies. A case in point is Saudi Arabia, where the level of income per capita more than halved, from $16,650 in 1980 to $7,239 in 2000.[12] Although this fall coincided with a prolonged slump in oil prices, and was followed by a period of enormous capital accumulation during the 2003–08 oil boom, it failed to mask fully the disparities, which are creating a new underclass of 'have-nots' in the region. These divergent trajectories are potentially destabilising because in many cases they follow fissures within society. These may overlay sectarian divisions, as in Bahrain or Saudi Arabia where absolute and relative rates of poverty are interlinked with the politics of uneven development, or they may exist between citizens and expatriates.[13] Both fault-lines reveal considerable tensions and societal pressures that may become systemic if they are not addressed in a comprehensive and sustainable manner.

In Yemen, meanwhile, the human development challenge is exacerbated by its poor performance across myriad indices of development. These include low quality of, and access to, education and the fifth largest gender gap in the world, a continuing mismatch in the labour market and restrictions on entry into GCC labour markets, institutional blockages that hinder the development of the private sector and reduce employment opportunities for Yemeni youth, and broader macroeconomic and political problems that have steadily eroded governmental authority and legitimacy. The cumulative result is the exclusion of a large proportion of youth from a formative age, and who subsequently will lack the basic skills to compete in labour markets and face lifelong difficulties in accessing the resources and support they require to productively participate in society.[14]

In Bahrain, pockets of extreme poverty and socio-economic deprivation exist within sight of the gleaming towers of the Manama Financial Harbour and World Trade Centre, in a visible reminder of the uneven development patterns inside the Kingdom.[15] Anti-ruling family slogans painted on walls and frequent outbreaks of low-level violence, which occasionally escalate into more serious trouble, attest to the simmering tensions that provide volatile kindling for future unrest.[16] Although the sectarian tension in Bahrain is atypical and unlikely to be replicated elsewhere in the GCC, with the potential exception of the Eastern Province of Saudi Arabia, it does reveal the challenges facing governments if the social contract binding state and society begins to break down. Rising levels of un- and under-employment, and the emergence of relative and absolute economic hardships, will increase regimes' vulnerability to societal pressure and political contestation, as witnessed in the previous period of low oil prices and economic difficulties in the 1990s.[17] This requires governments in the GCC, and (not least) Yemen, to find measures to accommodate the generational change and youth bulge without it becoming a risk to internal stability. Nevertheless, the persistence of highly stratified dual labour markets complicates this approach, and poses special obstacles to strategies to increase the rate of employment of citizens in national and region-wide labour markets.[18]

Dual Labour Markets

Elsewhere, the primary division in the incidence of poverty is between the citizen and expatriate communities. The existence of dual labour markets for these two categories of workers is the major distinguishing factor that marks the GCC out from other world regions. As of 2002–3, expatriate labourers provided the majority of the labour force in each of the six GCC states, ranging from 60 per cent in Saudi Arabia and Bahrain to 65.7 per cent in Oman, 80 per cent in Kuwait, 89.5 per cent in Qatar and 90 per cent in the UAE.[19] More broadly, expatriates constituted 37 per cent of the total population in the GCC in 2007, forming absolute majorities in Kuwait (66 per cent of the total), Qatar (75 per cent) and the United Arab Emirates (83 per cent), in addition to substantial minorities in Oman and Saudi Arabia (25 per cent) and Bahrain (40 per cent).[20] This has given rise to highly-stratified labour markets in which divisions between citizen and expatriate labour largely follow the public and private sector lines. Kuwait provides the clearest instance of this almost binary division of labour, where 92 per cent of Kuwaitis in work in 2005 were concentrated in the public sector, leaving the private sector almost exclusively peopled by expatriates.[21]

Such levels of stratification hold important implications for labour security on multiple levels. Expatriate labour communities in the Gulf have a heightened vulnerability to the inequalities and marginalisation described in the previous section. This is evidenced in Qatar, where a 2002 study found that more than 40 per cent of expatriates live below the poverty line compared to less than 1 per cent of Qatari nationals.[22] Similar disparities exist in the other GCC states where expatriate labour migrants comprise the majority community. Human Rights Watch has issued a number of reports listing serious exploitation of migrant labourers in the United Arab Emirates, including extremely low wages, labourers' indebtedness to recruitment agencies, low-quality housing conditions in labour camps, and a lack of enforceable contractual guarantees for basic human and working rights.[23] Kuwait has come in for similar criticism from international human rights organisations for the exploitation of the domestic and expatriate workers that constitute 70 per cent of the total labour force.[24] This reached such proportions that in June 2009 the former President of the Philippines, Joseph Estrada, called for a ban on sending Filipina workers, mainly female domestic staff, to Kuwait until working conditions improved.[25]

The presence within GCC societies of large numbers of migrant labourers with no civil or political rights and very few economic rights is another potent source of human insecurity. At a time when the notion of 'human security' is gaining voice in the Arab world, as elsewhere, the very concept of 'security for whom' becomes critically important in this particular context. If 'human security' in its GCC-specific context is taken to refer to the security of citizens only, it cannot by definition be classed as a population-centric approach that embraces the security of all communities within a defined polity. Conversely, the absolute and relative size of the expatriate population, particularly in the United Arab Emirates, Qatar and Kuwait, but also in the other GCC states, means that regimes are faced with a dilemma should their marginalised and disenfranchised labour migrants ever make a claim for civil or political rights in the future.[26] Already, significant (by GCC standards) labour unrest occurred in Dubai, Bahrain and Kuwait in 2007–8. The unrest coincided with the beginning of the global financial and economic crisis, and rising inflationary and cost-of-living pressures. Noticeably, it was this potential for economic unrest that worried governing officials in the GCC as it jeopardised their developmental models and called into question their ability to honour their side of the ruling bargain.[27]

These anxieties feed into a broader sense of unease felt by many GCC nationals at a dilution of their identity, as articulated by the commander of Dubai police force, Major-General Dahi Tamim Khalfan, in November 2008, when he said that the ongoing construction boom in the UAE would eventually come at the cost of the country losing its identity.[28] Later, in August 2009, the Bahraini Minister of Labour and Social Affairs, Dr Majeed Al-Alawi, stated apocalyptically that 'The issue of expatriate labour is not a time bomb; it is a bomb that has already gone off. It must be dealt with and suitable solutions must be put in place at present, otherwise the future of Gulf states will be at risk.'[29] Throughout the GCC states, a continuing reliance on expatriate labour, even during times of rising indigenous unemployment, contains the seeds of considerable future discontent. This remains the case even though lingering rentier mentalities mean that many GCC citizens would not, in any case, contemplate doing the hard manual tasks performed by the majority of the unskilled expatriate labourers.[30]

Unemployment and Weak Institutionalisation

Within the GCC, unemployment is regularly cited as the primary long-term challenge facing regimes. This goes alongside a widespread perception that officials lack the political courage and capital to formulate effective strategies for tackling the structural roots of the imbalanced labour market.[31] Doing so would require the dismantling of public attitudes and official policies toward the dual labour market system. It would also necessitate the ending of government strategies that created a depoliticised and controlled labour force consisting of imported labourers from South and East Asia. However, recent evidence does not indicate that regimes' pragmatic strategies of survival extend to making the deep, structural changes necessary to realign their labour markets with local educational systems in order to meet the challenge of domestic un- and under-employment. In addition, GCC states' citizens remain unwilling to forego lucrative public sector careers and enter the private sector, which retains a negative social stigma intertwined with deeply-embedded notions of entitlement.[32] These trends point toward a potential future breakdown in the social contract in its guise of cradle-to-grave welfare for citizens in the GCC, under the twin pressures of demographic change and inability to provide sufficient public-sector jobs to absorb all citizens willing and able to enter the labour force.[33]

The issue of unemployment is intertwined with the broader socio-economic challenges arising from the over-stretch of existing state capacity to meet rising demand for utilities, health care and education, in addition to job requirements. Nor is it confined to those states facing more imminent transitions to a post-oil future, such as Bahrain, Oman and Yemen, or to Saudi Arabia, where rapid population growth has eroded the state's redistributive capabilities. Especially in 'extreme rentiers,' such as Kuwait and the UAE, the situation is distinctly unfavourable to the wide-reaching reforms that will be necessary to transition the economic and labour markets onto long-term, sustainable bases.[34] In these examples, where bountiful oil reserves do not impose anything like the same urgency to diversify economically, problems of overstaffing and under-performing in the public sector remain essentially unchanged. A study conducted by the *Al-Watan* newspaper in November 2009 estimated that 30,000 public sector employees in Kuwait had not reported for work for several years, and that another 20,000 worked for no more than an hour or two each day, while receiving full pay in both cases.[35] Simultaneously in the UAE, an announced 70 per cent rise in the basic salary of Emiratis working for the federal government illustrated the importance of the public sector as another lucrative form of wealth redistribution in rentier systems, and the continuing temptation for ruling elites to use lavish pay increases as an instrument to maintain short-term favour with their citizenry.[36]

This notwithstanding, the problem of unemployment is more acute in the 'lesser rentiers' whose capacity for continued rent redistribution is much reduced. A study conducted by the McKinsey consultancy group in November 2007 laid bare the scale of the challenge posed by mounting unemployment. The report estimated that, contrary to official claims of much lower rates, real unemployment in Bahrain, Oman and Saudi Arabia exceeded 15 per cent, and that the figure rose to 35 per cent for those aged between sixteen and twenty-four. It also found that the saturated public sector was no longer able to guarantee employment to citizens entering the job market. Furthermore, it identified severe deficiencies in local education systems that meant that most entrants into GCC labour markets lacked the requisite qualifications to enter the private sector.[37] The situation is bleaker still in Yemen, where overall unemployment rates are between 35–40 per cent, amid the continuing reluctance of GCC states to admit unskilled or semi-skilled Yemeni labour migrants in place of workers from non-Muslim, Asian countries.[38]

The McKinsey report confirmed the findings of an earlier study commissioned in 2004 by the Crown Prince of Bahrain, Sheikh Salman bin

Hamad Al-Khalifa. This predicted that unemployment in Bahrain would reach 35 per cent by 2013, by which time the number of Bahraini nationals within the labour market was expected to be double its 2003 level.[39] In his capacity as chairman of the Economic Development Board in Bahrain, the Crown Prince subsequently prioritised economic reforms designed to modernise and update the Bahraini economy in line with a strategic *Vision 2030* project of economic diversification.[40] Specifically, the Board introduced measures to tackle corruption, increase the range of opportunities available to young people, encourage foreign direct investment and private-sector development, and embed the values of transparency and accountability in the corporate governance culture.[41]

Many of these reforms became entangled in an internal power struggle within the ruling Al-Khalifa family. This pitted the younger, reform-oriented Crown Prince against his conservative great-uncle, the long-serving Prime Minister Sheikh Khalifa bin Salman Al-Khalifa in an inter-generational and familial contest.[42] The latter appeared to be resolved in favour of the Crown Prince in 2008, although the Prime Minister continued to exert a powerful constraining influence on further political reform in Bahrain following the initial opening initiated by the new Emir (later King) Hamad bin Isa Al-Khalifa in 2001–2.[43] This in-fighting is particularly damaging because of the magnitude of the socio-economic challenges facing Bahrain. The intersection of sectarian-based tension, poverty, unemployment and economic marginalisation, coupled with the urgency of the looming depletion of oil reserves, mean that there is no margin for further delays to the reform process.

The Bahraini experience, in which reform was initiated (as in Qatar) by a newly-enthroned ruler in a generational shift from his predecessor, demonstrated one of the limiting factors on local reform movements. This is the lingering personalisation of reforms in light of the comparative youthfulness of national bureaucratic institutions in the GCC. The corollary of this is weak institutionalisation attributable to the ongoing consolidation of the structures created during the formative state-building era, as well as the enduring strength of personalised networks and vested interests that form a nexus of political-economic ties cemented by intra-familial and tribal relationships.[44] Together they ensure that reforms remain potentially tied to a particular individual or faction, and open to reversal at a future date. This is certainly the case with the reforms of the judiciary and higher education initiated by

King Abdullah bin Abdul-Aziz Al-Saud in Saudi Arabia since his accession in 2005.[45] A more conservative successor, such as the second-in-line Prince Nayef bin Abdul-Aziz Al-Saud, might well reverse them, as noted by Hassan Al-Husseini, a former administrator at the King Fahd University of Petroleum and Minerals, in observing that 'when something is established by royal edict, then that same thing can be reversed by another royal edict. It's not like you have legal protection for such things in Saudi Arabia.'[46]

Somewhat similarly, the unfolding economic crisis in Dubai revealed much about the personalisation of power and weakness of legal-rational authority as it gathered pace in 2008–9. These trends became visible in the run-up to and immediate aftermath of, Dubai World's request for a six-month moratorium on repayment of an Islamic bond due in December 2009. Dubai's ruler, Sheikh Mohammed bin Rashid Al-Maktoum, played a high-profile role in attempting to deflect rumours of a problem, describing the global financial crisis as a 'passing cloud that will not stay longer' in September 2009, and infamously telling critics of Dubai to 'shut up' and 'do their homework' in early-November.[47] However the enduring damage to Dubai's credibility came when officials obfuscated over the emirate's backing of government-linked institutions such as Dubai World.[48] This reversed several years of state-sanctioned hints at a full sovereign guarantee for these state investment and holding companies, and revealed the state-business nexus that hitherto had underpinned their growth to be hollow in times of difficulty.[49] It also exposed the considerable opacity and lack of accountability concerning the separation of power between ruler and state in Dubai's institutional structures.[50]

A combination of socio-political and economic factors therefore point to an imminent reformulation of the existing social contract in the GCC and Yemen, away from notions of citizen entitlement come what may. Central to this looming crunch is the growing overstretch of existing state capacity to meet rising demand for public utilities, including health care and education, and access to jobs. These are interlinked, and risk marginalising an entire generation of young people who lack the requisite skill sets and language abilities to compete with cheaper sources of expatriate labour.

The following section considers the implications of education and knowledge deficits in the GCC before a final section in this chapter examines the patchy record of economic diversification. Collectively, they expose the underlying issue, which is the comparative failure of Gulf States' strategies to resolve the systemic structural imbalances or fully address the 'crisis of education' at all its primary, secondary and higher forms.

Education and Knowledge Deficits

Education and access to knowledge are the great dividers in the modern information-based society. They encompass a range of tangible and intangible dimensions that feed into broader discourse on the transition toward knowledge-based economies that form such an integral part of the national visions and plans that populate the regional economic landscape. On the surface, a revolution has taken place in higher education in the GCC states since the turn of the twenty-first century. Between 2003 and 2007, more than forty foreign branches of Western universities opened in the UAE and Qatar, and over 100 universities and colleges formed in Saudi Arabia. The GCC emerged as the major academic player in the broader Middle East North Africa (MENA) region as the scale of investment into higher education and research became clear.[51] The trend was capped in 2009 by the opening of the King Abdullah University of Science and Technology (KAUST), in Saudi Arabia, and the Masdar Institute of Science and Technology (MIST), in Abu Dhabi. Meanwhile, the formation of NYU Abu Dhabi was a landmark move, involving the construction of an entire research university, including a fully-integrated liberal arts and science college in Abu Dhabi, rather than the importation of a single faculty or school, such as the Georgetown School of Foreign Service in Qatar.[52] Elsewhere, the Qatar Foundation led the way in creating Education City and the Qatar Science and Technology Park in collaboration with leading Western academic institutions, while in Oman the Knowledge Oasis Muscat brought together more than sixty international companies, including Microsoft, Oracle, HP and Motorola, to directly facilitate cooperation between higher education, business, industry and government.[53] These innovative developments established hubs of agglomeration for knowledge-intensive goods and services, bringing research and business together in a regional model of industry-university collaboration.[54]

These flagship institutions provide world-leading platforms for cutting-edge research and collaboration with leading Western institutions, including the University of Cambridge and Stanford University, both of which established collaborative initiatives with KAUST, Imperial College London, which founded a joint research initiative with the Qatar Science and Technology Park, and Harvard University, which established the Dubai Initiative in connection with the Dubai School of Government.[55] Particularly in the Saudi example, the co-educational KAUST model pushes out the social boundaries concerning the role of women and education, and, in the opinion of Osama Tayeb, president of King Abdulaziz University in Jeddah, is designed to 'accelerate scientific, technological, cultural, economic and social progress…all over the Kingdom.'[56] It also benefited from the strong personal support and funding of King Abdullah, although, as the previous section made clear, this raises the possibility that in the future, monarchs may not be so tolerant.[57]

Nevertheless, in spite of these considerable achievements, and the lavish expenditure devoted to higher education reform in the GCC states, significant gaps remain in educational standards and the acquisition of knowledge. One recent study of higher education in the GCC concluded pessimistically that the trends toward importing foreign (predominantly American) campuses perpetuated a dependency culture in which the Gulf States remained consumers, rather than producers, of knowledge, which continued to be generated externally. The authors, which included a former Minister for Higher Education (and current Chair of the State Council) in Oman, added that the influx of foreign institutions of higher education risked becoming 'a valuable economic and political cargo for the sellers/exporters but of little educational value to purchasers/importers.'[58]

Important though KAUST and Education City undoubtedly are, they are carefully-managed enclaves which, in the case of KAUST, is eighty kilometres from the nearest large city. It is thus effectively sealed off from Saudi society, and the possibility of any overspill of its social mixing is further diminished by the low number of Saudi students enrolled there and the tight controls of access to the campus.[59] Outside these enclaves, the substantial expansion in institutional facilities and expenditure has yet to be matched by a transformation in the quality of education made available.[60] Nor has the project to embed regional campuses of North American higher education been an unqualified success, as the difficulties experienced by the George Mason University campus in Ras al-Khaimah (which closed in 2009) and Michigan State

University attest. This divergent trajectory between quality and quantity highlighted a broader educational deficiency found in many countries in the Middle East and North Africa.[61] Particular weaknesses in the sciences, engineering and language skills, attested by low scores in international benchmarks such as TIMSS (Trends in International Mathematical and Science Study) translate into poor levels of knowledge generation, and an accelerating gap in value-added wealth creation between the developed and developing worlds.[62] For all their spending on educational reform and targeting of higher education, no indigenous universities in the GCC featured in a global ranking of the top 500 academic institutions in 2008.[63]

Different strands of these deficiencies occur in varying degrees within all the GCC states. In 2007, a study undertaken by the State Planning Council in Qatar identified a substantive disconnect between the education system and the labour market as constituting the major underlying obstacle to the country becoming a knowledge-based economy.[64] This is a feature common to all of the oil-producing states of the Arabian Peninsula, particularly the 'extreme rentier' states of Kuwait and the UAE, and resolving it will be critical to the success or otherwise of eventual transitions toward productive, post-oil economies.[65] Overcoming it requires the long-term reform of curricula from pre-school upward in order to align the quality of education on offer with the current and future needs of labour markets and knowledge-intensive economies.

However, local education standards in the GCC states have not improved significantly, and may even be falling further behind. This was the conclusion of a World Bank report on the UAE issued in 2007, which found that its knowledge-based sector had actually shrunk since 2005 owing, the report argued, to deteriorating standards in domestic education.[66] Meanwhile Bahrain's *Economic Vision 2030* implicitly criticised the existing educational system as it argued that educational reforms were mandatory to make it 'relevant to the requirements of Bahrain and its economy' in order to develop 'an education system that provides every citizen with educational opportunities appropriate to their individual needs, aspirations and abilities.'[67]

A second obstacle to reforming curricula and raising the standard of primary and secondary education is social and religious conservatism, particularly in Kuwait and Saudi Arabia. The rise of Islamism in the GCC states has its roots in the 1970s and mirrored in part the decline of Arabism and left-wing political currents as viable oppositional alternatives in the wider Arab world.[68] Schooling and curricula emerged as critical sites of contestation between regimes and Islamists, and cut to the heart of the ideological battle for the control of Gulf polities. In Kuwait, sustained Islamist pressure led to the segregation of formerly co-educational institutions in 1996, and parliamentary deadlock over proposed measures to reform educational standards.[69] In Saudi Arabia, three decades of religious clerical control over the Ministry of Higher Education left a legacy of emphasis on religious instruction over liberal arts or sciences. The opening of more than 100 institutions of higher education since 2003 demonstrates the scale of change now underway in Saudi Arabia, although it is notable that KAUST developed as a personal project of King Abdullah under the aegis of Saudi Aramco, rather than through the Ministry itself.[70]

The obstacles that face policymakers in the GCC states are common, to a greater or lesser extent, to the Middle East and North Africa region. The broader parameters of the problem of education were outlined in detail in the World Bank's seminal report, *The Road Not Traveled: Education Reform in the Middle East and North Africa*, published in 2007. It found that the region as a whole shared the GCC states' lack of alignment between standards and the skills sets required in modern labour markets. The report highlighted the tenuous linkages between investment in education and economic and social development in MENA countries as compared with similarly-placed countries in Latin America and East Asia.[71] Significantly, it also emphasised the importance of transitioning toward knowledge-based economies, as well as the dangers of falling further behind, as it concluded that modern global competitiveness 'depends on firms that employ a well-educated, technically skilled workforce and are capable of adopting new technologies and selling sophisticated goods and services.'[72]

The importance of developing knowledge-based economies was further reiterated by a high-level international conference organised by the Islamic Educational, Scientific and Cultural Organization in December 2009. In its concluding *Tunis Declaration on 'Building Knowledge Economies'*, the participants drew attention to the urgency of transforming their economic base:

In view of the pressing need of States to start preparing for the post-petroleum and post-carbon future, as well as for major water, energy, food, and climate change in the decades to come…the majority of States need to diversify their economies instead of over-dependency on petroleum revenues for some countries, or on the agricultural sector for others.[73]

As comparatively high-income developing nations, the GCC states are better positioned than other MENA countries to address these shortcomings in educational standards. This is evidenced in part by the proliferation of institutions of higher education outlined above, as well as the higher rates of literacy in each GCC state.[74] In addition, local discourse on the knowledge-based economic transition has entered policymaking debates and informed new approaches that seek to embed it in strategies of human capital development.[75] Nevertheless, reforms will need to go much deeper into the structure of education and align it with local labour markets in order to have any chance of proving effective over the longer-term. If regimes are indeed serious about transforming their economic base into a knowledge-intensive one, they will need to address systemic issues of dual labour markets, public sector crowding out of the private sector and, crucially, the dismantling of rent-seeking modes of behaviour that currently permeate GCC polities.[76]

Quick-fix solutions, such as importing satellite Western universities, fail to address the core problems. Tangible investment in campus infrastructure is insufficient on its own to deliver intangible benefits, such as a productive culture that directly links educational achievement to professional advancement.[77] Nor does it tackle the deeper issues posed by unproductive patterns of rent-seeking behaviour, or the structural deficiencies that underlay the highly-distorted labour market patterns in the Gulf States.[78] Moreover, they are vulnerable to shifting political and economic currents that complicate efforts to create a lasting and deep-rooted educational legacy. Financial strains, budgetary disagreements with the government of Ras al-Khaimah, and insufficient student take-up led George Mason University to close its campus after just three years' operation in 2009, while the bursting of Dubai's speculative bubble hit Michigan State University hard as it coincided with the opening of its Dubai campus in August 2008.[79] Moves to overhaul the culture of educational attainment also face vested political and socio-cultural obstacles to implementation, as seen in the mobilisation of political, largely Islamist-led, opposition to Kuwaiti plans to create a knowledge-intensive sector in the 1990s.[80] Transitioning toward knowledge-based economies therefore carries profound implications for the political economy of rentier and post-rentier systems of governance. These revolve around the question of whether a knowledge-based economy can co-exist within, or alongside redistributive structures in neo-patrimonial states. Moreover, any move toward a productive economy would necessitate the thorough reformulation of labour markets and the very basis of the redistributive mechanisms that have underpinned the social contract in the Gulf States for four decades.[81]

Changes of this sort would be transformative in their impact on models of governance and political participation, and critical to the unfolding transition to post-oil political economies. If successful, GCC state-led efforts to promote knowledge-based economies would fit into their record of pragmatic strategies of survival through updating their polities and bases of legitimacy. However, while reforms to education and knowledge-acquisition do fit into broader patterns of political liberalisation and economic diversification currently underway, the risk to GCC regimes is that a better-educated and higher-skilled workforce may emerge as agents of transformative change.[82] After three decades of depoliticising and disempowering their labour forces, it may appear counter-intuitive for regimes to promote policies that might facilitate the growth of politically-engaged elements within their own polities. Nevertheless, sustained processes of change will be more likely to succeed if they are measured and consensual, and undertaken in a spirit of partnership rather than confrontation between state and society.

Economic Diversification and Development

The encouragement of educational reform and the acquisition of knowledge constitute cornerstones of the ambitious projects of economic diversification launched in each GCC state during the 1990s and 2000s. Beginning in the mid-1990s, a plethora of national 'visions' and plans set out targets and objectives for diversifying GCC economies and expanding the productive base. Perhaps unsurprisingly, this occurred first in Oman and Bahrain, as it is in these countries that oil reserves will draw down earliest. Policymakers in both countries adopted reforms designed to broaden their economic and industrial base in order to lessen their reliance on hydrocarbon revenues and minimise the potential risks to internal security. In Bahrain, a package of measures included labour market reform, economic reform, and educational and training reform, in addition to the strengthening of its aluminium sector and the creation of the Economic Development Board to promote a pro-business agenda based around the branding of *Business Friendly Bahrain*.[83]

Meanwhile, officials in Oman were the first in the GCC to formulate an economic diversification plan with the launch of *Oman 2020: Vision for Oman's Economy* in June 1996. This comprehensive approach was designed to run in conjunction with an ongoing series of five-year development plans that focused directly on economic diversification and expanding the private and non-oil sectors. The Vision aimed to reduce the oil sector's share of Omani GDP from 41 per cent in 1996 to 9 per cent in 2020 while raising the share of gas and non-oil industry from under 1 per cent to 10 per cent and from 7.5 per cent to 29 per cent respectively. It also sought to improve the quality of human development among Omani citizens, particularly women, to equip them with the skills and qualifications to compete in the private sector against cheaper expatriate labourers.[84] However, results were very mixed as the plan entered its second decade. The share of oil revenue in GDP actually increased between 1995 and 2005, although this was attributable to the surging price of oil rather than an increase in production, which actually fell from 0.972 million barrels per day in 2000 to 0.754 million in 2004.[85] It demonstrated the extent of the Omani economy's continuing dependence on oil in spite of the attempt to diversify and broaden the economic base. Similarly slow progress marked the attempt to 'Omanise' the private-sector labour force. As of 2008, only 15.9 per cent of private-sector jobs were filled by Omani workers, set against the *Vision's* target of increasing the proportion from 7.5 per cent in 1996 to 75 per cent in 2020.[86]

Although Oman and Bahrain were early-movers in diversification, their efforts have since been surpassed in order of magnitude by Qatar, Saudi Arabia, and the United Arab Emirates. In 2008, the General Secretariat for Development Planning in Qatar unveiled its ambitious *Qatar National Vision 2030*. This outlined five major challenges facing Qatar, including meeting the needs both of current and future generations and aligning economic growth with social development and environmental management. It recommended four interconnected pillars, focusing on human, social, environmental and economic development, to meet these challenges.[87] This emphasis on human and sustainable development is evident in the rapid expansion of Ras Laffan Industrial City. Since its launch in 1996, Ras Laffan has emerged as one of the fastest growing industrial cities in the world and an integrated hub for the production and export of liquefied natural gas (LNG) and gas-to-liquid (GTL).[88] Already by 2009 it employed more than 100,000 people in twenty-two local and international companies, and developed a reputation for one of the world's leading green industrial zones through its focus on clean gas technologies.[89] It also set up a fully integrated port that ships LNG around the world in specially constructed Q-Max carriers that are among the largest ships ever built, with 80 per cent greater capacity than conventional carriers.[90]

Qatar's utilisation of its natural gas reserves demonstrates the geostrategic dimension of economic diversification. The supply of LNG to leading industrialised and emerging countries, including the United States, United Kingdom, South Korea, Japan and China, thickens the web of interdependences with powerful external actors with a direct stake in Qatari stability and security. Similarly, on a regional level, the piping of Qatari LNG to the United Arab Emirates and Oman as part of the Dolphin Project is a mechanism to strengthen political ties with these countries and enhance Qatar's regional status within the GCC, although it could also become a source of tension should baseline prices rise or Qatar move to reallocate supplies in the future.[91] Qatar's booming economy also has the potential to alleviate the socio-economic challenges in neighbouring Bahrain by opening its labour market to Bahraini workers and strengthening bilateral trade links, particularly after the scheduled opening of the 40 km long Friendship Bridge between the two countries in 2012.[92]

Economic diversification programmes in Saudi Arabia have followed a two-pronged approach. One dimension focuses on creating economic cities as hubs of agglomeration and the creation and diffusion of knowledge, while the other emphasises the development of a sophisticated downstream petrochemicals industry. Within the first strand, the major series of initiatives involve the construction of six economic cities, including the showpiece King Abdullah Economic City on the Red Sea coast north of Jeddah, containing an integrated seaport, industrial centre and financial sector.[93] These form the core of the Kingdom's strategy of economic diversification and job creation, and build on Saudi Arabia's long-delayed accession to the World Trade Organisation in 2005 and the privatisation of key economic sectors by the Supreme Economic Council in order to attract foreign investment.[94] More importantly, the cities are also designed to bypass cumbersome and ossified bureaucratic structures by creating parallel economies based on regulatory frameworks conducive to private sector investment.[95]

This strategy is consistent with the growth of what Steffen Hertog has identified as 'islands of efficiency' embedded within the Saudi state and bureaucratic apparatus. These are well-managed, technocratic enclaves, including Saudi Aramco, the Saudi Arabian Monetary Agency (SAMA), the Saudi Arabian Basic Industries Company (SABIC) and the Central Bank.[96] Significantly, the King Abdullah University of Science and Technology falls under the aegis of Saudi Aramco rather than the Ministry of Higher Education (the only higher education establishment in Saudi Arabia to do so), and tackles many of the socio-cultural taboos in Saudi society.[97] They include the intermixing of men and women in a coeducational environment, and allowing women to go unveiled and drive on campus.[98] The creation, and gradual widening, of such enclaves of modernisation, may be seen as a way of sensitising Saudi Arabia to the inducement of change in carefully-controlled environments before mainstreaming such reforms into Saudi society at large.

Massive investment in, and development of, downstream petrochemical products and capacity is the second pillar of economic diversification in Saudi Arabia. By 2009, the Kingdom was the fastest growing market in the Middle East for the petrochemical, printing, plastics and packaging industries, and accounted for 70 per cent of petrochemical production in the GCC. During the year, Saudi officials announced plans to consolidate their position as one of the biggest players in the global petrochemicals industry through the launch of three of the most ambitious petrochemicals projects in the world: the Ras Tanura Integrated Project, construction of the world's largest integrated petrochemicals facility in Jubail Industrial City, and an upgrading of the Petro Rabigh Refinery into one of the most sophisticated integrated oil refining and petrochemical facilities of its kind. The three initiatives aim to expand Saudi Arabia's range of petrochemical products and substantially increase its global market base, in addition to creating 150,000 skilled engineering and technical jobs.[99]

The scale of ambition and financial resources devoted to economic diversification in Saudi Arabia are impressive. Between 2009 and 2014, these large-scale projects are expected to generate 10.8 million jobs within the Kingdom. However, a report compiled by the National Bank of Kuwait in 2009 estimated that suitably-qualified Saudi workers would only fill about half, or 5.45 million, of the positions, leaving the remainder to expatriate labourers.[100] Ongoing lags in Saudi indices of human development exist alongside other constraining factors on the pace and extent of Saudi diversification. These include the dense networks of familial political-economic alliances that complicate the transition to a market economy with high standards of corporate governance.[101] These linkages and the business culture that they represented became clear during the sudden debt restructuring announced by two Saudi conglomerates (Saad Group and Ahmad Hamad Algosaibi and Brothers) in May 2009.[102] This affected more than eighty domestic, regional and international banks, including Citigroup and BNP Paribas, but the lack of transparency and inadequate disclosure of information over the degree of exposure demonstrated the obstacles to overcoming an older way of conducting business on the basis of a family name.[103]

Issues of 'political-economic families' and poor corporate governance are not Saudi-specific, but exist to varying degrees throughout the Gulf. Their continuing salience is clearly evidenced in the trajectory of economic diversification in the United Arab Emirates and Kuwait. Within the UAE, policymakers in Dubai fast-tracked a grandiose, government-led development model that repositioned the emirate as an international hub for the service and logistics industries.[104] Their approach constituted the most radical attempt in the Gulf to move toward a post-oil economy, and initially it succeeded in reducing the oil sector's contribution to GDP to 5.1 per cent by 2006.[105] This notwithstanding, the spectacular implosion of the Dubai business model in 2008–9 carried a cautionary warning for proponents of economic diversification in the Gulf States. The onset of the global financial downturn revealed the economic basis for the Dubai model to be little more than a mirage based on an unsustainable expectation of a constant supply of easy credit and rising real estate prices.[106] In November 2009, the circumstances of Dubai World's opaque announcement of a six-month moratorium on repayment of a $4 billion Islamic bond laid bare the illusory framework of corporate governance in the emirate.[107] In addition, and especially damaging to Dubai's international credibility, years of implicit guarantees of state backing for the government-owned investment company melted away in the face of official disassembling about the location of the nodes of power and responsibility in 'Dubai Inc.'[108]

Dubai's failure to create a sustainable non-oil economic base epitomised the barriers to effective economic diversification in the GCC states. Only a series of emergency injections of funds from oil-rich Abu Dhabi saved the emirate from financial meltdown, and came at a significant cost to Dubai's autonomy within the UAE. This was symbolised by the dramatic, last-minute decision to rename the world's tallest man-made structure the *Burj Khalifa*, after the ruler of Abu Dhabi and in lieu of its previous name of *Burj Dubai*, shortly before its opening in January 2010.[109] Similar to the emerging linkages of dependency between Bahrain and Saudi Arabia, the move underlined how unequal hierarchies of power are reshaping the intra-regional relations of the Gulf States as the distinction between hydrocarbon-rich and resource-poor states becomes more pronounced.

Kuwait remains the outlier and the regional laggard in moving toward diversifying its economy and broadening its sources of government revenue. Its participatory political system has delayed successive large-scale projects and plans for the past two decades, beginning with a joint study conducted by Harvard and the Massachusetts Institute of Technology (MIT) in the early-1990s. It recommended adopting a high value-added strategy based on building up human capital and expanding the financial sector in order to create jobs for well-educated Kuwaiti citizens.[110] It was followed by a recommendation in 1999 to create science and technology parks 'as a driving force to the economic development and welfare of Kuwaitis.' However, both initiatives failed to take off, owing to what the 1999 study described as a 'tendency toward too much politicisation of issues leading to indecision and inaction.'[111] More recently, in 2007 the Central Bank of Kuwait partnered with McKinsey to produce *Vision 2020*, and in March 2010 ex-British prime minister Tony Blair presented the 'Blair Report,' entitled *Vision Kuwait 2030*, to the government for consideration. This stated bluntly that 'Kuwait cannot sustain its current path,' and called for a 'thorough, deep and radical set of changes' that would turn Kuwait into the pre-eminent trading, energy and logistics hub for the northern Gulf by 2030.[112]

The primary problem facing the implementation of these various strategic visions is one unique to Kuwait in the Gulf States, with the partial exception of Bahrain. This is the participatory political system that has produced a succession of stand-offs between a comparatively weak government and strong parliamentary body. Political polarization increased markedly after the mini-succession crisis in January 2006, with three dissolutions of parliament between 2006 and 2009 alone.[113] Political battling negatively impacted the diversification process as it resulted in the delay or cancellation of a number of large-scale projects, including a $17.4 billion joint venture between the Petro-chemical Industries Company of Kuwait and the Dow Chemical Company, the construction of a fourth oil refinery by a Japanese-South Korean consortium, and a plan to attract foreign investment and external financing into the northern Kuwaiti oilfields through Project Kuwait.[114]

The cancellation of the K-Dow and fourth refinery deals occurred after members of parliament accused the government of irregularities and a lack of transparency in the tendering process, and inflicted significant damage on investor confidence in Kuwait.[115] Important questions also remain unresolved about the source and amount of funding for the projects of diversification earmarked in the Kuwait Four-Year Development Plan, announced in 2010. They underscored the sensitivity and intense suspicion between the government and the parliament over the ownership and direction of development of Kuwait's oil reserves.[116] The result has been a damaging erosion of international investors' confidence in the Kuwaiti regulatory and political environment. This has translated into remarkably low inflows of foreign direct investment (FDI) in Kuwait. In 2008, inflows reached a mere $58 million as compared with $1,794 million in Bahrain, $2,928 million in Oman, $6,700 million in Qatar, $13,700m in the United Arab Emirates, and $38,223 million in Saudi Arabia.[117] This astounding gap reflects the poor enabling environment in Kuwait and lays bare the scale of the challenge facing policymakers as they seek to compete in a dynamic and crowded environment that already boasts (multiple) regional financial, trading, aviation and maritime hubs.

The Limits of Reform

The political infighting in Kuwait provides a highly-visible example of the difficulties inherent in moving toward meaningful economic diversification in the Gulf States. True reform would involve a decisive shift away from notions of citizens' entitlement and have profound socio-political implications for the future of redistributive states.[118] It would also require the rebalancing of the public and private sectors, together with a fundamental reshaping of state-business relations. In addition, the measures would necessarily encompass the unbundling of the nexus of intertwined political and economic stakeholders, as embodied in the power and reach of the merchant family conglomerates.[119] Reforms thus need interlinking with comprehensive reform of educational systems and labour markets, and the move toward incentive-based and performance-linked structures. Moreover the underlying pivot should be an acknowledgment that the value of investment in human capital is limited without contemporaneous attitudinal shifts toward more sustainable patterns of development. This is particularly important in the industrialization projects that form a pillar of economic diversification, as they have added greatly to already-overstretched demands for power and water, as detailed in the next chapter.

This is not to imply that no progress at all has been achieved in the GCC states. On the contrary, the lavish expenditure on education and industrial mega-projects in recent years has produced tangible results, albeit at the paradoxical cost of enhancing aspects of resource insecurity. Significantly, an incipient bourgeoisie has begun to emerge in Saudi Arabia and the United Arab Emirates, whose wealth is based on some productive value-added rather than the mere redistribution of rent.[120] Furthermore, the pattern of state expenditures during the second oil boom (2002–8) differed qualitatively from that of the first in the 1970s and early 1980s. Dubai excepted, the GCC economies adopted more careful fiscal policies during the second boom that allowed them to pursue countercyclical policies that blunted the impact of the downturn that followed. This period also saw the formative growth of a private sector that served a greater private demand and became less dependent on state spending for its survival, while several private-sector companies, such as Zain or Agility in Kuwait, developed into regional champions, although both ran into difficulties in 2009.[121]

Nevertheless, programmes of diversification will remain cosmetic at best if they do not involve a shift in the balance of economic power or attitudes to development and private sector employment within Gulf polities. It is undoubtedly the case that the regimes in each of the Gulf States have embraced the concept of diversification and translated it into strategic visions and plans. However, it is unclear whether they have properly assessed the myriad implications of this choice if it were to be implemented in full. The economic downturn in 2008–9 and the problems in corporate governance that emerged in Saudi Arabia and Dubai indicate that the underlying issues remain largely unresolved. The same goes for the attempts to stimulate a knowledge-based economic transition in the Gulf States. Money and resources have been channeled toward tangible objectives, such as research collaboration with, and the opening of branches of, leading international universities. Yet it is the intangible shift in values concerning educational attainment and a productive culture that will be pivotal in embedding a qualitative shift in any successful transition to a post-oil economy.[122]

5

THE POLITICAL ECONOMY
OF RESOURCE INSECURITY

This chapter broadens the concept of security to encompass the political economy of resource distribution in the Gulf States and Yemen. It examines the long-term strategic dimensions of ensuring security of access to sufficient food, water and energy supplies. This is critical to meeting the challenges of rapid economic and demographic growth described in the previous chapter. Officials in the GCC states have taken innovative steps to meet the requirements of food security, in particular, but water supplies and power generation capabilities remain a challenge. These leave the Gulf States vulnerable to the contestation of resources if scarcities interact with the politics of uneven development. It is in this context that the political economy of access to resources holds the potential to sharpen existing fault-lines within Gulf polities and create additional fissures. Competition over dwindling natural resources can accentuate traditional and emerging tensions between individuals and communities both within societies and between states, if perceptions of unequal access or exploitation arise.

The first half of this chapter focuses on the measures being taken to address resource security in the Gulf States. It emphasises the politically expedient choices being made by GCC regimes to increase output, rather than the more difficult and unpopular steps that address the causes of unsustainable consumption. The chapter then examines three case studies of previous instances in which localized scarcities and uneven access to resources led to domestic tension and instability.

These are the Shiite-led unrest in Saudi Arabia in 1979 and Bahrain between 1994 and 1999, as well as the exploitation of Yemeni oil rents by patronage networks linked to President Ali Abdullah Saleh since the 1990s. Together, they demonstrate how the concentration of resources in one privileged grouping while scarcities persist elsewhere has been a major driver of internal conflict. Resource shortages may therefore develop into intractable threats to security if they become intertwined with the politics of marginalisation within Gulf societies or if they call into question the state's capacity to deliver essential goods to its citizen population.

A burgeoning academic literature explores the phenomenon of the 'oil curse' and the interaction of rent-seeking behaviour between state and non-state actors at the local, national, regional and international levels.[1] This is complicated in the Gulf States by the patterns of subsidisation that have become embedded in the fabric of state-society relations over the past four decades. Political leaders and officials in the GCC states fear the potential unrest that could ensue from the scaling back of these subsidies, particularly during times of comparative hardship. The street riots in Yemen in 2005 that followed government efforts to abolish subsidies on diesel provide a case in point.[2] So, too, did the surge in commodity prices in 2007–8, which left states in the GCC, as elsewhere in the Middle East, vulnerable to social unrest and simmering discontent at the rising cost of living.[3]

The drawdown of subsidy regimes and the search for resource security is consequently fraught with difficulty. For this reason, stability of access to resources is intertwined with the maintenance of social order, especially in the theoretically depoliticised polities of the Gulf. If well-managed, resources can become valuable assets of development, as evidenced most successfully in Norway in the decades following the discovery of North Sea oil and gas.[4] However, the record of experience in the chapter's case studies indicate how the perception of uneven access to declining resources can rapidly emerge as a source of contestation. A multiplier effect may then develop that feeds off other points of tension to exacerbate fractures within polities and heighten their vulnerability to exogenous shocks to the system. The longer the Gulf States put off the politically sensitive issues of reformulating the subsidy regimes and the social contract, the harder it will become to wean citizens off such mechanisms that increasingly are taken for granted. Hence the maintenance of resource security is a pillar of internal security in the short- to medium-term, and the way that governments address it will determine the nature of the transition to the post-oil era in the Gulf.

Food and Water Security

During 2007 and the first half of 2008, food prices and inflationary pressures escalated in the Gulf States, as elsewhere around the world. This negatively impacted the human security of the many blue-collar workers in the Gulf, for whom spending on food absorbed a high proportion of their disposable income. The increase in food costs hit these groups hard and triggered rioting by migrant labourers in the United Arab Emirates and Bahrain, while in Yemen more than seven million people (approximately one-third of the total population) suffer from chronic hunger, with a further 1.2 million requiring food aid. These include vulnerable refugees from Somalia and a generation of Yemeni children for whom the lack of sufficient food impacts their physical development and health.[5] Moreover, the rising price of food coincided with rapid increases in the cost of fuel and other commodities, and led to spiralling inflation that eroded the already-thin margins of subsistence for many communities and individuals.[6] Further demonstrations in July 2008 by Indian workers in Ras Al-Khaimah and Bangladeshi workers in Kuwait in support of improvements to their pay and standard of living underscored the linkage between inflation and social unrest, and the capacity for food shortages and complications of access to trigger discontent with states' responsive measures.[7]

Food security in the GCC is therefore complicated by the existence of large numbers of low-paid migrant workers as well as the countries' substantial dependence on imported supplies. This raises the vulnerability of the United Arab Emirates, Kuwait and Qatar to the impact of food costs on lower-income groups as expatriates, mostly low-wage labourers, form a majority of their populations.[8] Meanwhile, the Food and Agricultural Organisation of the United Nations estimated the level of import dependence in the GCC to exceed 60 per cent in 2010, while 15 per cent of all imports in Saudi Arabia are food items.[9] These two trends expose Gulf polities to the risks of external shocks that officials are powerless to control. The unrest in 2008 demonstrated regimes' susceptibility to popular frustration morphing into a backlash at their perceived inability to take effective remedial measures. Officials in all six GCC states subsequently began to consider innovative new steps to meet their food security requirements through strategic agricultural investments and tie-ups with food-producing countries.

The dilemma facing the Gulf States is that previous attempts to attain food security by promoting agricultural productivity have paradoxically made the problem worse. These policies have neither been successful in increasing food self-sufficiency and reducing reliance on imported foodstuffs, nor sustainable in their careful managing of scarce water resources. Agriculture accounted for a mere 6.5 per cent of GDP in Saudi Arabia and a total of 1.6 per cent throughout the GCC, but nearly 60 per cent of total water consumption usage in 2000.[10] This far outstripped industrial and domestic usage and represented an unsustainable utilisation of resources in what was already one of the most arid regions in the world. In 2006 Kuwait ranked as the most water-scarce country in the world, and three other GCC states featured in the top ten, with the United Arab Emirates third, Qatar fifth, and Saudi Arabia eighth.[11] A prominent example of the disjuncture between agricultural use and water scarcity is the Al-Safi Dairy Farm in Saudi Arabia. This is the largest in the world and more than double the size of the biggest dairy farm in the United States, with 37,000 cows producing more than 58 million gallons of milk each year, at an average water cost of nearly 2300 gallons of water per gallon of milk.[12]

Belated recognition of the intertwined problems of water and food security led Saudi Arabia to announce in February 2008 that it would cease producing grain by 2016. Officials attributed this abrupt reversal in food policy to the impact of climate change, drought and the depletion of fossil water. All of Saudi Arabia's wheat depended on central pivot irrigation that drew its water from fossil reserves. The drawdown of these reserves clashed with Saudi industrialisation plans and rapid population growth, both of which significantly increased the demand for scarce water supplies. This contributed to the policy shift away from three decades of state-sponsored agricultural development programmes. These policies, laid down in the 1970s, aimed to increase the Kingdom's self-sufficiency in selected food items, and raised wheat production from 3,000 tons in 1970 to a peak of 3.4 million in 1991, before falling away to 2.5 million tons by 2008.[13]

Unsustainable agricultural production has therefore resulted in overexploitation of fossil water reserves and the depletion of underground aquifers throughout the Arabian Peninsula. This is evidenced most bleakly in Yemen, where the water table has fallen by two metres in recent years, and nineteen of the country's twenty-one aquifers are no longer being replenished. Indeed, rates of extraction in Sana'a run at an estimated four times that of replenishment, while water basins elsewhere have either collapsed or are close to collapse.[14] It is part of a broader trend throughout the Middle East, although the rapidity of population growth and industrial development underway in the Gulf States exacerbated its effects. The full extent of the regional problem became clear in November 2008 in a report issued by the Islamic Development Bank. This found that average annual water availability per capita in the Middle East had declined by two-thirds since 1960, and is projected to halve again by 2050 to leave the entire region acutely water-scarce.[15]

Elsewhere on the Arabian Peninsula, the mining of fossil water from deep trans-boundary aquifers provides another potentially potent flashpoint. Much as Iraqi accusations of Kuwaiti slant drilling of oil from the shared Rumaila field formed an important pretext to, and (flawed) justification of, the August 1990 invasion, the unilateral draining of the shared aquifers under the Arabian Peninsula could become drivers of conflict if water resources continue to dwindle and decline in quality as salinity increases. An extensive regional aquifer system known as the Eastern Arabian Aquifer extends from central Saudi Arabia to Bahrain and Qatar, while the Kuwait Group Aquifer is hydraulically connected with the Dammam Foundation of the Hasa Group in eastern Saudi Arabia.[16] Beginning in the 1990s, Saudi Arabian over-exploitation of its aquifers for agricultural use began to reduce the water availability and agricultural potential in Bahrain and Qatar.[17] These trends contain the seeds of future political tension and an emerging conflict over trans-boundary water resources on the peninsula, particularly as cooperation between GCC member-states on utilising and managing joint aquifers has been negligible.[18]

Responses to these pessimistic prognoses have varied. At one extreme, in Yemen, a chaotic free for all 'tragedy of the commons' has developed as individuals and groups have rushed to extract as much water as possible to translate into short-term profit through the cultivation of qat before supplies run out.[19] The scale of the problem of private extraction from unregulated wells became clear when the Ministry of Water and Environment estimated that 99 per cent of all extraction in Yemen was unlicensed.[20] By contrast, officials in the GCC states formulated concerted strategies to alleviate the strain on water supplies. These primarily involved the outsourcing of food production and the conclusion of strategic agro-investments. The scale of human and financial resources devoted to these projects indicated the seriousness that policymakers attributed to the potential threat posed by resource insecurity to the internal stability of their polities.[21]

In Saudi Arabia, officials reacted to the food price rises in 2008 by announcing plans to set up a new investment fund to purchase agricultural land overseas. It prioritised investment in wheat and rice stocks to meet internal market demand and initially targeted land acquisitions in Pakistan, Sudan and Thailand.[22] Officials also established the King Abdullah Initiative for Saudi Agricultural Investment Abroad, and set up a food security panel affiliated to the Chamber of Commerce and Industry in Riyadh. This identified wheat, barley, corn, soybeans, maize, rice and sugar as strategic crops for investment.[23] In addition, the state-owned Saudi Industrial Development Fund began to grant financing facilities to firms exploring agricultural investments abroad. In February 2009, the Hail Agricultural Development Company announced a two-year investment of $45.3 million to develop 9000 hectares of farmland in Sudan, while in September it emerged that Saudi Arabia was negotiating with Pakistan to lease 202,400 hectares of farmland, an area nearly twice the size of Hong Kong. Significantly, the Pakistani Ministry of Agriculture stated that it would deploy special security forces to protect the farmland, and claimed that 'the land we will provide Saudi Arabia will be divided among the four provinces and they will be using it to grow a variety of produce such as wheat, fruits and vegetables.'[24] This introduces a fascinating albeit disturbing element, and a potentially new flashpoint of internal tension, into internal discussions of security and sovereignty in Pakistan and other recipient states.

Saudi Arabia is by no means alone in following this dual strategy of overseas land acquisitions and agro-investment. Qatar agreed in July 2008 to establish a joint holding company with the government of Sudan that would direct Qatari investment toward boosting the production of wheat, corn, animal fodder and oilseeds in Sudan.[25] Qatar also actively sought deals in 2009, and commenced a strategic dialogue with Thailand covering greater cooperation and joint investment opportunities in the energy and food sectors.[26] For its part, the United Arab Emirates examined the possibility of acquiring farmland in Pakistan, Egypt and Yemen, while the Abu Dhabi Fund for Development launched a large-scale agricultural project in Sudan in 2008–9.[27] The country also undertook strategic purchases of land in Tanzania, Mozambique and Ethiopia.[28] In the summer of 2008, the Emirates' Economy Minister, Sultan bin Said Al-Mansuri, acknowledged that investment in agriculture abroad formed 'part of our strategic investment in general,' and the issue was discussed during a visit by President Khalifa bin Zayed Al-Nahyan to Kazakhstan in July 2008.[29]

The range and frequency with which deals were being pursued in 2008–9 reflected the urgency of the problem as perceived by GCC policymakers. It also revealed an emerging alignment between the Gulf States' interest in food security and the energy security requirements of food-producing states in Africa and Asia. This 'oil for food' nexus dominated the inaugural joint meeting of foreign ministers from the GCC and Association of Southeast Asian Nations (ASEAN) states in June 2009. The ASEAN Secretary-General, Suring Pitsuan, explicitly told a news conference that 'You have what we don't have, and we have plenty of what you don't have, so we need each other.' The joint-meeting also initiated discussions about moving toward constructing a trade bloc based on food and oil that targeted the energy and food security needs of both groups of states.[30] Bilateral negotiations in 2009 between Saudi Arabia and Angola also centred round an oil-food nexus, with potential Saudi assistance in boosting Angola's refining capacity being discussed.[31]

These moves into foreign farmland acquisition are reshaping the international relations of the GCC states, especially with emerging partners in Africa and Asia. They represent one aspect of the internationalisation of the Gulf and the broader eastward and southern repositioning in the global order. This introduces another dimension into the changing regional security equation set out in chapter three, namely potential competition for access to farmland with China. The GCC and China were the two largest-scale movers into the farmland market in 2008, with Chinese policies being guided by its aggressive 'Go Abroad' outward investment strategy. This resulted in more than thirty agricultural cooperation agreements throughout Asia and Africa that gave China access to 'friendly country' farmland in exchange for Chinese technologies, training and infrastructural development funds.[32]

The Chinese approach stoked considerable local resentment and carries a warning for the Gulf States. Tension focused on local cultivators' perceptions that their land and labour were being diverted to meet Chinese requirements with little benefit to themselves. In this context, it is in the Gulf States' interest that they structure their engagement to ensure that both producing and consuming states—and particularly host societies and communities—benefit from the agreements.[33] The interlocking interests between food and energy security may well provide the level of mutual benefit that ensures that the Gulf States do not make the same missteps as the Chinese. So, too, might enhanced GCC investment flows to host societies, particularly when they overlap with an ideational and religious appeal to fellow Arab and Islamic states, in whose countries many of the agro-investments have occurred.[34] It is nevertheless the case that agro-investments in Asia and Africa expose the Gulf States to potential tensions ranging from local backlashes to regional and international competition for scarce resources in the future.

Food security provides an example of specific and targeted actions that informed and subsequently influenced policy planning in the Gulf States in response to an identified threat to internal stability. The outsourcing of food production increased their adaptive capacity and enabled the continuation of the subsidisation regimes that form an intrinsic part of the ruling bargain in the Gulf.[35] However, policy did not focus on the underlying trends of rapid demographic growth and unsustainable exploitation of limited natural resources in daily life. To the extent that access to food and water became securitised at all, it was in response to the short-term phenomena of high commodity and fuel prices that triggered social unrest in 2007–8. It did not represent part of a coherent re-conceptualisation of the meaning and object of security. Instead, thinking remained ad hoc and short-term and was not integrated into broader debates on the sustainability of patterns of urban and industrial development in the region.[36]

Energy Security and Power Generation

Energy security operates at two interconnected levels in the Arabian Peninsula states. Internally, privileged access to resources through policies of widespread subsidisation constitute powerful centripetal mechanisms and pillars of regime legitimation. Externally, governments' ability to provide these resources to their citizenry is intimately bound up with (and vulnerable to disruption to) the constant and unimpeded flow of revenues from hydrocarbon exports. This, in turn, feeds into a third dimension, which is the energy security requirements of the oil-consuming nations that purchase their oil and gas from the Gulf region. The internal and external dimensions are interlinked as any disruption to one heightens the vulnerability of the other, as the two are contingent on the smooth functioning of each. This was evidenced in Al-Qaeda in the Arabian Peninsula's specific targeting of the core of regime legitimacy in Saudi Arabia through its attack on the Kingdom's oil-processing facilities at Abqaiq in February 2006.[37]

Power generation and energy availability represent another dimension of resource insecurity in the Gulf States. Both approached peak capacity during the second oil boom as the accelerating pace of regional development and mega-projects placed existing facilities under severe strain. High (and increasing) reliance on energy-intensive desalination plants for water supplies compounded the problem, as the proportion of desalinated water reached 99 per cent of total demand in Qatar, 96.5 per cent in Kuwait, 92 per cent in Bahrain and 85 per cent in the United Arab Emirates in 2005. These shares were considerably higher than their 1990 equivalents, and only Saudi Arabia and Oman met the majority of their water demands from renewable sources.[38] Blackouts became a common feature in many Gulf cities, particularly during the hot summer months owing to soaring demand for air conditioning.[39] In Bahrain alone, energy consumption doubled between 2006 and 2008 and demand for energy was forecast to grow a further 65 per cent to 2014.[40] The onset of the global economic downturn and the delay or cancellation of a number of major development projects temporarily alleviated the strain on existing capacity. Yet all of the Gulf States, with the sole exception of Qatar, face current and future shortages in power generation caused by high population growth, over-demand and under-pricing.[41] This complicates strategies to promote sustainable development as it challenges embedded notions of subsidised consumption that inform perceptions of the social contract.

Officials in the Gulf States have adopted ambitious measures to meet the spiralling demands of power generation. In 2009, the GCC estimated that its power consumption was rising by 8–10 per cent each year, making it one of the highest rates of recorded growth in the world. At a collective level, the inauguration of the GCC Interconnection Authority in July 2009 was especially important. It represented the completion of the first of two phases connecting GCC electricity networks in a single grid by 2010. When fully connected, the grid will allow the GCC states to supply each other with electricity from their own grids in the event of localised shortages.[42] Significantly, the power exchange and trading agreement represented a landmark instance of pan-Gulf cooperation as ownership and division of supplies are shared proportionately among the six member-states.[43] It also marked a step forward in intra-regional cooperation from the Dolphin Project to connect the national gas grids of Saudi Arabia, Kuwait, Bahrain and the United Arab Emirates into a single integrated bloc, which experienced persistent political disagreements, territorial disputes and Saudi Arabian opposition that hindered and eventually downsized its eventual implementation.[44]

Once again, and similar to the analysis outlined in the previous section on food security, the measures addressed the symptoms rather than the roots of the problem. Gas consumption in Saudi Arabia, Qatar, Kuwait and the United Arab Emirates surged by 50 per cent between 2002 and 2008 yet barely kept pace with competing demands from electricity generation, water desalination and energy-intensive industrialization into petrochemicals and aluminium.[45] These reflect the linkages between economic diversification, security of access to resources, and environmental degradation and climate change. In particular, water desalination plants are energy-intensive, environmentally harmful, and central to the political economy of subsidisation in the GCC. So, too, are cheap electricity prices, which (as with the price of water) neither reflect global norms nor encourage sustainable consumption. Electricity is provided free to citizens in Qatar, while elsewhere tariffs rise to a regional high of 5.5 cents per kilowatt hour (KwH) in Dubai, compared to an average charge of 12 cents per KwH in the United States and 16 cents in the United Kingdom.[46] Meanwhile, Kuwaiti plans to quadruple its own gas production to more than 4 billion cubic feet per day by 2030 may become a new source of cross-border tensions in the future. Plans announced in 2010 anticipate the development and extraction of non-associated gas from the Neutral Zone that Kuwait shares with Saudi Arabia, and from the Dorra gas field that it shares with Iran. The latter, in particular, may become a flashpoint or driver of instability, as Kuwait and Iran have still to resolve ongoing differences over its development that date back to the 1960s.[47]

Government-led policymaking therefore focused on diversifying the sources of energy rather than addressing patterns of unsustainable consumption. Led by Abu Dhabi, investment into renewable and alternative forms of energy increased substantially after 2004. These included Abu Dhabi's flagship carbon-neutral Masdar City project and the prioritisation of research into solar and alternative energy science in the King Abdullah University of Science and Technology in Saudi Arabia. Abu Dhabi was also selected as the headquarters of the newly-created International Renewable Energy Agency (IRENA) in 2009, and plays host to the World Future Energy Summit each year.[48] Together with the launching of the Masdar Institute of Science and Technology in September 2009, the initiatives enabled Abu Dhabi to brand itself as a world leader in cutting-edge research into renewable and sustainable energy.[49] In support of this branding initiative, officials in Abu Dhabi in January 2009 set an ambitious renewable energy target of 7 per cent of the total energy mix by 2020, although subsequent policy pronouncements have indicated that a figure of 5 per cent is more realistic.[50]

Somewhat at odds with the focus on renewable energy, and to the public displeasure of IRENA, the UAE also took the lead in developing a civil nuclear energy programme, with plans to construct up to 20 gigawatts (GW) of nuclear power station capacity to assist in meeting a projected national energy demand of 40GW by 2020.[51] In light of the international concern over the intent and capability of Iran's nuclear programme, the UAE cooperated intensively with the International Atomic Energy Agency (IAEA) to ensure that its plans meet the highest standards of transparency, safeguarding and monitoring.[52] This gained it the support of the international community in general, and the United States in particular. Congressional approval for the thirty-year nuclear cooperation deal in October 2009 sent a powerful signal of geopolitical support for the UAE as a responsible regional actor and a model for other Middle Eastern states seeking a nuclear energy capability.[53] The '123 Agreement' for bilateral US-UAE peaceful nuclear cooperation subsequently went into force in December 2009 and established a legal framework for commerce in civil nuclear technology between the two countries.[54] In the same month, the UAE signed a landmark $20.4 billion agreement with an international consortium led by the Korea Electric Power Company (KEPCO) to build and operate four nuclear reactors in Sag Baraka, an area of coastal desert near the border with Saudi Arabia. The first reactor is scheduled to begin generating electricity in May 2017 and the remaining three are projected to open by 2020, all using fuel that will be supplied by the Korea Nuclear Fuel Company.[55]

International support for the UAE nuclear programme nevertheless raises the possibility of a regional proliferation cascade. In December 2006, GCC leaders, meeting at their annual heads of state summit in Riyadh, announced plans to undertake a study for a joint programme that would focus on nuclear technology for peaceful purposes. It was followed by a feasibility study conducted by the IAEA in 2007 on the benefits of centralising nuclear power production in one location in the GCC.[56] These developments raised more questions than answers, including any mechanism for deciding where to site any facilities in light of the considerable intra-GCC tensions over leadership and location. However the joint plan later became moot as it was superseded by the decision of individual governments to move forward with unilateral plans of their own. The UAE moved first, but during 2009 Kuwait and Oman also unveiled plans to seek civil nuclear energy for peaceful purposes and in full cooperation with the IAEA. Officials in both countries framed their decisions as vital to meeting heightened demands for power generation for electricity and water desalination.[57] This was followed in April 2010 by the announcement of the creation of the King Abdullah City for Nuclear and Renewable Energy in Riyadh, a move interpreted as a strong signal that Saudi Arabia was actively considering a civilian nuclear power programme to reduce its heavy reliance on oil for power generation.[58]

These civil nuclear energy initiatives do not in themselves hold any immediate threat to the non-proliferation regime, particularly as the nuclear fuel will be imported rather than produced domestically. Instead, it is the strategic context of current and future inter-regional rivalry with Iran that injects an inherent proliferation risk and note of strategic uncertainty into the nuclear fuel cycle in the Gulf. A perceived or actual Iranian breakout in its nuclear weapons capability might tip the GCC states toward seeking a regional nuclear deterrent of their own. This would not necessarily be welcomed by the smaller GCC states, particularly if it involved the prospect of a 'Saudi bomb.' A nuclear-capable Saudi Arabia would risk reinforcing the smaller states' suspicions of the Kingdom's hegemonic designs on the Arabian Peninsula. It would likely be resisted by the United Arab Emirates and Qatar, and potentially trigger a costly and destabilising regional arms race, both among the GCC states and with Iran.[59] This builds upon and complicates the shorter-term issue posed by the range of policy responses open to the international community should it perceive that

Iran needed to be prevented from gaining nuclear weapons capability. This appeared to be gathering momentum in the months that followed President Ahmedinejad's contested re-election in June 2009 as the uncovering of a clandestine enrichment facility near Qom in September 2009 was followed by a defiant Iranian announcement in November of its intention to construct a further ten enrichment plants. Subsequently, in February 2010, Ahmedinejad formally declared Iran a 'nuclear power' and announced plans to raise the enrichment level of its uranium from 3.5 per cent to 20 per cent This prompted the IAEA to release a report warning (for the first time since the Iranian nuclear file began in 2002) that Iran's 'past or current undisclosed activities related to the development of a nuclear payload for a missile.'[60]

Increasing power generation capacity is one side of the coin and hitherto the preferred route for GCC states. The emphasis on supply-side expansion has enabled them to avoid taking politically sensitive demand-side changes that would tamper with the social contract in its current format. On the other side of the coin, the measures introduced to address the root causes of the problem of unsustainable consumption have been very limited. One solution involved the introduction of basic charges for utilities but limited to expatriates only. This was the case with electricity charging in Qatar as well as the introduction of a charge for water use in Dubai in 2008.[61] Both measures represented a tentative move in the direction of heightening consumer awareness of the cost of consumption and the need for efficiency. However, the exemption for citizens noticeably left untouched the group within society most likely to combine a high standard of living with wasteful patterns of consumption.[62] Until such tariffs are extended to citizens, and more closely aligned with market rates, their impact will remain limited and the systemic problems engendered by subsidy regimes will continue to distort utilities markets in the region.

Officials and policymakers are not unaware of the scale of the problem at hand. On the contrary, they frequently cite subsidies as one the key issues that need overhauling as part of the broader move toward a post-redistributive form of governance. Senior officials in Kuwait, for instance, acknowledge that 'the state cannot continue to offer a blank cheque without imposing responsibility,' but recognise that 'there are at present too many incentives and motivations for people to remain rent-seekers.'[63] Meanwhile, a prominent academic in Bahrain warned bluntly that 'the system must change or transform itself but this is very difficult and probably they [the government] cannot do it.'[64] Elsewhere in the GCC, the numerous governmental visions and plans for economic diversification also attest to the need for expanding the productive economic base to wean economies away from reliance on the income from hydrocarbons.

The fundamental problem is that awareness of the problems of transition is matched by a realistic understanding among officials of the difficulties involved in tampering with the redistributive mechanisms that underpin the social contract in the GCC states. The complexity of unbundling the layers of subsidy that are intertwined in the social contract thus explains governments' reluctance to take on the issue, particularly during times of relative economic hardship.[65] Their failure to commit to a sustained process of structural reform between 2002 and 2008 signified a lost opportunity to take action during a favourable economic climate. It increases the likelihood that governments will have to attempt the potentially painful changes during times of comparative economic difficulty, or when the transition toward a post-oil economy can no longer be put off, and when rapid socio-economic change is more likely to be contested rather than consensual.[66]

Three Case Studies: Saudi Arabia, Bahrain and Yemen

The steps being taken by governments to attain food, water and energy security are important in themselves. Nevertheless, a more intractable problem facing several GCC states and Yemen comes from the interaction of dwindling levels of resources with the persistence or shapening of unequal patterns of distribution. Moreover, the pace of resource depletion will accelerate in the face of demographic pressures and economic growth. In numerous comparative instances elsewhere, the concentration of resources in one particular or privileged grouping while scarcities exist elsewhere has been a demonstrated source of sub-national—and occasionally cross-border—conflict.[67] This has also occurred in the Arabian Peninsula, as documented by three case-studies from Saudi Arabia, Bahrain and Yemen. They demonstrate how uneven access to resources became politicised and a driver of domestic instability by sharpening latent tensions between ethnic, tribal or sectarian groups within society. The case-studies emphasise the ties that interlink the trajectories of resource depletion and demographic growth with the choices of political and societal actors, and the persistence of patterns of unequal access to, and distribution of, increasingly-scarce resources.[68]

In November 1979, the Eastern Province of Saudi Arabia experienced seven days of prolonged and bloody clashes between thousands of Shiite protestors and state security forces. The violence had multiple causes, and was sparked by harsh state-sanctioned repression of the Ashura festival commemorating the martyrdom of Imam Hussein. It overlapped with the occupation of the Grand Mosque in Mecca by extremist Sunni rejectionists of Al-Saud rule, as well as the ongoing Islamic Revolution in Iran. The convergence of these contemporaneous crises rocked the Saudi elite as it appeared to face systemic challenges to its legitimacy from both its Sunni core and the peripheral Shiite communities that populated its oil-rich Eastern Province.[69] The Iranian revolution, in particular, presented a two-fold warning to the Sunni regimes of the Gulf of the dangers of popular anger cascading out of control and the potential linkage of pan-Shiite empowerment with patterns of relative marginalisation and uneven development within their own polities.[70]

The political economy of resource distribution provided the contextual parameters for the anger felt by Saudi Shiites toward what they perceived as unfair and discriminatory government policies. Shiites' resentment at contracting water resources and failing water systems in the Eastern Province oases of Qatif and Al-Hasa was a major cause of the violent clashes with security forces in both regions. Tensions were exacerbated by protestors' anger at the apparent inability of local municipalities to alleviate the worsening situation, which was impacting agricultural yields and depleting the water table through unregulated extraction. These feelings tapped into broader currents of grievance at the perceived marginalisation of Shiite communities in Saudi Arabia and the politics of uneven development that denied basic services to the towns and villages in the Eastern Province.[71]

Developments in Bahrain since the 1990s illustrate the tensions that arise from differential levels of access to resources and employment. Economic deprivation and government discrimination against the majority-Shiite population formed the basis for recurrent bouts of internal unrest. Seven separate episodes of tension between 1921 and 1975 provided the background to the sustained and organised uprising that occurred between Shiite-led protestors and the regime between 1994 and 1999.[72] During the 1990s, the sectarian imbalance between

Sunni and Shiite communities became interlinked with the country's socio-economic problems and high levels of unemployment and marginalisation among Bahraini Shiite communities.[73] This potent combination of economic decline, uneven distribution of oil wealth and a disadvantaged Shiite population carried worrying implications for Saudi officials lest the unrest spread to the Eastern Province.[74] It also accounted for the unprecedented levels of solidarity between the Al-Saud and the Al-Khalifa ruling families and the determination of the former that the latter not be allowed to fall at any cost.[75]

The uprising in Bahrain ended in 1999. It was followed by a period of reconciliation marked by the accession of the new Emir (later King) Hamad bin Isa Al-Khalifa, in 1999, and the symbolic repeal of the draconian State Security Law. A series of political reforms culminated in a new constitution and a bicameral National Assembly under the framework of a National Action Charter. These developments introduced a participatory mechanism that oversaw quaddriennial elections to the Council of Representatives (the lower house) beginning in 2002.[76] Nevertheless, the government of Bahrain continued to face persistent accusations of attempting to manipulate the Kingdom's ethnic and sectarian composition in order to tighten its grip on power. The so-called 'Bandargate' issue, which surfaced in September 2006, two months before the elections to the Council of Representatives, was one of these.[77] It concerned an alleged plan, uncovered by Salah Al-Bandar, a British-Sudanese advisor to the government, concerning an apparent high-level plan systematically to undermine Bahrain's Shiite communities by increasing naturalisation of Sunnis from other countries, infiltrating Shiite civil society organisations, and establishing fake non-governmental organisations during the election period.[78]

These allegations were never proven and Al-Bandar fled to the United Kingdom, while the government of Bahrain imposed a blanket ban on media reporting of the issue. The 'Bandargate' affair heightened internal divisions in Bahrain, both within the Shiite communities and with the government.[79] The largest Shiite political society (Al Wefaq National Islamic Society) reversed its 2002 decision to boycott the elections, and entered the political process. In the November 2006 elections, it picked up seventeen of the Council's forty seats to emerge as the largest oppositional group in the new parliament.[80] Yet its MPs walked out of a parliamentary debate in May 2008 in protest at the unexpected announcement of a 41 per cent increase in the population during 2007.[81] This, they alleged, was due to government attempts to dilute the Shiite majority on the islands through in-migration of Sunnis from Syria, Jordan and Saudi Arabia. More than 10,000 families were naturalised in this way, and used to staff the security services, from which Bahraini Shiites have long been excluded from leadership positions.[82] The new arrivals also elicited cross-sectarian concern at the strain they placed on already-overstretched services such as housing, education and the energy grid.[83]

Bahrain's experience highlighted the danger facing Gulf elites and society from dashed expectations of political reform processes. If the reforms are perceived merely as cloaking an old emperor in new clothes they risk generating popular disillusionment with, and disengagement from, the political process. This has already happened in Bahrain, where opposition groups struggle to explain to their constituents how their participation in the 2006 elections produced any tangible benefits.[84] Notably, this disillusion with the political process extended beyond Shiite Islamist groups to include more secular, left-wing organisations such as the National Democratic Action Society (NDAS). In September 2008, the NDAS hinted that it and other oppositional groups might boycott the 2010 elections.[85] This trend poses a potential threat to internal security and stability should oppositional groups decide that insufficient scope for redress exists within an inflexible political system, and channel their demands through violence instead.

Developments in Yemen since reunification in 1990 illustrate how differential access to resources can sharpen existing fault-lines and create new fissures within society. The discovery of oil in the southern province of Hadramawt shortly after reunification injected a potent and lucrative rent-seeking dimension into intra-regional tensions between the northern and southern provinces of Yemen. Many of these lingered from the pre- and post-occupation era and reflected existing imbalances in power relations and access to resources between the former provinces of northern and southern Yemen. In particular, officials and businessmen belonging to the powerful (northern-based) Rashid tribal confederation of President Ali Abdullah Saleh were perceived to benefit unduly from their links to the regime and preferential access to oil rents.[86]

This played on the systemic weaknesses in governance that penetrated Yemeni state institutions. It faciliated an endemic misuse of oil rents that increasingly propped up the extensive networks of patronage that

regulated inter- and intra-tribal and state-society relations.[87] It also reinforced powerful feelings of marginalisation and alienation from the
central government felt by local sheikhs and tribal leaders in southern
provinces. This tapped into anger at the inequitable distribution of
post-1990 political and economic power in Yemen, and with the political pattern laid down after the brief civil war in 1994. Such feelings
played on, and deepened, the lingering regional tensions and were a
contributory cause (although not the proximate one) of the southern
secessionist movement that rapidly gained momentum after 2007.[88]

The nature of the interconnected crises of governance and legitimate
political authority facing Yemen means that drivers of conflict cannot
be considered in isolation from each other. Nevertheless, the introduction of rent-seeking behaviour permeated state institutions that had
already been weakened by corruption and patronage. New networks
of inequality emerged that further eroded the fragile legitimacy of
Yemeni state institutions in the eyes of its many detractors. The pro-
ceeds from oil extraction also enhanced the regime's ability to remain
in power without embarking on sustained or credible reform initiatives, even as it faced violent contestations of its power and authority.
Oil rents thus operated both as a driver and multiplier of existing tensions and fault-lines that sustained a faltering political economy, while
obstructing moves to prepare for the looming post-oil transition. With
the imminent depletion of oil reserves within the coming decade, the
legacy of resource inequality is already manifesting itself in the contraction of state services and the erosion of regime legitimacy and state
authority in both violent and non-violent ways.

Fragile Resource Bases

The three case studies of Saudi Arabia, Bahrain and Yemen demonstrate how states and societies that contain numerous fault-lines can
become susceptible to internal tensions and conflict. Gulf polities contain many such fissures, including ethnic, sectarian and tribal splits,
differences between citizens and expatriates, and between different
classes of citizens themselves. These divisions both reflect, and interact
with, differential levels of access to resources. Together, they heighten
regime vulnerability to future politicisation and contestation if resource
scarcities develop and persist. Were this to happen it would also erode
regime credibility and societal confidence in the ruling bargain, based

as it has been on the redistribution of goods and services in lieu of extensive participatory mechanisms.

Any breakdown of social cohesion would jeopardise the web of social relationships that bind together the many different communities and groups within the highly-stratified Gulf polities. Alternatively, the implementation of inclusive counter-measures to promote and strengthen internal cohesion will increase the likelihood of a consensual and non-violent transition toward post-oil political economies. For this reason, leaderships, particularly in the richer GCC states, have invested large amounts of time and money in attaining food and energy security and attempting to delay the moment when the carrying capacity of their rapidly-expanding populations exceeds the boundaries of economic, social and environmental sustainability. Yet these represent short-term initiatives to boost supply rather than the politically more difficult yet long-term more sustainable measures to regulate demand through the introduction of market pricing or progressive dismantling of subsidy regimes. As such, they merely postpone the eventual reckoning and introduce the possibility that it will not come about as the result of the regime's choosing in a controlled and orderly top-down manner.

Internal tensions and fault-lines also weaken states' capacities to absorb and overcome external shocks, such as the danger of abrupt or irreversible changes arising from environmental degradation or climate change. The following chapter will examine this in detail. Already the Yemeni experience indicates how easily inequitable levels of resource allocation can become drivers and multipliers of conflict. Furthermore, the direction of Gulf States' initiatives to boost capacity rather than change habits of unsustainable consumption provides a visible indication of the difficult political choices that must be confronted at some point. Here, the core issue at stake is the updating of the social contract to bring it into line with sustainable and long-term patterns of consumption and production. Yet the danger that faces Gulf policymakers is that their failure to roll back subsidies and patterns of wasteful consumption in times of comparative plenty will mean that reforms will instead occur during periods of relative hardship. This, in turn, enhances the possibility that change, when it occurs, will be contested and violent, rather than consensual and incremental.

6

CLIMATE SECURITY AND ENVIRONMENTAL CHALLENGES

The existence of unequal resource distribution and socio-economic challenges such as population stresses described in previous chapters increase a society's vulnerability to external shocks.[1] Moreover, they hold the potential to sharpen the disruptive effects of any subsequent dislocation or natural disaster, such as rising sea levels or a decisive move away from carbon-emitting fossil fuels in the industrialised world. Particularly in the low-lying coastal zones of the Arabian Peninsula, the direct and indirect impact of long-term climate-change could profoundly impact long-established patterns of human settlement and urbanisation.[2] Furthermore, these pressures have already placed the fragile ecosystem of the Peninsula under great stress, and reduced its resilience to any external shock. The interaction of these environmental scarcities and stresses with systems of perceived or actual inequalities in access to dwindling resources thus represents a potent future threat to internal stability in a climate-stressed world.[3] Already, climate change and environmental degradation have emerged as threat multipliers and drivers of conflict in Darfur and are doing so in Yemen, where they are overlaid on existing points of weakness.

There is, nevertheless, a growing disjuncture between international and Gulf-centric discourses on the environmental and security dimensions of climate change. Interlocking power circles and interest networks play a critical role in determining how perceptions of climate change in the Gulf States feed through to policy formulation.[4] These are dominated by policymakers' concern for the stability and continuity of the revenues from oil exports. Hence, issues of environmental degradation and climate change barely feature in regional security discussions, which remain overwhelmingly focused on short-term 'hard' threats to security and stability, and officials in the Gulf States (in common with other Arab states in the Middle East) still do not perceive climate change as a threatening factor in spite of mounting evidence to the contrary.[5] There is very low availability of information on, and public awareness of, these issues, and their mainstreaming into policy-making and implementation has been extremely low.[6] On the contrary, the processes of energy-intensive industrialisation and prestigious mega-projects that dominate the economic landscape of the GCC have contributed to among the highest levels of per-capita energy consumption and carbon emissions in the world.[7] This fits in the pattern of subsidised and ultimately unsustainable patterns of consumption highlighted in the previous chapter.

Climate change and environmental degradation are global issues whose effects will accelerate in the twenty-first century and present a serious and enduring threat to human (as well as state) security. Their effects will be trans-boundary and cannot be resolved without a comprehensive and multilateral approach. This marks them out as bellwethers of the profound shift in global politics in which problems and responses transcend national borders and rigid distinctions between domestic and international policy.[8] Recent research into their security implications has positioned climate change in the nexus between conflict and resource scarcity outlined in the previous chapter. Furthermore, academics and analysts have connected it to heightened vulnerability to internal instability and conflict, as well as state failure in its most extreme case.[9] Underlying these linkages is the importance of socio-political and cultural awareness that shape the institutional context in which adaptation and mitigation strategies evolve. Yet it remains the case that the institutional context in the Gulf States is dominated by their continuing reliance on revenues from the extraction and export of oil. This drives official scepticism about the effects of human-induced climate change and an unwillingness to consider or address its environmental or security dimensions.[10]

The Emergence of Climate Security

Beginning in the post-Second World War era but accelerating rapidly in the 1990s, the concept of political community became re-conceptualised into a distinctive form of 'global politics.' This developed in order to explain the intensity and extensity of global interconnections and states' enmeshment within trans-national frameworks and issues.[11] This had a security dimension, as the ending of the Cold War triggered a major rethinking of traditional concepts of security. This involved a move beyond the 'national security' of states, as hitherto defined, toward a broadening definition that encompassed both military and non-military threats. It tied into the growing awareness of global inter-dependencies based on international cooperation and multilateral frameworks of international governance. These interconnected link-ages required a cognitive shift in thinking about global security.[12] Many new security discourses appeared in the 1990s, including human security, environmental security, and climate security. All of these para-digms challenged the distinction between the internal (domestic) and external (foreign) policy dimensions that had dominated Cold War, realist perspectives on security.[13]

The early chapters of this book analysed how and why no such cog-nitive shift occurred in the Gulf, where policymaking remained focused on hard military threats to security and continued to be couched in zero-sum, balance of power terms.[14] Nevertheless, during the 1990s and accelerating in the 2000s, the threat from ecological disruption and human-induced climate change emerged as key components in the shifting global security paradigm. The concept of 'environmental secu-rity' officially became recognised as early as 1987 in the Brundtland Report (*Our Common Future*) published by the United Nations World Commission on Environment and Development. This path-breaking report introduced the notion of sustainable development and empha-sised the interlocking nature of the crises facing the planet.[15] It also paved the way for the 1992 Earth Summit, the Rio Declaration and the creation of the Commission on Sustainable Development, and the 1995 UN Commission on Global Governance with its emphasis on 'planetary security.'[16]

In 2004, the United Nations High-Level Panel on Threats, Chal-lenges and Change broadened the focus of security policy to include non-conventional threats such as poverty, infectious diseases and envi-ronmental degradation, in addition to conflict within and between states. It also made a powerful case for a new security consensus based on collective and cooperative action as it argued that 'in the twenty-first century, more than ever before, no State can stand wholly alone…

today's threats recognize no national boundaries, are connected, and must be addressed at the global and regional as well as the national levels.'[17] Three years later, in March 2007, the new UN Secretary-General, Ban Ki-Moon, urged the reframing of the debate over climate change from an environmental to a development and security issue.[18] The following month saw the first UN Security Council discussion on the international security implications of climate change. It identified a range of potential threats to security, including flows of environmental refugees, potential conflict over access to resources and energy supplies, as well as societal stresses and humanitarian crises.[19]

Recent research and policy discourse have disaggregated climate change into its direct and indirect impacts and focused on how it might reformulate the international security and geopolitical spectrum. Nick Mabey argued that if it is not slowed, climate change will become the primary driver of conflict within and between states, and that the pattern of violence in Darfur demonstrates how access to resources in times of environmental stress can become politicised and exacerbate existing communal conflicts. This linked both the direct and indirect dimensions as the stresses imparted by the former exacerbated existing divisions and created new ones. Moving from the micro- to the macro-level, he also predicted that climate change will link old problems in new ways and change the nature of strategic interests, alliances, borders, comparative advantages and inter-state cooperation.[20] Meanwhile, Jeffrey Mazo highlighted the multiplicative and interactive causality of climate change as a stressor on more proximate drivers of conflict in Darfur, such as access to water, which he termed 'the first modern climate change conflict.[21] Paul Smith made a similar comparative point that climate change has emerged as a new variable of international security in the twenty-first century.[22]

Moving toward an assessment of the likely implications in the Middle East, Oli Brown and Alec Crawford of the International Institute for Strategic Development examined the security challenges of climate change in the Levant. They agreed with the assessments (above) that climate change is likely to aggravate existing tensions and constitute one (of numerous) drivers of future conflict over access to scarce resources, food insecurity, and the changing availability of water resources. The indirect impact of climate change was thus particularly important in the conflict-afflicted region of the Middle East, where numerous actual and latent tensions and inter- and intra-state fault-lines abound. Their sobering conclusions highlighted the possibility that climate change may hinder economic growth and thereby exacerbate social instability and potential societal breakdown. Furthermore, they emphasised the danger that political and popular perceptions of resource shrinkage might lead to the militarisation of access to, and control over, strategic natural resources.[23]

In the specific context of the Arabian Peninsula and the GCC states, such research as has occurred has mostly originated from outside the region. A notable exception is the research carried out by Mohamed Raouf at the Gulf Research Centre in Dubai. His work has mapped the changing institutional and policymaking perspectives on climate change-related issues in the GCC states. Although his finding of a subtle shift in perspective has been corroborated by external analysts,[24] remedial policy has taken the form of energy diversification rather than tackling environmental awareness and unsustainable consumption. This ties into the previous chapter's emphasis on Gulf States' preference for boosting capacities to obviate the need to undertake difficult and politically sensitive reforms to the social contract.[25] Finally, speaking at the annual Manama Dialogue regional security summit in Bahrain in December 2008, the then UK Secretary of Defence John Hutton listed climate change as one of the new threats to Gulf security, alongside the proliferation of weapons of mass destruction and the existence of terrorist havens in failed states.[26]

Climate security has therefore embedded itself in global security discourse. It straddles a dangerous intersection between development, governance and sources of conflict. This vulnerability operates both at the intra-societal and inter-state levels. It is consistent with recent patterns of conflict indicating that outbreaks of violence are more likely to take place within societies rather than between states.[27] However, its position on the fuzzy margins between domestic and global politics complicates strategies to address it. While human-induced climate change already poses a hard security threat in certain manifestations and locations, its full effects will become apparent over decades rather than months and years. These will require concerted and multilateral solutions that tackle both its environmental and security aspects.[28] Yet the disappointing outcome of the December 2009 United Nations Climate Change Conference in Copenhagen demonstrated the difficulties inherent in reaching even a global consensus, let alone agreement, on climate change.[29] It also highlighted the paradoxical disjuncture between the growing urgency of global challenges and the continuing inability to arrive at global solutions to these interconnected problems.[30]

Perceptions of Climate Security in the Gulf States

Climate change and environmental degradation present multi-dimensional threats to internal and regional security in the Gulf region. These range from rising sea levels to the impact on already-fragile ecosystems and more highly contested access to food and water resources, alongside a potential shift toward a de-carbonised world economy that might depress global demand for Gulf oil. In all of these instances, climate change may exacerbate existing tensions and create new drivers of conflict within and between societies. Although regional perspectives on these issues have shifted subtly in recent years with the launch of several high-profile renewable and clean energy initiatives, awareness of, and adaptation to, the impacts of climate change has been very low.[31] This is evidenced in the paradoxical contrast between Abu Dhabi's patronage of the Masdar clean energy initiative and successful bid to host the headquarters of the International Renewable Energy Agency (IRENA) while boasting the world's largest ecological footprint per capita.[32]

The anthropogenic causes of human-induced climate change are manifold, and encompass political, economic, socio-cultural and demographic factors. These include population growth, demographic shifts, economic and technological development, cultural values and belief systems, and governance and institutional structures. Underlying all of these, and interlinking them, is the destructive interaction between human societies and their ecosystems and the incompatibility of current models of economic growth with sustainable development.[33] This is a challenge confronting states and societies across the world, but in the Gulf States it is compounded by regional political economies that depend on oil revenues for their survival and stability. Previous chapters demonstrated how policies of wasteful, subsidised consumption form a core of the social contract in these rentier systems. These trends skew institutional structures and political willpower against substantive reformulation of these patterns of unsustainable growth. They also resulted in GCC states occupying the top four global rankings in carbon dioxide emissions per capita, with Qatar's figure being more than double that of the United Arab Emirates in second place and over three times that of the United States.[34]

What is lacking in the GCC is a coherent sense of the emerging climate-security nexus as described above. Only in Oman has widespread awareness of sustainable development and climate change mitigation entered policymaking discourse at a high level, with the formation of a dedicated Ministry of Environment and Climate Affairs in 2007.[35] This is unsurprising in a regional context lacking even an internal consensus on the environmental aspects of climate change. This was evidenced in successive rounds of international climate change negotiations leading up to the 2009 Copenhagen Summit. With the notable exception of Oman, GCC states earned a reputation for obstructionist tactics focusing on the (negative in their perception) economic implications of a climate-changed world rather than the environmental impacts of climate change itself.[36] In March 2009, Mohammed Al-Sabban, head of the Saudi delegation to the United Nations Framework Convention on Climate Change (UNFCCC), stated clearly that strict global proposals to mitigate climate change by cutting carbon emissions and dependence on oil represented a 'very serious [threat] for oil producing countries and in particular Gulf producing countries,' which 'stand to lose out to such policies that are biased against oil producers.'[37]

During the run-up to the Copenhagen Summit, Al-Sabban also seized on the revelation that scientists in the United Kingdom had allegedly manipulated data to support their argument that the planet is warming up to cast doubt on the broader validity of climate science. He added that 'the size of [economic] sacrifices must be built on a secure foundation of information, which we found now is not true.'[38] His comments demonstrated the extent to which policymakers in the Gulf view potential moves toward a de-carbonised world as the greatest potential climate change-linked threat to security. They also reflected the Gulf States' sense of defensive protectiveness toward their use of oil reserves, both directly as generators of revenue and stability, and indirectly as the facilitator of economic diversification initiatives. It is through this powerful lens that climate-related perspectives are refracted.[39]

It is against this backdrop of concern for their own security that the Gulf states' considerable efforts to become world leaders in renewable and alternative energy must be viewed. Abu Dhabi campaigned hard to host the headquarters of IRENA at its flagship carbon-neutral Masdar City.[40] The Masdar Initiative also encompasses the annual World

Future Energy Summit, which launched in 2008, and the Masdar Institute of Science and Technology, which opened in September 2009. Together, they provide a world-leading platform for advanced research into renewable and sustainable energy and enabled Abu Dhabi to brand itself, somewhat improbably in light of its ecological footprint, as a global leader in the field.[41] Nor was Abu Dhabi alone in seizing the initiative; in Saudi Arabia, the $10bn-endowed King Abdullah University of Science and Technology, which also began operating in September 2009, included a dedicated research track examining resources, energy and environment issues with a particular emphasis on clean combustion technologies and solar and alternative energy science.[42] Meanwhile in Qatar the Al-Shaheen Oilfield Gas Recovery and Utilisation Project became the first registered Clean Development Mechanism (CDM) project in the Gulf in May 2007, and other CDM initiatives are currently underway in the renewable energy, waste, cement and aluminium smelting sectors.[43]

These initiatives in part represented attempts to divert the focus of international attention away from blunt criticism of the Gulf States' policies toward climate change and environmental issues. Regional positions on climate change (such as they exist) have been dominated by the economic impact of adaptation and mitigation and the issue of financial compensation to offset economic losses caused by developed countries' response measures, rather than on the science itself.[44] As rentier states dependent on the extraction of oil and redistribution of its revenues, policymakers in the GCC states fear that any global move away from oil will disproportionately impact their own political economies. In this context, official and public opinion views the environmental and climate security dimensions as secondary to the primary challenge of maintaining intact their major source of revenue. Strategies of pragmatic and political survival thus explain the regional distinctiveness of Gulf conversations on these global issues.

Environmental and Security Threats From Climate Change

The Gulf States are nevertheless highly exposed to the effects of climate change and environmental degradation on already-stressed ecosystems and patterns of habitation. The UK Meterological Office Hadley Centre predicts a progressive rise in the long-term average temperature in the Middle East by 3.2 degrees Celsius from 1990–2070. It also warned that increasing water stress and salinity and further degradation of soil quality will adversely affect crop yields and make the region still more reliant on imported foodstuffs.[45] These findings have been corroborated by other studies that also predict a significant long-term increase in temperature (as well as humidity) as well as a decrease in long-term precipitation in the Arabian Peninsula. Richer provides a summary of the range of predicted rises of between 3 and 5.9 degrees Celsius over the course of the twenty-first century.[46] Meanwhile, the interaction of rising temperatures with falling precipitation will intensify still further the competition for already-scarce resources of food and water, and open them up for potential contestation in times of hardship.

Moreover, trajectories of human and urban settlement are imposing additional extra-systemic stress factors on the fragile ecosystems of the Arabian Peninsula. These are exacerbated by the energy-intensive models of economic development and diversification that are underway throughout the GCC states. Together, the trends interact with the prevailing value-systems and behavioural culture outlined in the previous section. The result is a continuation of the short-term and traditional 'hard' security approaches, which have not started to factor in the possible medium- to longer-term threats and potential societal disruption arising from climate and environmental security. On a societal level, if left unchecked, the trends will also render the land progressively less suitable for further development, and heighten the value (and potential contestability) of existing resources. This is already unfolding in Yemen, where dwindling water reserves, partially caused by falling precipitation, are heightening local tensions and leading to a rush to extract as much water as possible before supplies run out.[47]

As a hyper-arid region with few natural resources other than oil (and gas) reserves, the Arabian Peninsula presents myriad difficulties to large-scale human activity. These include food insecurity and water stress (as examined in the previous chapter), both of which reflect a historically narrow margin of subsistence over the land. More than 90 per cent of the limited arable land on the Peninsula already suffers from overgrazing and land degradation, leading to further desertification of the already-limited regions of non-desert.[48] The scale of the problem is evidenced in Kuwait, where studies have shown an average annual loss of 285 square kilometres of productive land to desertification.[49] This creeping desertification is matched by an increasing salinity of depleting fossil water reserves. Saltwater intrusion into groundwater has resulted in massive increases in salinity levels in Qatar, in particular, and is directly attributable to unsustainable over-exploitation of underground aquifers.[50] This problem is at its most acute and urgent in Yemen, as the following chapter makes clear, where water tables have been dropping by as much as ten feet each year and water basins have started to dry up altogether.[51]

Coastal patterns of settlement and development in the GCC states render them especially vulnerable to changes in sea levels arising from climate change. In February 2009, the World Meteorological Organisation warned that a 5 centimetre rise in sea levels would have major consequences for marine life and coastal development around the world.[52] This compares to predictions of sea level rises of anything between 18 and 59 centimetres by 2100 (depending on different carbon emissions scenarios and trajectories) made in the *Fourth Assessment Report of the Intergovernmental Panel on Climate Change* in 2007.[53] Moreover, the report predicted with very high confidence that 'Many millions more people are projected to be flooded every year due to sea-level rise by the 2080s,' and added that 'The unavoidability of sea-level rise, even in the longer-term, frequently conflicts with present-day human development patterns and trends.'[54]

These alarmist predictions clash directly with the ambitious land reclamation and prestigious mega-projects that have become features of the Arabian Peninsula coastline. While some overly-ambitious developments such as 'The World' archipelago in Dubai have fallen victim to the global financial downturn, the rapid pace of urbanisation and land development projects elsewhere magnify the threat from climate change and rising sea levels. The concentration of urban and human development in low-lying coastal areas also complicates and heightens any future financial and social cost of adaptation to a climate-changed environment.[55] This is particularly pertinent for the thirty-three islands that constitute the Bahrain archipelago even without factoring in the prestigious new groups of artificial islands in the Durrat al-Bahrain and Amwaj luxury residential projects. However it is also applicable to the major urban conurbations and coastal development projects in all other GCC states, with the partial exception of Saudi Arabia.[56]

Changing patterns of temperature, precipitation and sea levels represent the tangible effects of climate change that have already started to occur in the Gulf, as elsewhere. These trends, to a high probability, are expected to accelerate over the course of the twenty-first century and constitute an increasingly direct challenge to security and stability. Although current awareness is low throughout the GCC, the tangible manifestations of climate change do at least hold the potential to be targeted by adaptive counter-measures to mitigate some of their effects.[57] This is particularly the case in the high-income developing states in the GCC, which enjoy greater levels of material resources than most other developing world-regions. Hence, the issue is more one of the lack of political willpower and institutional agency (at least in the short-term) rather than lack of material resources that is at stake.[58] In poorer states, such as Yemen but also potentially including Bahrain and Oman in the near-future, the capability to undertake expensive adaptation and mitigation projects is likely to be far more limited, and this may magnify the negative impacts arising from exogenous shocks and internal disruption.

Rather more difficult to predict is the intangible impact of the processes of climate change over the medium- and longer-term. The variable lies in the interaction of internal and external stressors that may arise with political, economic and socio-cultural behaviour. These will play out over the coming years and decades and their effects cannot be predicted with any certainty. Nevertheless, it is possible to pinpoint the major dynamics that will shape the contextual parameters within which this interaction will take place. Of these, the most important (as previously described) are heightened competition for increasingly scarce resources and a lack of political will or capability to take effective measures of mitigation and adaptation. It is this symbiosis that is most vulnerable to exogenous shocks to the system if redistributive mechanisms begin to falter or societal stresses threaten to become unmanageable.

Here, the issue of combating and mitigating climate change becomes bound up with the maintenance of the social contract in its current redistributive guise. As stated above, this presents policymakers with difficult and potentially painful choices. The paradox facing officials is that while the advocacy of adaptive measures or changes to unsustainable patterns of living carries its own risks, the long-term consequences of inaction are likely to be much higher. This will be magnified still further if they become intertwined with depleting oil reserves and states' declining ability to redistribute wealth toward their societies in times of comparative economic hardship. Here, the unpalatable factor facing Gulf policymakers is that they will eventually face this shift toward a post-oil era at some point in coming decades, although this will occur at different speeds in each country. The common denominator is that the predicted acceleration of climate change represents an exogenous stressor during a time of vulnerable transition. Once again, however, regimes have, and will continue to, put off these decisions until they can no longer be delayed. The absence of concerted efforts to change mindsets and raise awareness of climate security raises the possibility that eventual adaptive mechanisms will become marked by contestation rather than consensus.

The vulnerability of, and scale of investment in, man-made islands and other elaborate coastal development projects provides regimes with incentives to study carefully the local and regional impacts of climate change. Moreover, measures to bridge the gap between popular awareness of climate change and its range of likely impacts may lessen societal vulnerability to insecurity arising from exogenous shocks to the system. This is particularly important in states and societies characterised by existing fissures that then become susceptible to fragmentation or rupture under pressure. In this context, the broadening and deepening of the concept of what, and for whom, the idea of security involves becomes relevant to regional political economies, as they evolve under the twin pressures of long-term climate change and transition toward a post-oil era. A human security approach, focused on the needs of communities and individuals, may provide the optimal policy instrument for strengthening societal cohesion and state-society relations during times of profound and rapid change and possible upheaval.

A further factor that can be expected to take on critical importance is the need for some form of regional collaboration on trans-boundary issues. The Gulf's troubled history of inter-state conflict reflects and overlays the geo-political fault-lines that criss-cross the region. The growing competition for increasingly scarce resources that is anticipated to be a feature of a climate-stressed world contains the seed of potential tensions and conflict if policymaking continues to follow a unilateral rather than collective commons approach. For this to be obviated, however, political and popular awareness of the validity and urgency of climate change must first undergo a profound shift. In addition to promoting policies that encourage conservation and sustainable development, an appreciation of climate security and its potential implications for internal and external stability will be cornerstones of any new and inclusive attempts to tackle the threat from climate change. This challenges political and security officials proactively to broaden their conception of security and adopt a long-term, non-military view encompassing direct threats to the sustenance of human communities and patterns of settlement.

Threats From Environmental Degradation

A second, partially interlinked, threat to the fragile ecosystem of the Arabian Peninsula and the marine environment of the Gulf comes from environmental degradation. Again, this is magnified by the coastal patterns of settlement and development that have proliferated over recent decades and placed increasing strain on local ecosystems. This enhances their vulnerability to future natural and man-made disasters. The most urgent, and potentially damaging, threat comes from any accident at the Iranian nuclear reactor in Bushehr. If this were to occur it would have devastating ecological and human consequences for surrounding countries as the reactor lies within the internationally-agreed 500 kilometre radius of settlements.[59] Officials in the GCC states point out that the reactor is closer to Kuwait, Qatar and Bahrain than Teheran and that the counter-clockwise currents in the Gulf would result in the Arabian coastline bearing the brunt of any irradiation of water supplies.[60]

The effect of irradiation on water supplies would also be devastating to human and urban settlements throughout the Gulf littoral. As outlined in the previous chapter, regional water scarcities and the over-use of renewable and fossil water reserves has left the GCC states' over-reliant on desalinated water drawn from the Gulf. Desalinated water currently meets up to 99 per cent of total water demand in Qatar and 96.5 per cent in Kuwait, with only Saudi Arabia and Oman being able to draw on extensive non-desalinated supplies.[61] Moreover, the share of desalinated water will increase over time as existing fossil reserves become exhausted. Consequently, any contamination of water supplies in the Gulf would be catastrophic, particularly were it to have prolonged, long-term effects. This is a cause of constant anxiety to policymakers in the GCC states, who express concern at the broader weakness of international safeguards and monitoring systems in Iran's controversial and secretive nuclear programme.[62]

Gulf coastlines and water supplies are also highly vulnerable to actual and potential oil spillage. Even before taking into account the possibility of leakage or accidents, an estimated equivalent of 1.2 million barrels of oil are discharged into Gulf waters by oil tankers each year.[63] In 1991, retreating Iraqi forces inflicted enormous environmental and material damage as they set Kuwaiti oil wells ablaze. The smoke and carbon fallout from the more than 700 fires interfered with weather patterns in the northern Gulf and dramatically decreased the quality of air, causing respiratory hazards for inhabitants in the afflicted areas.[64] In the short-term, it inflicted irreparable harm on the biodiversity and natural habitat of Gulf coastlines and damaged fish, shrimp and other marine wildlife stocks. It also opened up a range of health security impacts that may only become apparent over the longer-term, including the residual effects of smoke inhalation on susceptibility to lung cancer and birth defects.[65]

This vulnerability to exogenous and unpredictable events is a potential trigger of instability in the Gulf States. If a disruptive event were to occur it would jeopardise the human security of entire communities and the physical security of urban settlements and coastal developments. The political fall-out would strain state-society relations to breaking-point if it were to bring into question the political economy underpinnings of development models. Yet, aside from lingering memories in Kuwait of the oil fires that led to a resurgence of interest in environmental protection and Oman's regional-leading approach to awareness of sustainable development, environmental degradation barely features in regional discourse.[66] This seemingly surprising omission (given its manifold vulnerabilities) is primarily attributable to the emphasis on energy-intensive industrialisation and urbanisation projects that have formed the cornerstone of economic diversification programmes in the GCC.[67]

Successive *Living Planet* reports issued by the World Wildlife Federation laid bare the scale of environmental disregard in the GCC. The reports deconstruct the changing state of global biodiversity into the Living Planet Index and the Ecological Footprint. The latter is a measure of human demand on the natural ecosystems that support human activity. The 2008 report found that the UAE had an ecological footprint of 9.5 global hectares per person. This was marginally ahead of the United States (9.4) and Kuwait (8.9), but much higher than both the global average (2.7) and the median for high income countries (6.4).[68] These figures revealed the unsustainable growth patterns relative to resources in the Gulf States, and must be seen in light of the previous chapter's analysis on the political economy of resource distribution and emerging scarcities in key areas.

Although the global financial and economic crisis slowed the pace of expansion, the underlying business and development models mean that the pressure on natural resources will continue to grow while the already-thin margin of subsistence over the natural environment continues to erode. To these diverging trajectories must be added a lack of appreciable or strong civil society organisations that focus on ecological issues. These building blocks of public education could assist in embedding the values of environmentalism and sustainable development in policymaking frameworks and popular consciousness.[69] Their comparative absence, notwithstanding a small presence in Kuwait and Bahrain and the work of the Emirates Environmental Group in Dubai, reduces the likelihood of meaningful changes to behavioural values or the institutionalisation and mainstreaming of environmental awareness.[70] Here, as with climate security, the relationship between power, knowledge and interests actively shapes the direction of policymaking and determines which issues make it onto national and regional security agendas. With these agendas remaining fixated on short-term, 'hard' security challenges, discussion of the threat (and of its level of severity) to livelihoods and to the basic human security of communities has yet to feed into the public or political arena in any meaningful way.[71]

Longer-Term Challenges

As oil-based economies heavily reliant on the hydrocarbons sector for approximately 50 per cent of regional GDP and 80 per cent of fiscal and export revenues, the GCC states would be adversely impacted by any fall in global demand for oil or changing energy mix.[72] The dramatic fall in oil prices and government revenues in 2008–9 demonstrated the Gulf States' vulnerability to external and sector-specific volatility. In Oman, government revenues fell by 21.3 per cent to the year ending June 2009 on the back of a 33.3 per cent decline in net oil revenues, while in Yemen, government oil receipts plunged by nearly 60 per cent in 2009 owing both to declining reserves and the fall in price.[73] While oil prices recovered thereafter, the dramatic swing exposed the inherent uncertainty that complicates regional budgetary planning and policy implementation, with knock-on implications for the economic prosperity and socio-political stability of all Gulf States.

In addition to the security implications of climate change and environmental degradation discussed in previous sections, a further dimension is specific to oil-producing states. This is the potential implication that may arise from a shift in global energy demand in a climate-stressed and increasingly environmentally aware world.[74] During the course of the twenty-first century, the accelerating pace of technological innovation, research and development is expected to result in significant advances in alternative and renewable energies. Oil will remain important but likely constitute only one of several options, particularly in post-industrial Western economies. The defensive posture adopted by Saudi Arabia and Kuwait in international climate change negotiations and Abu Dhabi and Qatar's spearheading of renewable and greener energy initiatives do suggest that policymakers in the GCC recognise the possibility of a gradual move toward a de-carbonised economy in coming decades.[75] This perception informs their objective interests in the issues of climate change and environmental degradation, and it emphasises how these interests reflect intersubjective understandings about the means required to project power, influence and wealth.[76]

Concern for the maintenance of their revenue streams is therefore intertwined with questions of political and economic stability and the durability of the social contract in the Gulf States. Domestic interests coalesce around this nexus to produce public and political acquiescence for the continuation of models of economic development that increasingly will prove more and more difficult to sustain. This will make the eventual dismantling of the patterns of subsidised lifestyles more difficult and painful. It also raises the risks of the transition being accompanied by societal stresses and internal instability, particularly if the resource insecurities and unequal patterns of distribution described earlier persist. Nevertheless, with the challenges of climate change and environmental degradation predicted to become more acute and multi-dimensional, the costs of inaction in the short-term are likely to be heavy in the medium- and longer-one.

Climate change and environmental degradation thus contains important implications for the future security paradigm of the Gulf States. These will impact socio-political and economic patterns and will be contemporaneous to, and embedded within, the unfolding post-oil economic transition. Their trans-national character will also inject new potential sources of tension into intra- and inter-state relations, particularly if they interact with existing inequalities and societal fault-lines in an interconnected cycle of instability and predatory contestation. All of this will play out over years and decades and thus has not been accorded priority in national and regional security agendas. Yet pre-emptive and preparatory research into the security implications of climate change and environmental degradation can assuage (if not eliminate) some of the more indirect effects that may be expected to occur. These include raising public awareness and political will in order to strengthen institutional capacity to draw up and implement adaptation and mitigation measures. Above all, regional security paradigms need to integrate the study of climate and environmental security into research on failing and contracting states, such as Yemen. This would interrogate the overlaying of climate change and environmental degradation as additional stress points and drivers of conflict on fractured polities and examine their implications for states already teetering on the edge of failure.

PART THREE

7

YEMEN'S CONTESTED TRANSITION

The previous three chapters tracked the emergence of a range of longer-term and non-military challenges to regional security in the Gulf. These form part of the broadening and deepening of the concept of security to encompass a human dimension in addition to older frameworks of 'national' security. This final section shifts the focus of analysis to study the interlinking of these multiple sources of insecurity and causes of state weakness in Yemen. It extends the assessment of the trans-national dimensions of Yemeni-based terrorism in chapter two to address the interconnected socio-political, economic, environmental and trans-national challenges afflicting domestic conditions in the country. Collectively, these amount to a crisis of governance and regressive political implosion that constitutes the single most dangerous short-term challenge to the security and stability of the Arabian Peninsula. It also raises a number of worrying comparative issues for the GCC states to consider as they gradually move toward the delicate task of disentangling the layers of patronage and rent-seeking networks inherent in moves to a post-oil political economy.

Yemen faces a combination of underlying challenges, each of which, on its own, would be profoundly destabilising. These include a military rebellion in the northern province of Sa'dah that has flared intermittently with six rounds of fighting since 2004, a growing southern secessionist movement that challenges the post-1990 reunification settlement, as well as the reconstitution of Al-Qaeda in the Arabian Peninsula following the merger of its Yemeni and Saudi wings in January 2009. Underlying all of these hard threats to security is the imminent depletion of oil and water reserves, and the erosion of regime legitimacy and state capacity to govern effectively or even fairly. Across the Gulf of Aden, state collapse in Somalia has facilitated destabilising flows of men, money and material between Somalia and Yemen. This has injected the multiple drivers of conflict and insecurity in the Horn of Africa into the Gulf's regional security equation. The result is a failing political economy and fragmenting society on the south-western flank of the Arabian Peninsula that can no longer be contained within Yemen itself.

The systemic crises of imminent resource depletion, environmental degradation and the reformulation of regime legitimacy during a period of profound political and economic transition demonstrate the interlocking challenges to security described in previous chapters. All of these issues will, in some combination, also face the GCC states over the course of the twenty-first century. As this chapter will show, the downward spiral of developments in Yemen demonstrates how each can exacerbate the other and lead to a transition that is marked more by violence than consensus. Further, these tangible manifestations of insecurity exacerbate the intangible breakdown of social relations and erode the nexus of rules, consent and popular legitimacy that is critical to the maintenance of state-society relations and the latter's confidence in the regime's continued rule. Consequently, Yemen's downward trajectory toward failing statehood provides a worrying bellwether of the difficult changes that confront its neighbours on the Arabian Peninsula as they too embark on the processes of rapid transition during periods of declining resources and burgeoning socio-economic challenges.

Systemic Crises and Interlocking Challenges

Yemen is one of the poorest countries in the Arab and Islamic world with a fragmentary and relatively brief history as a unitary state that reflects the powerful centrifugal, partially tribally-based, pressures that militate against strong centralised control. These pressures have undermined Yemeni unity since the unification of North and South Yemen in 1990 and led to a brief yet bloody civil war in 1994. Unified Yemen is a very low income country highly dependent on a single source of (oil) revenue and also has one of the highest rates of population growth in the world. In 2009 its GDP per capita of $2500 ranked it 173rd in the world according to the *CIA World Factbook*, while the perils of over-reliance on volatile oil prices became clear as oil revenues, which constituted approximately 70 per cent of total government revenue, halved in 2008–9.[1] The impact of these figures is sharpened by demographic and socio-economic problems arising from population growth of 3.7 per cent per annum and poverty and unemployment rates of more than 40 per cent.[2] Rapid rates of resource depletion and the imminent exhaustion of oil reserves by 2017 lend an air of urgency to efforts to reformulate the country's political economy. Yet Yemen has no obvious route of transition to a post-oil economy, notwithstanding the less-than-anticipated revenues resulting from the delayed launch of liquefied natural gas exports in November 2009.[3]

An absence of credible and sustainable alternative sources of government revenue, together with endemic corruption and parallel networks of patronage crucially diminishes the capacity of the central state to maintain political or economic legitimacy. It also contributes to a crunch whereby faltering distribution of revenues and government services diverge from the basic and humanitarian needs of an increasingly impoverished population.[4] Broader structural factors, such as the weak rule of law and limited political legitimacy of public institutions, exacerbate the social conflicts and systemic economic difficulties caused by rapid resource depletion. Multiple drivers and dynamics of conflict thus operate at individual, societal and provincial levels and contribute to the erosion of state authority and centralised political control.[5] Their cumulative impact has been to devastate Yemen's already-fragile economy and divert scarce resources away from humanitarian assistance and societal needs to feed a flourishing war economy.

A widening chasm has therefore opened up between the capacity of the state to govern and the socio-economic and demographic pressures facing it. In September 2009, Mohamed Abulahoum, former head of the government's foreign relations and economic development departments, argued that 'the economy is the number one challenge, it is the number two challenge, and it is the number three challenge. This is the cause of every problem that we have in Yemen.'[6] This viewpoint downplays the importance of the political choices made by President Ali Abdullah Saleh in manipulating tribal and patronage networks to maintain power since 1978. It nevertheless draws out the myriad economic pressures, which include declining oil revenues and widespread food and water insecurity, a depreciating exchange rate, inflationary pressures, political reliance on food and fuel subsidies, rampant corruption, and insufficient capacity to absorb external developmental assistance.[7] Government attempts in 2005 to reduce fuel subsidies by increasing the price of gasoline, diesel and kerosene had to be reversed following riots that killed twenty-two people and injured more than 300.[8] Weak institutional and governance capabilities diluted the disbursement of $4.7 billion of development pledges made at a donors' conference in London in 2006. This included more than $4 billion offered by the GCC states, but by January 2010 a mere 7 per cent had actually been spent.[9]

Yemen's contracting economic base constitutes the underlying cause of current and future instability. Their effects are exacerbated by the other dimension of the faltering political economy, namely the erosion of already-weak state legitimacy and authority and the weakness of the social contract and rule of law. The lack of a consensual political settlement within Yemen has reactivated latent feelings of post-1990 marginalisation and alienation among groups and tribes excluded from the circles of power and patronage.[10] It has also sharpened socio-political tensions and complicated and undermined periodic regime efforts at conflict resolution and reconciliation as embedded networks of patronage became the visible symbols of uneven access to, and distribution of, public goods and state resources.[11] Previous reform initiatives failed to change either the locus or structure of political power and the mechanisms through which it is exercised, or eliminate the significant obstacles to reform stemming from the system of personalised power and patronage networks that buttress the political survival of the regime. A comprehensive National Reform Agenda drafted by the Ministry of Planning and National Coordination in October 2006 initially promised much but ultimately delivered little in the way of meaningful change. Although it aimed to reduce corruption, enhance transparency, strengthen press freedoms and work toward reform of the judiciary and a separation of powers, most of the agenda was never subsequently implemented.[12]

The National Reform Agenda demonstrated the limitations posed by a weak state and its inadequate institutional capacity to move from the identification of problems to their actual implementation. This tempers the prospects for the next round of political reforms unveiled in June 2008 and endorsed by Saleh in August 2009. This Ten-Point Program amounted to an exercise in prioritising the ten most urgent areas for reform. These included overhauling the civil service and bureaucracy, enforcing government authority and the rule of law, reducing subsidies without raising prices and risking societal unrest as happened in 2005 when fuel prices were increased, finding urgent solutions to water issues and land ownership problems, and creating a fast-track initiative for further oil and gas exploration.[13] These proposals won international acclaim from then British Foreign Secretary David Miliband and US Secretary of State Hillary Clinton when they were presented at the London conference on Yemen in January 2010.[14] However they must be balanced against other political developments that underscore the continuing absence of a comprehensive political settlement. Notably, parliamentary elections scheduled for 2009 were postponed until 2011 after opposition parties threatened to boycott them in the belief that they would neither be free nor fair.[15]

Meanwhile, a genuinely inclusive national dialogue also faltered as the government refused to include Houthi rebels or southern secessionists in it. Indeed, Yemen's Prime Minister signalled a toughening stance against political opponents of the regime in April 2010 as he alleged that 'Those who call themselves the opposition...have entered into suspicious alliances with groups outside of the system, the law and the constitution.'[16] The chasm separating the two sides became evident in subsequent remarks by a prominent representative of the Southern Movement, Yahia Ghalib, as he rejected Saleh's call for a dialogue to discuss the formation of a national unity government, stating that 'Our problem is a political and legal problem; the south is under siege and lives in a state of emergency. Our peaceful struggle will continue, as the unity they are talking about ended in the 1994 war. What is happening now is an occupation.'[17] As will be discussed at length in the next section, Yemen's internal fragmentation is approaching a tipping-point of no return in which a negotiated solution is becoming increasingly unlikely in the face of entrenching positions and hardening rhetoric.

Such discouraging results from previous reform initiatives and attempts to fashion a national dialogue of sorts do not augur well for the prospects for a consensual transition of the Yemeni political economy away from oil. Unfulfilled pledges and veiled and actual threats to political opponents sap the government's credibility and erode its reputation as an honest arbiter at a critical period of rapid change. Furthermore, the widespread perception that the political arena is fundamentally rigged undermines the motivation and results that opposition groups might expect to gain from entering the political process.[18] This has profound implications for Yemeni stakeholders as they prepare to address the systemic challenges to governance and security. Powerful feelings of mutual distrust reinforce lingering memories of bitterness and conflict arising from the reunification era and the civil war in 1994. Accordingly, the chances for a peaceful solution to Yemen's interlinked problems become more remote with every setback in the reform process. As the next section makes clear, the unravelling of the Yemeni polity has already begun as converging challenges from northern rebels and southern separatists present an existential threat to the survival of a unitary Yemeni state.

Political and Violent Contestation of Power

The resilience of Yemeni power structures to meaningful reform complicates strategies to address the interlocking socio-political, economic and demographic challenges. The regime's inability to impart or construct any significant consensus on the direction and pace of change has facilitated the emergence of opposition movements that directly challenge the authority and legitimacy of the state in its present formation. This has been most apparent in southern Yemen, where a secessionist Southern Movement has grown considerably since 2007, in large part in response to perceived governmental missteps in accommodating and channelling demands for reform. The movement began as a moderate call for equality and an end to the political marginalisation and economic exploitation of the former South Yemeni provinces by tribal and patronage groups linked to the northern elite around President Saleh. Thus, it initially focused on achieving equality with citizens in the north, greater influence over local decision-making, and more control over southern economic resources, including the Hawdramati oilfields.[19]

Initial moderation notwithstanding, the regime's mishandling of the movement's demands now threatens the political settlement that reunified the country in 1990 and survived a brief yet bloody civil war in 1994. This taps into the political economy of unequal resource distribution as examined in chapter five. The majority of Yemen's oil receipts issued from the country's largest oilfield at Al-Maseela in Hadramawt province. The majority of the revenues, however, accrued to northern-based patronage networks linked to President Saleh's powerful Hashid tribe, and did not percolate down to local communities. This acted as a powerful stimulant to southern disaffection with the balance of power within Yemen. The lock on political, economic and security power exercised by the circle of officials around Saleh reinforced the feelings of frustration at the government's apparent lack of sincerity in its reform initiatives.[20]

Southern perceptions of marginalisation and alienation interacted with emerging scarcities as the state's capacity to govern became over-stretched, and the arrival of tens of thousands of refugees from Somalia added to the burden on the limited resources that were available. By the time that sporadic and initially uncoordinated protests against the regime began in May 2007, the government had very little remaining credibility among southern Yemeni political or popular opinion. Attitudes of mutual distrust between the protestors and the security forces contributed to a cycle of dissent and repression that led in March 2008 to mass protests at governmental economic policies in southern cities. These erupted into widespread urban rioting and were only quelled by a coercive security crackdown that lasted throughout the spring.[21] Nevertheless, the protests continued to gather momentum during 2009 and 2010 and survived recurring government attempts to suppress them as they morphed into a fully-fledged secessionist movement. This change in discourse and objectives was accompanied by the appearance of flags and other insignia from the former People's Democratic Republic of (South) Yemen in a visible rejection of Saleh's rule.[22]

The emergence and growth of the secessionist movement in southern Yemen occurred contemporaneously to the violent contestation of regime authority in the northern province of Sa'dah. Beginning in September 2004 with the state-sponsored killing of their clerical leader, Hussein Badr Eddin, the Houthi rebellion pitted Shiite Zaydi tribesmen against state security forces in periodic bouts of intense fighting. These successive rounds of violence claimed thousands of lives, shattered civilian infrastructure, and inflicted great hardships on the local population.[23] An early Qatari attempt at mediation between the Houthi and the government in 2007 produced a fragile and temporary six-month cessation in the fighting and a short-lived political reconciliation. This quickly broke down during the spring of 2008 as each side claimed that the other was not serious about making peace, amid an endemic lack of trust that undermined the implementation of agreements covering the release of prisoners and the handover of arms.[24] Consequently the violence returned in the summer of 2008 when fighting flared and an estimated 150,000 people were displaced, or again in August 2009 as Saleh launched *Operation Scorched Earth* designed to 'uproot this cancer that exists in Sa'dah province.'[25]

This sixth round of conflict lasted until an uneasy truce was declared in February 2010, although acts of violence on both sides continued to occur thereafter.[26] It became notable for dragging Saudi Arabia into a messy three-month border conflict after Houthi rebels conducted a cross-border raid that inflicted casualties on Saudi personnel in November 2009. The kingdom responded with a full-scale artillery and air assault led by Prince Khaled bin Sultan, assistant minister of defence and aviation. Nevertheless, Saudi forces experienced considerable difficulties in clearing the border region and took relatively heavy casualties of more than 500 killed, wounded and missing in the three months' fighting that followed.[27] The military campaign was unprecedented in modern Saudi history as it marked the first occasion since the Kingdom's foundation in 1932 of unilateral (as opposed to coalition-based) military action beyond its boundaries.[28] It reflected the Kingdom's mounting concern at the threat of overspill of instability from the Houthi rebellion and the increasing incidence of trans-national terrorist infiltration, following the attempted assassination of Prince Mohamed bin Nayef in August 2009.

The failure to end the persistent fighting in northern Yemen has had numerous deleterious results. It has strained the Yemeni military and security forces and exposed their limitations whilst demonstrating their weaknesses to other putative and actual domestic challengers. The six rounds of conflict have also had devastating economic consequences and accelerated the drawdown of the country's limited financial reserves at a time of falling government revenues. Estimates drawn up by Christopher Boucek of the Carnegie Endowment for International Peace suggest that the Yemeni government spent more than $1 billion in hard currency reserves during the sixth round of fighting in 2009.[29] This diversion of scarce expenditure risks entrapping the Yemeni regime in a vicious cycle of conflict whereby the war economy erodes the capability of the government to provide even the basic levels of services and public goods necessary for updating and reformulating state legitimacy within a fragmented and conflict-afflicted polity.

During 2009, the growing threat from Al-Qaeda in the Arabian Peninsula (AQAP) was inserted into this maelstrom of political and violent contestation of power and dwindling regime legitimacy. The existing dynamics of oppositional rejection provided opportunities for AQAP to attempt to form tactical alliances with oppositional group-ings. Thus, in May 2009, a leading figure in AQAP, Nasser Al-Wahayshi, expressed his support for the southern secessionist movement and his desire for an independent Islamic state in southern Yemen that would provide AQAP with a new base of operations.[30] Although AQAP's objectives and worldview differ radically from those of the southern movement, and there is no record of the latter's acquiescence with AQAP goals, the coalescing of organisations opposed to the mainte-nance of the status quo in Yemen is significant on two levels. One is that the emerging security gaps and scaling back of centralised control in Yemen creates a vacuum within which extremist groups can operate. These 'ungoverned spaces' have been constructed as threats to security by officials and analysts in the United States, who argue that they con-stitute 'breeding grounds for terrorism and criminal activities and as launching pads for attacks against the United States and Western interests.'[31] The Christmas Day failed bombing in 2009 appeared to validate and confirm these fears, and catapulted Yemen to the top of Western counter-terrorism agendas.

The second implication of AQAP's declaration of affinity with the southern movement is that it reinforced regime-sponsored narratives that label oppositional movements as 'terrorist' threats to Yemeni secu-rity. This played into President Saleh's long-established strategy of 'divide and rule' as a means of balancing and playing off different fac-tions within Yemen against each other. Significantly, it also tapped into hegemonic Western discourse on the 'war against terror' by portraying the Yemeni government as a 'front-line state' deserving high-priority Western support for its role in countering the overspill of terrorism to the geo-strategically vital GCC and Gulf of Aden.[32] A similar motiva-tion lay behind the regime's (unfounded) allegations of Iranian involve-ment in supporting the Houthi rebellion in autumn 2009, with Information Minister Hasan Ahmad Al-Lawzi referring darkly to a campaign of 'financial and political support to acts of terrorism and destruction which are aimed at the heart of the security and stability of Yemen and especially Sa'dah.'[33]

Regional and International Involvement

The efficacy of this approach became evident both in Saudi Arabia's military intervention on behalf of the Saleh regime and in a letter written by US President Barack Obama to Saleh in September 2009. Both developments emphasised the regional and international securitisation of the threat from AQAP and emerging consensus that Saleh was fighting a common foe in its own 'fight against terrorism.' Obama's letter, in particular, stated that 'Yemen's security is vital to the security of the United States' and pledged that the US would 'stand beside Yemen, its unity, security and stability.'[34] Visits to Yemen by CENTCOM commander General David Petraeus carried similar messages of support, as well as a doubling of US security assistance from $70 million to $150 million in the aftermath of the attempted Christmas Day attack on Detroit that originated in Yemen.[35] The pragmatic realities of American support for Yemeni counter-terrorist operations extended to tacit acceptance of a new wave of repressive crackdowns and curtailment of freedoms that were launched by the regime in 2010. A doubling in security assistance also reflected the Obama administration's troubling prioritisation of counter-terrorism over issues of bad governance and human rights abuses within Yemen.[36]

The high-level meeting in London in January 2010 and its follow-up in Riyadh on 28 February brought the GCC states into the centre of the international policy response toward countering the threat to security arising from Yemen. The Gulf States also led the way in creating the Friends of Yemen informal network, with the United Arab Emirates taking the lead in one of its two working groups, focusing on the economy and governance.[37] In part, this emphasis on regional engagement and leadership made clear to GCC stakeholders their interest in stabilising Yemen to avoid the overspill of insecurity and cross-border tension. It may also assist in unblocking the financial assistance pledged by the GCC states at the London donors' meeting in 2006 which remains largely undistributed. Gulf States' developmental assistance to Yemen dwarfs the amounts pledged by Western donors, with Saudi Arabia pledging $1.25 billion in 2009 as compared to an American figure of $63 million. Saudi concerns that Yemen's interconnected crises may spill over to its own southern provinces, which share close tribal, familial and socio-cultural, translate into strong support for President Saleh and his maintenance of centralised authority and control. Hence the Kingdom has in recent years channelled additional and undisclosed sums of money co-opting support and buying political influence among key tribal figures.[38]

Saudi support for Yemen thus concentrated on strengthening the military and security capabilities of the Saleh regime in order to better protect its own security from the overspill of Yemeni instability. This came at the expense of a more nuanced approach focusing instead on Yemeni political and socio-economic issues or encouraging mediation in the multiple internal conflicts taking place within Yemen. It was further characterised by a lack of coherence or coordination across a range of formal and informal Saudi donors often competing for influence.[39] Furthermore, its prioritisation of Saudi interests highlighted the gap between regional and international approaches to Yemen. Security officials in Saudi Arabia may share with their American counterparts the view that regional security is best served by upholding a secure and unified Yemen.[40] However, the marked difference in policy approaches and maintenance of parallel and informal channels of aid distribution will undermine the evolution of the Friends of Yemen process of international engagement as set out in the London meeting in January 2010.

This introduces a new set of issues over the transparency and motivations of donors, in addition to the channelling of non-state financial and security assistance to manipulate and strengthen selected informal power structures inside Yemen.[41] The securitisation of Yemen as a counter-terrorism issue in Western and GCC policymaking circles is troublesome on several counts. Framing the issue of the contraction of regime power and legitimacy in these terms marginalises the root socio-political and economic causes of the contestation of governmental authority. Neither does it offer practical and urgently-needed solutions to the socio-economic threats to human development through humanitarian initiatives designed to combat the high incidence of poverty, unemployment and malnutrition, In Sa'dah, the Houthi rebellion originated in frustration at a combination of historical grievances, perceived socio-economic inequalities, competing sectarian identities (exacerbated by the overspill of fundamentalist Salafism from Saudi Arabia), and regional under-development.[42] Abdul-Malik Al-Houthi has described the conflict as a fight for rights, but the government has responded militarily, in part to send a message to other opposition movements, particularly the southern secessionist movement, that dissent will not be tolerated.[43] This is matched in southern Yemen by the regime's unwillingness to address the underlying causes of alienation from, and disaffection with, the Yemeni polity in its present guise. In both cases, the government's uncompromising position has exacerbated local grievances, accelerated the underlying political and economic crises, and made less likely the possibility of a negotiated and consensual solution.

Increasing support for the Saleh regime through the prism of counter-terrorism is at best a short-term and an ad hoc solution to Yemeni insecurity. It notably does not address the deep-rooted socio-economic problems within Yemen, as the GCC states remain loathe to opening their labour markets to substantial numbers of Yemeni economic migrants. More than 850,000 Yemenis were expelled from Saudi Arabia and the other GCC states following Saleh's decision not to support the international effort to liberate Kuwait in 1990–91. Yemeni re-entry into labour markets closed off to them since 1991 would run counter to GCC strategies to depoliticise and control their labour forces through replacing Arab with Southeast Asian workers. Fears for their own labour security tie into GCC policymakers' concern that shared linguistic and cultural bonds might result in Yemeni labourers becoming conduits of unrest and domestic instability.[44]

Both the GCC states and the international community face an unpalatable challenge in their policymaking toward Yemen. This is that in the absence of meaningful domestic reforms, any measures to extend the central government's power and authority are likely to sharpen existing centrifugal tensions and leave untouched the vested interests and entrenched networks of patronage that have become the objects of such vigorous contestation.[45] Neither do they realistically consider the possibility that President Saleh's government may actually constitute a part of Yemen's interconnected problems, rather than an impartial participant in any solution. The central security paradox in Yemen is the misalignment between the Saleh regime and the international community's focus on combating the threat from Al-Qaeda in the Arabian Peninsula, and the existential challenges to the legitimacy and survival of the Yemeni polity posed by the Houthi and Southern Movement which both reject his continued rule. For his part, Saleh follows an uneasy balance between accepting American security and military assistance and being perceived as too closely identified with the United States in the eyes of his opponents, both violent and non-violent.[46] Hence, the securitisation of Yemeni-based terrorism risks exacerbating the disintegration of state control and widening the ungoverned zones that facilitated the emergence of the security gaps and spaces for Al-Qaeda in the Arabian Peninsula to operate in the first instance.[47] Moreover it does nothing to repair the existing and latent fissures within Yemeni society by tackling the socio-economic and political root-causes or taking measures to reverse the contraction of state authority and control beyond the short-term enhancement of Saleh's contested coercive apparatus.

Seen from the perspective of policymakers in the GCC states, the case for supporting regime survival in Yemen stems from a number of interconnected factors. One of the most important internal considerations is a pragmatic instinct of their own political survival on the part of regional elites and ruling families. The political downfall of a long-standing ruler, however peripheral to the GCC states, would nevertheless constitute a very visible and awkward reminder of a previous era of intense intra-regime struggles for power in the Arabian Peninsula.[48] The loss of Saleh would also strip the GCC states, particularly Saudi Arabia, of their existing leverage over, and capacity to influence developments in Yemen. Gulf States' predilection for bilateral deals and informal distribution of aid has enmeshed them within networks of patronage and influence and created a situation that would be difficult to extricate from, aside from the uncertainties that a total collapse of governance in Yemen would bring, both for Yemen's immediate neighbours and the international community at large.[49]

More problematic for officials in the Arabian Peninsula is the worrying portent that Yemen holds for the breakdown of social cohesion under the pressure of the interlocking challenges to security at their most basic human level. Should it occur, regime failure in Yemen would indicate that the magnitude of these internal and external problems had become unmanageable in their cumulative and corrosive effects on domestic conditions. It is this security dilemma that cuts to the heart of the Gulf States' socio-political and economic trajectories over the course of the twenty-first century. Social cohesion as the intangible bond that holds members of any society together and facilitates co-existence represents the foundation-stone of the sustainability and survival of any polity. In addition to acting as a safety net for vulnerable members of society, it is an integral part of socio-economic development by strengthening mechanisms that can limit the damage of exposure to endogenous and exogenous shocks alike. Conversely, relations between and within communities and individuals break down when elemental aspects of food and water and physical protection from violence and depredation can no longer be assured.[50]

The example of Yemen demonstrates how intractable can be the reformulation of governance and the basis of state-society relations in periods of rapid and profound transition. It also highlights the tensions between the reconstruction of failing institutions and the reconstitution of social relations when these begin to break down under the strain of internal and external stresses. Renewing state legitimacy in Yemen by channelling regional and international support to the Saleh regime will considerably complicate the social reconstruction of the Yemeni polity. Empowering the capacity and reach of an already-contested governing structure will sharpen the centrifugal forces fragmenting state-society relations within Yemen and further weaken what little social cohesion currently exists.[51] For all of these reasons, Yemen provides a deeply alarming yet prescient case-study of how rapid socio-economic transitions may overwhelm fragile state capacity and intersect with eroding political legitimacy to produce a 'perfect storm' of a systemic crisis of governance and breakdown of legitimate political authority.

Canary in the Mine

Both the regional and international communities hold important stakes in preventing the complete unravelling of governance and security in Yemen. The physical manifestation of the overspill of Yemeni-based insecurity to the GCC in 2009 prompted a strategic reassessment of their range of responses. This was evidenced in their participation in the London meeting and hosting of the follow-up in Riyadh in February 2010. Both meetings marked the beginning of a new phase of international engagement with Yemen and its regional partners, amid belated recognition that its neighbours were likely to bear the brunt of Yemen's increasing fragility in the absence of a new and comprehensive approach to regional security.[52]

The myriad trans-national and inter-regional dimensions of instability emphasise its central role in an emerging zone of insecurity binding the Horn of Africa with the Arabian Peninsula. This, in itself, holds profound implications for the security and stability of the GCC states, as documented in chapter two. It injects the problems of state collapse in Somalia and state failure in Yemen and the existence of hitherto-localised conflicts into the regional security equation. Moreover, the combination of these spokes of terror radiating outward from Yemen and the geo-commercial importance of the Arabian Peninsula and Gulf of Aden sea lanes magnifies the geopolitical significance of this regional instability. It can plausibly be argued that this presents at least as great a challenge as the international military intervention in Afghanistan, a landlocked country in central Asia of only marginal importance to the global economy. A frequent justification of Western involvement in Afghanistan is that this is necessary to safeguard their internal security from possible future terrorist attacks. Looked at in cold geo-strategic terms, though, it is Yemeni-based instability that has exhibited a genuinely trans-national and far-reaching threat both to its regional neighbours, as well as a global reach extending as far as the United States homeland itself.

Moving beyond the troubling securitisation of Yemen as part of the global struggle against terrorism, its interlocking crises carry worrying implications for the GCC states. Although the post-oil transition is a distant concern for Saudi Arabia, Kuwait, the United Arab Emirates and Qatar, they do need to overhaul entrenched subsidisation and redistributive mechanisms and expand their productive economic sector. Meanwhile, Bahrain and Omani oil reserves are projected to deplete within twenty years barring unexpected new discoveries. Both polities urgently face the need to renew the bases of their legitimacy to overcome the drawdown of the oil-wealth redistributive mechanisms that have characterised the social contract in these rentier states.

Transitioning toward a post-oil era in all GCC states will therefore involve painful socio-political decisions and the dismantling of decades of rent-seeking patterns of behaviour. From their perspective, Yemen's difficulties highlight the challenge of reformulating political legitimacy and building a sustainable and productive non-oil economy. The contestation of governmental authority in southern and northern Yemen visibly demonstrates how existing socio-economic discontent and regional marginalisation can fracture and fragment societal cohesion. Similar fissures and unequal patterns of access to resources exist in the GCC states and could become transmitters of conflict in the future. Gulf officials' uneasy awareness of their own looming transition may well be a contributing factor to their reluctance to engage too publicly or closely with Yemen's ills.

Yet this inconvenient truth clashes squarely with the ambitious developmental models that have been embraced so firmly in the GCC.

Moreover, the violent contestation of power in Yemen provides a visible example of how troubled the eventual transition may become. While it is undoubtedly the case that the GCC states possess greater material resources to buttress this shift, their dependence on oil has both been longer-lasting and deeper-rooted. In addition, short-term avoidance of the difficult decisions inherent in rolling back redistributive and subsidisation mechanisms and embedding sustainable post-oil structures of governance will make these harder to achieve over the medium- to longer-term. Yet the fundamental paradox facing policy-makers in the Gulf States is that they are reliant on precisely these mechanisms for their legitimacy and the continuance of the social contract for short-term internal security and stability.

The challenges facing Yemen and the GCC states alike were neatly encapsulated by Prince Hassan bin Talal of Jordan in an article written in 2009, arguing that:

Rent-seeking tends to lead to policy failure in the form of an intense political competition aimed at gaining short-term access to revenues and benefits, as opposed to political competition over what policies might be in the long-term public interest.[53]

This sums up the difficult policy options that lie ahead in the Arabian Peninsula as regional security challenges become more diffuse and interlinked with declining indices of human development. Here, the nexus between resource depletion, food and water insecurity, inadequate access to labour markets and rising levels of un- and under-employment becomes starkly apparent. The case-study of Yemen shows how the fragmentation of social relationships and the contestation of political authority accelerates the decline of regime legitimacy and increases the risk of state failure or, at least, protracted state weakness. This, in turn, poses a new, two-fold threat to the human security of individuals and local communities in the first instance, in addition to a secondary trans-national threat to the stability of neighbouring states. The two dimensions are linked as each can exacerbate the other and result in a collection of fragile states on the Arabian Peninsula when the oil revenues that underlay the social contract between state and society begin to fray.

8

CONCLUSION

A NEW APPROACH TO SECURITY

The future evolution of Gulf security will be framed by the need to find sustainable balances—between competing visions of the national and regional security architecture, between incremental changes to governing and economic structures and the deeper systemic problems that undermine long-term solutions, and between rising demands for, and falling supplies of, natural resources. At its core lies the balance between state and society and the reformulation of the social contract and frameworks of governing institutions to ensure as orderly a transition into the post-oil era as possible. In this regard, the management of dwindling oil reserves in Bahrain, Oman and Yemen will provide a barometer of the longer-term prospects for internal security and external stability in the Arabian Peninsula.

States in transition are more vulnerable than most to outbreaks of political violence and ideational and other sub-state challenges to legitimacy. The case of Yemen illustrates this troubling point and carries a warning to policymakers in the GCC states of the difficulties involved in stripping away the layers of vested interests and reconstructing the basis of political economy. It underscores how redistributive and patronage-based states are especially vulnerable to economic insecurity and the breakdown of mechanisms for spreading wealth and co-opting support. The socio-economic challenges and growing disparities of income and wealth within the GCC add further impetus and urgency to regimes' attempts to broaden their base of support and construct more inclusive polities. This is crucial to weathering the transitions that lie ahead and maximising the possibility that changes will be consensual and aggregated rather than contested and violent.

The concept of human security has gained considerable traction since the 1990s to describe a new, people-centred notion that focuses on the security of individuals and communities rather than of states. Regional debates on security in the Gulf, as well as the broader Arab Middle East, have begun increasingly to anchor new approaches in human security. This emerging awareness of the concept of human security could form an important element of a comprehensive approach to tackling the difficult underlying causes of the socio-economic challenges facing the transition to a post-oil political economy in the Gulf. Alternatively, ruling elites in the GCC may instead view their advocacy of human security as part of a strategy to update regime security and legitimacy, resulting in a 'half-way' house of stalled reforms that do not substantively shift the regional security architecture or paradigm. This is the turning-point that policymakers and regional stakeholders in the Gulf will need to address in the years and decades to come.

The Emergence of Human Security

Human security as a paradigmatic concept traces its roots back to Franklin D. Roosevelt's famous 1941 State of the Union Address in which he listed 'freedom from want' and 'freedom from fear' as the third and fourth of his Four Freedoms (the others being freedom of speech and freedom of religion.) Beginning during the Cold War itself, but accelerating during its immediate aftermath, a multidisciplinary approach to questions of what security denotes began to reformulate the concept and re-centre its referent point from the level of the state to that of the individual and the community. The 1994 *Human Development Report* issued by the United Nations Development Programme (UNDP) outlined the conceptual tenets of human security as it stated that:

For too long the concept of security has been shaped by the potential for conflict between states. For too long, security has been equated with the threats to a country's borders. For too long, nations have sought arms to protect their security...To address the growing challenge of human security, a new development paradigm is needed that puts people at the centre of development, regards economic growth as a means and not an end, protects the life opportunities of future generations as well as the present generations and respects the natural systems on which all life depends.[1]

The report further disaggregated the concept of human security into seven components of economic, food, health, environmental, personal, community and political security.[2]

Adopting and integrating a human security approach involves a paradigm shift from 'traditional' national security approaches to foreign policy. By broadening the question of what the notion of security should entail, and by placing the individual at the centre of its approach, advocates of human security argue that it is best equipped to address the complex and interlinked insecurities in the contemporary global era.[3] Critics argue that it is a fuzzy and all-encompassing approach that offers little in the way of new thinking in relation to the use of military force or intervention, while acknowledging that it provides a valuable perspective on how to address the indivisible and global issues that afflict people rather than states.[4] This notwithstanding, the concept of human security has entered the policymaking arena in the European Union in particular, spearheaded by the former High Representative for Common Foreign and Security Policy (1999–2009), Javier Solana.

The reformulation of the idea of 'for whom and for what' security should entail does provide a compelling antidote to more realist-oriented concepts of security in regions that have endured multiple inter- and intra-state conflicts in recent decades. Particularly in the Gulf region, the three major inter-state wars and incidence of internal unrest in Bahrain, Yemen, Saudi Arabia, Iraq and Iran since 1979 demonstrate its failure to share in the transformation toward cooperative security structures as occurred in Latin America or Eastern Europe. Moreover, its definitional elasticity has proven attractive to regimes and interest groups that selectively appropriate parts of the concept that fit into their own pragmatic strategies of political survival. In the Arabian Peninsula and the Middle East more broadly, it has resulted in the emergence of an oxymoronic discourse focusing on a top-down human security approach.

In recent years, debate amongst groups and organisations in the GCC and the wider Middle East have begun to recognise the value of human security as a foundation-stone for constructing a new security paradigm. In November 2008, the Arab Women's Organization, an intergovernmental body led by Arab First Ladies or their representatives, themed its biennial conference around women and human security. The delegates devoted the event, which took place in Abu Dhabi, to formulating a human security strategy that embraces women as equal participants and contributors.[5] They cast this in developmental terms, arguing that the interconnected crises afflicting the Middle East 'requires the total mobilisation of a nation's resources and capabilities, particularly the fuller participation of women in our societies...it is a national, regional and global necessity.'[6]

The Arab Women's Organization's top-down approach was followed by a decidedly more 'bottom-up' advocacy of human security in the fifth Arab Human Development report. This was entitled *Challenges to Human Security in the Arab Countries* and was published by UNDP in July 2009. Its focus on the symbiosis of human development and human security marked the logical culmination of the four previous Arab Human Development Reports, which identified the lag in key indices of human development, governance, and the political, economic and social empowerment in the Arab world.[7] The report adopted its own definition of human security as 'the liberation of human beings from those intense, extensive, prolonged, and comprehensive threats to which their lives are vulnerable.' It went on to address the rationale for shifting toward a human security approach to tackling regional issues:

In the Arab countries, widespread human insecurity relentlessly undermines human development. It is brought on by the depletion of natural resources under pressure, by high population, growth rates and by rapid climate change, which could threaten the livelihoods, income, food and shelter of millions of Arabs...the subject provides a framework for analysing and addressing critical hazards to which the region, at the time of writing, is increasingly vulnerable. These manifest themselves not only in direct threats to life in cases such as Iraq, Sudan, Somalia and the Occupied Palestinian Territory, but also in the indirect threats posed by poverty, hunger and environmental stresses.[8]

By linking human security with human development, the report added visible impetus to the hitherto-limited awareness of these concepts in the Arab world. This is reflected in the greater frequency with which the terms are entering regional discourse and debate, as, for example, in the West Asia North Africa Forum established by Prince Hassan bin Talal of Jordan in 2009. This five-year initiative places human security at the heart of its approach to seeking common solutions to common problems afflicting the region's peoples and communities rather than its states.[9]

The developments and high-profile advocacy of the concept of human security described above are indeed promising. They must nonetheless be tempered by a note of caution and a degree of scepticism as to whom the notion of human security is intended to apply, and whether it is conceptually possible to implement a partial or top-down approach at all. Both scenarios raise a number of problematic considerations, not the least of which is the presence in the GCC states of large numbers of non-citizen labourers with few civil, political, economic or human rights. In this context, any announcement of a strategy securing the rights and freedoms of individuals risks reinforcing intra-societal divisions and hierarchical stratifications if it merely creates an additional layer of differential treatment and access to resources. In Dubai, for example, a report issued by Human Rights Watch in November 2006 entitled *Building Towers, Cheating Workers* concluded that 'the UAE has abdicated almost entirely from its responsibility to protect worker's rights.'[10] Similarly, in 2009 the US State Department's annual report on human rights abuses harshly criticised the Kuwaiti government of not committing itself to even minimal standards toward the elimination of human trafficking. Troublingly, the report also suggested that most of the 500,000 women employed as domestic workers in Kuwait had been subjected at one time or another to forced labour, physical and sexual abuse, and non-payment of salaries.[11]

With this in mind, any top-down conception of a human security approach may be expected to differ substantially from the essence of the notion of a genuinely people-centred, bottom-up strategy to securing individual freedoms and rights. This was in evidence during the Arab Women's Organization's conference in November 2008, when delegates expressed unease at the appropriation of the concept of human security by the First Ladies and their representatives.[12] It remains to be seen how serious is the regional discourse on human security and whether or not it develops into a substantive redefinition of security in the GCC states. This notwithstanding, the idea of human security has become more visible and entered policymaking debates in recent years, and it does offer the intellectual building-blocks for a new vision on security should it develop a momentum of its own that takes it beyond the smothering embrace of the elite.

Intertwined with the rising awareness of human security are increasing references to issues of gender security. Alongside the United Arab Emirates, Oman and Qatar have led the way in publicising women's rights and placing women in visible positions of political and economic leadership. Prominent royals such as Sheikha Mozah of Qatar have

169

assumed a leading role in educational and cultural development through initiatives such as the Qatar Foundation for Education, Science and Community Development and the Arab Democracy Foundation, in addition to becoming more assertive in entering the policymaking arena and spearheading national and international development projects.[13] In Oman, Sultan Qaboos appointed nine women to the fifty-eight-strong State Council (*Majlis ad-Dawla*) in 2005, as part of a strategy designed to change public perceptions of the role of women in society, create role models for future generations, and extend his endorsement to the entry of women into public life.[14]

Similarly high-profile appointments in Bahrain included the first Arab woman to lead the UN General Assembly and first judicial appointment to the Higher Civil Court, both in 2006, and the first female Ambassador to the United States, in 2008.[15] Meanwhile in Kuwait, the historic election of four female members of the National Assembly in the May 2009 both reflected popular levels of frustration with the 'old guard' of Kuwaiti politicians and a desire for a new and more responsible approach to politics in the state.[16] In late-2008, the shifting paradigm of elite-led female empowerment was clearly enunciated by the United Arab Emirates' permanent representative at the United Nations. In a Security Council debate on 'Women and Peace and Security,' Ahmed Al-Jarman called for the 'efficient and integrated participation of women in all efforts made to maintain and promote domestic peace and security in their communities, including effective participation in decision-making processes, mediation, reconciliation and negotiation.'[17]

As with human security, the prioritisation of gender security provides an opportunity for policymakers to work toward an inclusive and empowering agenda that strengthens internal social cohesion. If this is allowed to take place, it can contribute both to human and national security by addressing the latent fault-lines and internal fissures that might otherwise be vulnerable to manipulation by external variables or stresses. Such an approach would also lessen the likelihood of political violence and social conflict accompanying the transition to post-oil forms of governance and political economy, as states in transition have historically been more susceptible than others to contestation and challenge. Much initially depends on the attitude of the ruling families as agents of change, as the nature of reform processes in the Gulf are initially top-down and state-controlled, at least in their early stages. Their actions will determine whether fledgling reforms or discursive shifts develop into a substantive commitment to the values of people-centred security without discrimination between individuals and communities, including those with interests distinct from those of the ruling elite.

Previous experience of the political reform projects that began in the 1990s suggests that the most likely outcome (at least in the short- to medium-term) is a stalled 'halfway house' whereby initial openings stagnate and do not expand into substantive changes. This was the case with the processes of incipient democratisation that have either resulted in a flawed 'status quo' in Kuwait and Bahrain or not translated initial promise into significant progress, as in Qatar, Saudi Arabia and the UAE. Instead, the limited decompressions that did occur fit into the ruling elites' record of pragmatically adopting strategies of survival that ease these non-democratic states through periods of intense transitions. However, over the longer-term, a stalled process is a dissatisfying outcome that ultimately satisfies neither the interests of the state nor those of individuals and groupings within society. There is little to suggest that current initiatives to create a genuinely new security paradigm will fare any differently if policymakers and regime elites suspect it will lead to a cascade of changes that could develop a momentum of their own.

A Regional Approach

Human security thus represents more of an aspiration than a probable outcome at the present moment, and would aim at strengthening internal social cohesion within existing polities in the first instance. In the more immediate-term and at a regional level, a series of concrete measures to formulate a workable balance toward regional security could do much to minimise the prospects of an accidental flare-up of tensions or even conflict between the states of the Gulf littoral. Of pressing urgency is the importance of finding a sustainable compromise between the GCC states' reliance on the United States as their external security guarantor and the creation of a regional security architecture that can provide greater stability within the Gulf than the existing balance of power dynamic. Regional states need to overcome binary visions of what a regional security infrastructure would entail and focus on addressing the multiple latent and actual sources of volatility. This may best be achieved through engaging economically and commercially with Iran and a potentially resurgent post-occupation Iraq while regulating their power through an inclusive security arrangement.

Such a framework need not entail the expansion of the GCC to include both Iran and Iraq. This scenario is unfeasible in the short-term and likely to remain so for the foreseeable future. Instead, it could take the form of a network of forums and mechanisms for comprehensive and cooperative security loosely modelled on the Organisation for Security and Cooperation in Europe.[18] Indeed, the high-level *Vision Kuwait 2030* report prepared by former UK Prime Minister Tony Blair for the Kuwaiti government in 2010 recommended the creation of an *Organisation for Security and Cooperation in the Gulf* as a framework for peacefully resolving regional differences.[19] The objective would be to raise the opportunity cost of further conflict to the level where mutual interdependencies and trade and investment flows provide sufficient economic incentives for cooperation rather than contestation. Any such alignment of security and economic opportunities would offer the best possible foundation for a sustainable and cooperative regional architecture. Similarly, the adoption of a range of confidence-boosting measures could prevent the outbreak of accidental conflict and boost mutual communication, interaction, verification and observation of each party to Gulf security structures.[20]

Nevertheless, this cooperative vision is complicated by the persistence of myriad sources of intra- and inter-regional instability. Hopes for a new phase, and possible thaw, in US-Iranian relations following presidential elections in the two countries in 2008–9 failed to materialise as the Obama administration's initial outreach was not reciprocated in Iran. On the contrary, the controversial and violently-contested re-election of President Ahmedinejad in June 2009 exacerbated the outlook for regional security by injecting a potent combination of internal unrest and external pressure into Iran's regional posturing. Moreover, the international community's continuing misgivings over the intent and capabilities of Iran's nuclear programme mean that military action against Iran cannot be ruled out, in spite of the grave consequences that might befall the GCC states. Although issues of maritime stability in Gulf waters might provide one area of mutual interest for limited US-Iranian cooperation to avoid any repetition of past skirmishes in Gulf waters, the current climate renders it exceedingly unlikely.

Globalising Transitions

This book has documented the changing parameters of Gulf security as states and societies face the coming transition toward a post-oil era. It has argued that a number of longer-term and increasingly non-military issues pose profound challenges to the security and stability of regional polities. Although the more traditional 'hard' and territorially-bounded threats to stability remain largely unresolved at the time of writing, the impact of the processes of globalisation have eroded the boundaries between the domestic and the international spheres and interlinked old problems in new ways. Indeed, the challenges of refor-mulating the social contract and transitioning the states of the Arabian Peninsula toward post-rentier forms of governance are taking place in an *intermestic* and inexorably globalising environment. Officials and individuals operate in an environment in which it is no longer possible to isolate the internal from the external, and in which the major sources of future insecurity are likely to be oriented toward the human rather than the state.

As the Gulf States interact with globalising trends and progressive resource depletion, the cross-border nature of many insecurities— ranging from food and water to energy and climate change—will require common solutions to common problems. Here, the record of intergovernmental cooperation on initiatives such as the United Nations Climate Change Conference in Copenhagen conference is not encouraging for advocates of a global and regional commons that pri-oritises multilateral cooperation over national interests. However, other issues must be addressed domestically and will involve politically difficult and painful decisions if they are not to become politically and economically disintegrative, as in the case of Yemen. A major conten-tion of this book has been that ruling elites and policymakers are aware of the challenges but hitherto have shied away from addressing their root causes.

This reticence is intertwined with acknowledgment that the social contract regulating state-society relations needs to be overhauled if a productive, post-oil political economy is to emerge. This will require the gradual stripping away of the layers of subsidy and the redistribu-tive 'rentier' mechanisms that have embedded an unproductive culture of entitlement among many Gulf States' citizens. The difficulty facing policymakers in the GCC states is how to achieve this without eroding their own bases of legitimacy and societal consent for their continued rule. To be sure, the Gulf States survived intact the transformative socio-economic transition when they entered the oil era in the 1960s and 1970s, and the monarchies survived against the predictions of many social scientists. Ruling elites' pragmatic instincts for survival should not be underestimated, particularly following four decades of socialisation and acculturation as nation-states. However, the primary differing variable in the shift to the post-oil future is that their capacity to co-opt support is likely to be limited both by socio-economic constraints and by the globalising flows of people, ideas and norms.

Difficult challenges lie ahead for the Arab oil monarchies and Yemen. The ruling elites must find a way of reformulating the welfare states constructed during times of low populations and high wealth per capita. The transition to post-redistributive governing structures will require them to address the systemic structural problems in their socio-political composition. Simultaneously, accelerating global enmeshments and their political and economic opening-up to cross-border and sub-state flows provide new material and ideational linkages that interlink the domestic and international spheres of security policy. The symbiosis between the two dimensions is evident in the need for the Gulf States to expand their support base and strengthen internal social cohesion in order to withstand the potential exogenous stresses and shocks that might arise from irreversible climate change or future scarcities in food, water or energy reserves.

The future of Gulf security will be framed by the search for sustainable balances—between competing visions of national and regional security frameworks, between incremental reforms to political economy structures and the deeper underlying problems that complicate and undermine long-term solutions, and between rising demand for, and falling supplies of, natural resources. At its core lies the balance between state and society and the looming transition toward post-oil political economies. The management of dwindling oil rents in Bahrain and Oman will provide an early barometer of the longer-term prospects for internal security and external stability in the Arabian Peninsula. Yet the contemporaneous slide of Yemen toward failing statehood illustrates the scale of the challenges inherent in maintaining state legitimacy and societal acquiescence while scaling back layers of subsidy and networks of patronage and facing the imminent depletion both of oil revenues and water reserves. Yemen's enduring significance will become apparent in the medium- to longer-term when the GCC states undergo their own transition to a post-oil era. The key question will be whether they can manage the processes of change in a more orderly and consensual manner, as the inconvenient truth confronting GCC policymakers is that they face similar systemic and structural obstacles to reform, and while they enjoy greater material resources to buttress the transition, their dependence on oil has both been longer-lasting and deeper-rooted.

POSTSCRIPT

As this book went to press a wave of popular protest was sweeping the Middle East and North Africa. Their size and contagious overspill demonstrated the urgency and potency of addressing the socio-economic and political challenges described in this book. The demonstrations were remarkable for their largely non-violent and inclusive nature. Demonstrators came from all sects, religions and classes and far exceeded the parameters of normal opposition. Their largely peaceful demands for change contrasted sharply with the repressive use of force deployed by the beleaguered regimes. Nevertheless the killing of fellow citizens constituted a red line that heralded the rapid demise of the Ben Ali and Mubarak regimes in Tunisia and Egypt and intensifying mass opposition to the Gaddafi regime in Libya. It also revealed the narrow social base of support underpinning these longstanding authoritarian rulers and their inability to rule once they lost the power of coercion or the threat of force.

Although the protests originated in North Africa following the self-immolation of Mohamed Bouazizi in Tunisia in December 2010, his plight resonated heavily among people across the region. It tapped into powerful feelings of helplessness and a perceived lack of prospects for a better future among youthful populations lacking sufficient opportunities for employment. In addition, it exposed the elderly, authoritarian regimes' absolute failure to manage or meet the demands of a younger generation in a rapidly changing global economy. Crucially, regional economies are falling further behind at a time of accelerating innovation and knowledge-intensive growth elsewhere. Human and social capital is being held back by sclerotic labour markets and uncompetitive and bloated public sectors. These risk marginalising an entire generation of young people and fostering the perception that no meaningful change is possible within existing political systems.

The above applies to the Gulf States just as much as it does the more populous and less resource-rich states in North Africa and the Mashreq. Political tensions in Bahrain and Kuwait escalated in the second half of 2010 and prompted heavy-handed government responses in return. In the run-up to the October 2010 elections to the Bahraini Council of Representatives (Majlis Al-Nuwab) dozens of opposition and human rights activists were arrested.[1] Many remained in detention for months thereafter and allegations of torture were widespread, awakening memories of the 1994–99 uprising. The clampdown highlighted enduring authoritarian patterns of behaviour in the face of a popular social movement against socio-political injustice and abuse of power. It also demonstrated the Bahraini regime's natural instinct to suppress, rather than engage with, an increasingly organised and vocal political opposition.[2]

More troubling, and part of the same currents of unrest, were signs that Kuwait's much-vaunted political and media freedoms were being rolled back. A series of incidents occurred in the last few months of 2010 which threatened Kuwait's reputation as the most open society in the GCC. In November, a prominent writer, Mohammed Abdulqader Al-Jassem, was convicted of slandering the Prime Minister and sentenced to one year in prison, before being released on appeal in January 2011. This prompted Amnesty International to label Al-Jassem a 'prisoner of conscience' who had been jailed 'solely for non-violently exercising his right to freedom of expression.'[4] Just two weeks later Obeid Al-Wasmi, a Kuwait University law professor openly critical of the ruling family, was also arrested and detained for three months before being released in February 2011.[5] Most spectacularly, state security forces attacked and forcibly broke up a demonstration in December 2010, during which four MPs and a number of other participants were beaten and injured. The incidents culminated in the death of a man allegedly tortured in police custody in January 2011, and the resignation of the Interior Minister shortly thereafter.[6]

The political temperature in the Gulf was therefore rising even before the outbreak of widespread demonstrations throughout the Middle East and North Africa. A worrying confluence of opposition demands and repressive counter-measures in Kuwait and Bahrain suggested a tinder box awaiting a spark. Moreover, in Saudi Arabia this period coincided with a vacuum in political leadership at the top level.

This was occasioned by King Abdullah's lengthy convalescence in Morocco after a back operation in New York, as well as Crown Prince Sultan's ongoing health problems. Sultan's absence impacted in particular on Saudi Arabia's policy toward Yemen as he had dominated the 'Yemen file' ever since his appointment as Minister of Defence and Aviation in 1962. Although Prince Khalid bin Sultan stood in for his father in his capacity as Assistant Minister, the uncertain results of the three-month military campaign against Huthi rebels in 2009–10 indicated the Kingdom's Yemen policy was in some disarray at a dangerously uncertain moment.[7]

For these reasons the unprecedented displays of popular anger and anti-government demonstrations that broke out in January and February 2011 did not take place in a vacuum. Rather, they constituted a major escalation of existing pressures with the galvanising added factor of momentum as protestors forced regimes into making unprecedented political concessions. The protests spread throughout the region following the toppling of the Ben Ali and Mubarak regimes in Tunisia and Egypt on 14 January and 11 February. Demonstrations reached the Gulf on 14 February with the organisation of a 'Day of Anger' in Bahrain. Although the first rallies only gathered several hundred people in scattered Shiite villages, the killing of two protestors by the security services transformed the nature of the protests. They swelled into a gathering in central Manama that quickly attracted up to 20,000 people, demanding meaningful political reform and the resignation of the unpopular and long-serving Prime Minister, Sheikh Khalifa bin Salman Al-Khalifa.[8]

Significantly, the crowd encompassed Sunnis as well as Shiites and reflected socio-economic frustrations that crossed sectarian lines: at corruption; at high youth un- and under-employment; and at the lack of basic freedoms. For many Shiite communities, these intersected with longstanding complaints of political marginalisation and discrimination in higher positions within the Bahraini labour market, demonstrating how push-factors can quickly latch onto latent and existing internal fissures to widen and magnify discontent. Moreover, the protests were characterised by non-violence and the voluntary organisation of basic services, in clear imitation of the Tahrir Square protests in Cairo that toppled Mubarak the week before. However, their numbers and social inclusiveness panicked the ruling Al-Khalifa family into a brutally repressive response as the army attempted to smash the protests before they got too large. The result—at least five dead and hundreds injured—signalled the end of the post-1999 period of political reconciliation, broke the bonds of trust between regime and society, and decisively altered the political dynamic in Bahrain, though it remains to be seen how this will play out in the longer term.[9]

Kuwait was the other Gulf State that experienced protests, perhaps predictably in light of the swirling contours of unrest. Although these protests were much smaller in scale than in Bahrain, and concentrated in the bedoon (stateless) community, the government reacted similarly in attempting to suppress, rather than to engage with, this show of opposition. In both countries, rulers had earlier tried to pre-empt any discontent by increasing the spread of wealth. The Kuwaiti government announced the gift of 1000 Kuwaiti Dinars (approximately $3600) and fourteen months worth of food rations to each Kuwaiti citizen. This attempt to financially co-opt citizens was quickly copied by the Bahraini government, which announced a gift of 1000 Bahraini Dinars (approximately $2660) to each of its citizens.[10] While this may work in the short term in Kuwait, where citizens arguably have more to lose than gain from any change to the status quo, it illustrates just how difficult will be the eventual reformulation and dismantling of rent-seeking mentalities.

Officials in the United Arab Emirates also attempted to pre-empt any potential demands for reform by announcing that an 'electorate' of 300 voters would elect half of the representatives to the Federal National Council.[11] This constituted an incremental increase in political participation from the limited political reforms announced in 2006. This cautious approach is possible in the affluent context of the UAE, which, like Qatar, benefits from the combination of a small national population and high resource levels, although much of this is concentrated in Abu Dhabi. However it may not prove sufficient to head off protests or demands for change in the smaller, poorer emirates. Nor does it apply to Saudi Arabia or Oman, whose larger citizen populations and lower per capita incomes mean that there are large numbers of nationals living in poverty and with few economic opportunities.[12]

Indeed, in the wake of the trouble in Bahrain, Prince Talal bin Abdul-Aziz, a half-brother of King Abdullah of Saudi Arabia, warned that political reforms were needed to avert a coming storm, and called for a constitutional monarchy and democratic development along the Kuwaiti model.[13] However, the rapid break-up of the first political party to form in the Kingdom (the Islamic Umma Party) and the arrest of its leaders showed that, like its Gulf neighbours, the process of widening and deepening political participatory mechanisms will neither be uncontested nor smooth. The key questions will be the ruling families' preparedness to make meaningful political concessions that transform the structures and hierarchies of power, and their capacity to maintain control over the transition to ensure it does not develop an unstoppable momentum of its own. Resolving the dilemma between top-down attempts to pre-empt substantial bottom-up challenges to power and authority will be critical factors in the looming transition in the Gulf.

The Gulf States are consequently far from immune to the winds of change blasting forcefully through the Middle East. Large numbers of disenfranchised and disempowered Gulf nationals could yet provide the lightning rod that fuses social and economic unrest with political discontent. It was precisely this intersection of the political and the economic that represented the transformative aspect of the demonstrations elsewhere in the Middle East and set them apart from previous outbreaks of domestic unrest.[14] Notably, the Gulf States share many of the same attributes—bulging young populations, high youth unemployment and sclerotic labour markets that cannot absorb sufficient numbers of them, and the reluctance of authoritarian regimes to open up to meaningful political reform—that characterised the protests in Egypt and Tunisia. Moreover, the intergenerational clash between elderly policy-makers and a young generation more politically aware and interconnected than ever opens important new spaces for oppositional mobilisation and debate.[15]

Existing and latent fissures run deep through Gulf polities, as documented in this book. The premise of its argument is that security is fragile and based on a transient stability linked to the possession of substantial reserves of hydrocarbons. These provided the ruling families with the ability to co-opt opposition and spread wealth, but they will not last forever. For this reason, the violence of the protests in Bahrain in February 2011 is a worrying indication of potential troubles ahead when the Gulf States make the transition toward the post-oil era. Moreover, fragmented societies or weakened states will be more vulnerable to possible exogenous shocks arising from irreversible climate change or environmental degradation. Already, the winds of change blowing through the Middle East have shown how external forces can interact with, sharpen and reconfigure internal fault-lines. Underpinning everything is the tension between a generation of young people who lack any point of reference with the pre-oil era and take for granted the redistribution of unearned income, yet feel they lack economic opportunities and a political stake in the transition to the post-oil era, and the older structures of political and economic decision-making and authority that have increasingly been unable to provide solutions to these pressing problems.

NOTES

INTRODUCTION

1. The Gulf Cooperation Council, hereafter also referred to as the Gulf States, was founded in 1981 by Bahrain, Kuwait, Oman, Qatar, Saudi Arabia and the United Arab Emirates. In addition, 'Gulf security' cannot be considered in isolation from Yemen, which occupies a strategic position on the southwest flank of the Arabian Peninsula, and Iran and Iraq, which together with Saudi Arabia have historically formed a triangular 'balance of power' in the Persian Gulf.

2. Anoushiravan Ehteshami, *Globalization and Geopolitics in the Middle East: Old Games, New Rules* (London: Routledge, 2007), p. 110.

3. F. Gregory Gause, *The International Relations of the Persian Gulf* (Cambridge: Cambridge University Press, 2010, pp. 3–6; Henner Furtig, 'Conflict and Cooperation in the Persian Gulf: The Interregional Order and US Policy,' *Middle East Journal*, 61(4), 2007, pp. 627–40.

4. Ibid.

5. Gerd Nonneman, 'Security and Inclusion: Regimes Responses to Domestic Challenges in the Gulf,' in Sean McKnight, Neil Partrick and Francis Toase (eds), *Gulf Security: Opportunities and Challenges for the New Generation* (London: RUSI Whitehall Paper Series 51, 2000), pp. 107–15.

6. Gerd Nonneman, 'Determinants and Patterns of Saudi Foreign Policy: "Omnibalancing" and "Relative Autonomy" in Multiple Environments,' in Paul Aarts and Gerd Nonneman (eds), *Saudi Arabia in the Balance: Political Economy, Society, Foreign Affairs* (London: Hurst and Co., 2005), pp. 315–51.

7. Christopher Davidson, *The United Arab Emirates: A Study in Survival* (London: Lynne Rienner, 2006), p. 87.

8. Notable recent contributions include Alexander Wendt, *Social Theory of International Politics* (Cambridge: Cambridge University Press, 1999), Barry Buzan & Ole Waever, *Regions and Powers: The Structure of International Security* (Cambridge: Cambridge University Press, 2003), and Rich-

ard M. Price, *Moral Limit and Possibility in World Politics* (Cambridge: Cambridge University Press, 2008).

9. Keith Krause, 'Insecurity and State Formation in the Global Military Order: The Middle Eastern Case,' *European Journal of International Relations*, 2(3), 1996, p. 325.
10. Anoushiravan Ehteshami, 'Reform from Above: The Politics of Participation in the Oil Monarchies,' *International Affairs*, 79 (1), 2003, p. 55.
11. Joseph A. Kechichian, *Power and Succession in Arab Monarchies: A Reference Guide* (Boulder: Lynne Rienner, 2008), p. 420.
12. Gause, *International Relations*, p. 9.
13. Arshin Adib-Moghaddam, *The International Politics of the Persian Gulf* (New York: Routledge, 2006), p. 5
14. Michael Dillon, 'Global Security in the 21st Century: Circulation, Complexity and Contingency,' in Christopher Browning & Paul Cornish (eds), *The Globalization of Security—ISP/NSC Briefing Paper 05/02* (London: Chatham House, 2005), p. 3.
15. Mary Kaldor, *New and Old Wars: Organized Violence in a Global Era*, 2nd edition (Stanford, CA: Stanford University Press, 2007), p. 32.
16. Keith Krause, 'Theorizing Security, State Formation and the 'Third World' in the Post-Cold War World,' *Review of International Studies*, 24(1), 1998, p. 135.
17. Christian Reus-Smit, 'Constructivism and the structure of ethical reasoning,' in Richard Price (ed.), *Moral Limit and Possibility in World Politics* (Cambridge: Cambridge University Press, 2008), p. 53.
18. Paul Aarts & Dennis Janssen, 'Shades of Opinion: The Oil Exporting Countries and International Climate Politics', in Nonneman, *Analyzing Middle East Foreign Policies in Europe*, p. 225.
19. Barry Buzan, Ole Waever and Jaap de Wilde, *Security: A New Framework for Analysis* (Boulder, CO: Lynne Rienner, 1998), p. 23.
20. Barry Buzan, 'Will the "global war on terrorism" be the new Cold War?', *International Affairs*, 82(6), 2006, pp. 1102–03.
21. Keith Krause, 'Insecurity and State Formation in the Global Military Order: The Middle Eastern Case,' *European Journal of International Relations*, 2(3), 1996, p. 319.
22. Fred Halliday, *The Middle East in International Relations: Power, Politics and Ideology*, (Cambridge: Cambridge University press, 2005), p. 150.
23. Munira Fakhro, 'The Uprising in Bahrain: An Assessment' in Gary Sick and Lawrence Potter (eds), *The Persian Gulf at the Millennium: Essays in Politics, Economy, Security and Religion* (London: Macmillan, 1997), p. 184.
24. Personal interview, Bahrain, October 2009.
25. Nicole Stracke, 'Where is the UAE Islands Dispute Heading?' (Dubai: Gulf Research Centre, 25 September 2008).
26. Morten Valbjorn and Andre Bank, 'Signs of a New Arab Cold War: The 2006 Lebanon War and the Sunni-Shi'i Divide,' *Middle East Report* 242, 37(1), 2007, p. 7.

1. HISTORY OF GULF SECURITY STRUCTURES, 1903–2003

1. House of Lords debate, 'Great Britain and the Persian Gulf,' 5 May 1903. Hansard, vol. 121, column 1348.
2. David Gilmour, *Curzon* (London, John Murray, 1994), p. 203.
3. Gary Sick, 'The United States and the Persian Gulf in the Twentieth Century,' in Lawrence Potter (ed.), *The Persian Gulf in History* (New York: Palgrave Macmillan, 2009), p. 298.
4. Although the body of water is officially known as the Persian Gulf, this nomenclature is contested by the Arabian Peninsula states, which use instead the term Arabian Gulf. This book utilises the neutral term 'the Gulf.'
5. João Teles e Cunha, 'The Portuguese Presence in the Persian Gulf,' in Potter, *Persian Gulf in History*, p. 210.
6. Personal interview, Qatar, December 2008.
7. Alan Villiers, *Sons of Sindbad* (London: Arabian Publishing, 2006), p. 26.
8. Beatrice Nicolini, 'The Baluch Role in the Persian Gulf during the Nineteenth and Twentieth Centuries,' *Comparative Studies of South Asia, Africa and the Middle East*, 27 (2), 2007, p. 396.
9. Thomas Metcalf, *Imperial Connections: India in the Indian Ocean Arena, 1860–1920* (Berkeley: University of California Press, 2007), pp. 9–12.
10. Michael Casey, *The History of Kuwait* (Westport: CT, Greenwood Press, 2007), p. 39; Fatma Al-Sayegh, 'Merchants' Role in a Changing Society: The Case of Dubai, 1900–90,' *Middle Eastern Studies*, 34(1), 1998, p. 87.
11. Sulayman Khalaf, 'The Nationalisation of Culture: Kuwait's Invention of a Pearl-Diving Heritage,' in Alanoud Alsharekh and Robert Springborg (eds), *Popular Culture and Political Identity in the Arab Gulf States* (London: Saqi Books, 2008), p. 60.
12. Jill Crystal, *Oil and Politics in the Gulf: Rulers and Merchants in Kuwait and Qatar* (Cambridge: Cambridge University Press, 1990), p. 4.
13. Rosemary Said Zahlan, *The Making of the Modern Gulf States* (Reading: Ithaca Press, 2nd ed. 1998), p. 14.
14. James Onley and Suleyman Khalaf, 'Shaikly Authority in the Pre-oil Gulf: An Historical-Anthropological Study,' *History and Anthropology*, 17(3), 2006, p. 193.
15. Lisa Anderson, 'Absolutism and the Resilience of Monarchy in the Middle East,' *Political Science Quarterly*, 106(1), 1991, p. 9.
16. Frederick Anscombe, *The Ottoman Gulf: The Creation of Kuwait, Saudi Arabia and Qatar* (New York: Columbia University Press, 1997), p. 172.
17. Reidar Visser, *Basra: The Failed Gulf State: Separatism and Nationalism in Southern Iraq* (Munster: Lit Verlag, 2005), p. 18.
18. Benjamin Slot, *Mubarak Al-Sabah: Founder of Modern Kuwait 1896–1915* (London: Arabian Publishing, 2005), p. 420.

19. Keith Neilson, 'For diplomatic, economic, strategic and telegraphic reasons: British imperial defence, the Middle East and India, 1914–1918,' in Greg Kennedy and Keith Neilson, *Far-flung Lines: Essays on Imperial Defence in Honour of Donald Mackenzie Schurman* (London: Frank Cass, 1997), p. 102.
20. J.E. Peterson, 'Britain and the Gulf: at the Periphery of Empire,' in Potter, *Persian Gulf in History*, p. 286.
21. Evidence of Sir Arthur Hirtzel to the Mesopotamia Commission of Enquiry, *The National* Archive (T.N.A.), London, CAB 19/8.
22. James Onley, *The Arabian Frontier of the British Raj: Merchants, Rulers and the British in the Nineteenth-Century Gulf* (Oxford: Oxford University Press, 2007), p. 64.
23. Philip Graves, *The Life of Sir Percy Cox* (London: Hutchinson, 1941), p. 93.
24. Peterson, 'Britain and the Gulf', p. 279.
25. 'Effect of the Baghdad Railway on our Relations with Persia and the Defence of India,' War Office General Staff Memorandum, 16 November 1904, British Library India Office Records (I.O.R.), London, L/P&S/10/87.
26. Telegram from Sir Edward Grey to Prince Lichnowsky, 4 April 1914, T.N.A., FO 424/252.
27. Charles Tripp, *A History of Iraq* (Cambridge: Cambridge University Press, 2000), p. 32.
28. Kristian Coates Ulrichsen, 'The British Occupation of Mesopotamia, 1914–1922,' *Journal of Strategic Studies*, 30(2), 2007, p. 349.
29. Ali Ansari, *Modern Iran: the Pahlavis and After* (Harlow: Pearson Longman, 2007), p. 31.
30. Christopher Davidson, *Abu Dhabi: Oil and Beyond* (London: Hurst and Co. 2009), p. 40.
31. Hanna Batatu, *The Old Social Classes and the Revolutionary Movements of Iraq* (Princeton: Princeton University Press, 1978), p. 1116.
32. Prominent examples of Iranian intervention in the 1960s and 1970s included the military assistance provided to Oman during the Dhofar rebellion, the seizure of three islands belonging to Ras al-Khaimah and Sharjah in 1971, and its longstanding territorial claim on Bahrain. See Fred Halliday, *Middle East in International Relations*, p. 103.
33. Wm Roger Louis, *Ends of British Imperialism: The Scramble for Empire, Suez and Decolonization* (London: I.B. Tauris, 2006), p. 893.
34. Fred Halliday, *Arabia without Sultans* (London: Saqi Books, 2nd ed. 2002), p. 456.
35. Simon Smith, *Kuwait, 1950–1965: Britain, the al-Sabah, and Oil* (Oxford: Oxford University Press, 1999), p. 116 and p. 120.
36. Telegram from the British Ambassador to Iran to the Foreign Secretary, 29 December 1970, T.N.A., FCO 8/1372.

37. Winspeare Guicciardi, 'Good Offices Mission Bahrain,' 24 April 1970, T.N.A., FCO 8/1370.
38. Christopher Davidson, *Dubai: The Vulnerability of Success* (London: Hurst and Co., 2008), p. 63.
39. Wm Roger Louis, 'The British Withdrawal from the Gulf, 1967–71,' *Journal of Imperial and Commonwealth History*, 31(1), p. 102.
40. F. Gregory Gause, 'The Persistence of Monarchy in the Arabian Peninsula: A Comparative Analysis,' in Joseph Kostiner (ed.), *Middle East Monarchies: The Challenge of Modernity* (London: Lynne Rienner, 2000), p. 186.
41. Anoushiravan Ehteshami, *Globalization and Geopolitics in the Middle East: Old Games, New Rules* (London: Routledge, 2007), p. 110.
42. Personal interview, Kuwait, October 2009.
43. The six founding members of the Gulf Cooperation Council were, and remain, Bahrain, Kuwait, Qatar, Oman, Saudi Arabia and the United Arab Emirates.
44. Mary Kaldor, Terry Lynn Karl and Yahya Said, *Oil Wars* (London: Pluto Press, 2007), p. 28.
45. The exception was Saudi Arabia, which had been locked in to the United States' military umbrella through a wide range of military agreements dating back to the 1940s.
46. Laurence Louer, *Transnational Shia Politics: Religious and Political Networks in the Gulf* (London: Hurst and Co., 2008), p. 155.
47. Abdulkhaleq Abdulla, 'The Gulf Cooperation Council: Nature, Origin and Processes,' in Michael Hudson (ed.), *Middle East Dilemma: The Politics and Economics of Arab Integration* (New York: Columbia University Press, 1999), p. 154.
48. Letter from the Defence Secretary in the Sultanate of Oman to the British Ambassador to Oman, 28 March 1972, T.N.A., FCO 46/947.
49. Ministry of Defence minute, 6 May 1974, T.N.A., DEFE 24/750.
50. Letter from the Permanent Representative of the People's Democratic Republic of Yemen to the Secretary-General of the United Nations, 26 November 1973, T.N.A., FCO 8/2037.
51. Steve Yetiv and Chunlong Yu, 'China, Global Energy and the Middle East,' *Middle East Journal*, 61(2), 2007, pp. 201–2.
52. Foreign and Commonwealth Office minute, 20 November 1972, T.N.A., FCO 8/1865.
53. Foreign and Commonwealth Office briefing note for the Prime Minister, 'British Military Assistance to Oman,' 1973, T.N.A., FCO 8/2117.
54. Davidson, *Dubai*, pp. 250–52.
55. 'Ras al-Khaimah's Links to Al-Qaida, not Iran, is the Real Issue,' Guardian, 6 June 2010.
56. Davidson, *The United Arab Emirates*, p. 66.
57. Personal interview, Dubai, October 2009.

58. Steffen Hertog, 'Shaping the Saudi State: Human Agency's Shifting Role in Rentier-State Formation,' *International Journal of Middle East Studies*, 39(4), 2007, p. 539; Marc Valeri, *Oman: Politics and Society in the Qaboos State* (London: Hurst and Co., 2009), p. 251.

59. J.E. Peterson, 'The Emergence of Post-Traditional Oman,' Sir William Luce Fellowship Paper No. 5. University of Durham, 2004, p. 5.

60. Anh Nga Longva, 'Neither Autocracy nor Democracy but Ethnocracy: Citizens, Expatriates and the Socio-Political in Kuwait,' in Paul Dresch and James Piscatori (eds), *Monarchies and Nations: Globalization and Identity in the Arab States of the Gulf* (London: I.B. Tauris, 2004), p. 134.

61. Tore Petersen and Richard Nixon, *Great Britain and the Anglo-American Alignment in the Persian Gulf and Arabian Peninsula: Making Allies Out of Clients* (Brighton: Sussex Academic Press, 2009), p. 133.

62. Yezid Sayigh and Avi Shlaim (eds), *The Cold War and the Middle East* (Oxford: Clarendon Press, 1977), p. 288.

63. Furtig, 'Conflict and Cooperation,' p. 628.

64. Charles Tripp, 'The Foreign Policy of Iraq,' in Raymond Hinnebusch and Anoushiravan Ehteshami (eds), *The Foreign Policies of Middle East States* (London: Lynne Rienner, 2002), pp. 175–76.

65. Telegram from the British Ambassador to Bahrain to the Foreign Secretary, 29 January 1977, T.N.A., FCO 8/2874.

66. Abdulla, 'Gulf Cooperation Council' (Op. Cit), p. 154.

67. Abdulla Baabood, 'Dynamics and Determinants of the GCC States' Foreign Policy, with Special Reference to the EU,' in Gerd Nonneman (ed.), *Analyzing Middle Eastern Foreign Policies* (London: Routledge, 2005), p. 147.

68. Anthony Cordesman and Khalid Al-Rodhan, 'The Gulf Military Forces in an Era of Asymmetric War: Qatar,' (Washington DC: Center for Strategic and International Studies, June 2006), p. 11.

69. Ahmed Abdelkareem Saif, 'Deconstructing Before Building: Perspectives on Democracy in Qatar,' in Anoushiravan Ehteshami and Steven Wright, *Reform in the Middle East Oil Monarchies* (Reading: Ithaca Press, 2008), p. 106.

70. The United Arab Emirate's sudden decision to withdraw from the GCC project of monetary union in May 2009 following the decision to site the Central Bank in Riyadh is the latest and most high-profile example of unresolved intra-regional tension.

71. Furtig, 'Conflict and Cooperation,' p. 627.

72. Andrew Rathmell, Theodore Karasik and David Gompert, 'A New Persian Gulf Security System,' RAND Issue Paper (2003), p. 2.

73. Thomas Hegghammer, 'Islamist Violence and Regime Stability in Saudi Arabia,' *International Affairs*, 84(4), 2008, p. 707.

74. F. Gregory Gause, *Oil Monarchies: Domestic and Security Challenges in the Arab Gulf States* (New York: Council on Foreign Relations Press, 1994), p. 90.

75. Adib-Moghaddam, *International Politics of the Persian Gulf*, p. 42.

76. Valeri, *Oman*, p. 78.

77. Davidson, *The United Arab Emirates*, p. 206.

78. Anthony Cordesman, 'Iran, Oil and the Strait of Hormuz,' Washington DC: Center for Strategic and International Studies, March 2007, p. 2.

79. Personal interview, Cambridge, July 2010.

80. Yahia Zoubir and Louisa Dris-Ait-Hamadouche, 'US-Saudi Relationship and the Iraq War: The Dialects of a Dependent Alliance,' *Journal of Third World Studies*, 24(1), 2007, p. 109.

81. Halliday, *The Middle East in International Relations*, p. 150.

82. Abdullah Al-Shayeji, 'Dangerous Perceptions: Gulf Views of the U.S. Role in the Region,' *Middle East Policy*, 5 (1997), p. 5.

83. Barry Buzan and Ole Waever, *Regions and Powers: The Structure of International Security* (Cambridge: Cambridge University Press, 2003), p. 201.

84. Gause, *International Relations of the Gulf*, p. 127.

85. John Duke Anthony, Jean-Francois Seznec, Taynar Ari and Wayne White, 'War with Iran: Regional Reactions and Requirements,' *Middle East Policy*, 15(3), 2008, p. 3.

86. Al-Shayeji, 'Dangerous Perceptions, p. 1.

87. 'Jihad Against Jews and Crusaders,' World Islamic Front Statement, 23 February 1998. http://www.fas.org/irp/world/para/docs/980223-fatwa.htm

88. Gwenn Okruhlik, 'Rentier Wealth, Unruly Law, and the Rise of Opposition: the Political Economy of Oil States,' *Comparative Politics*, 31 (3), 1999, p. 299.

89. Hegghammer, 'Islamist Violence,' p. 707.

90. Personal interview, Qatar, December 2008.

91. Nonneman, 'Security and Inclusion' (Op. Cit), p. 108.

92. Personal interview, Kuwait, May 2008.

93. Anoushiravan Ehteshami and Steven Wright, 'Political Change in the Arab Oil Monarchies: From Liberalization to Enfranchisement,' *International Affairs*, 83(5), 2007, p. 930.

94. Mary Ann Weaver, 'Letter from Qatar: "Democracy by Decree",' *The New Yorker*, 20 November 2000, p. 54.

95. Fifteen hijackers were from Saudi Arabia and two were from the United Arab Emirates, in addition to one each from Egypt and Lebanon.

96. Mahan Abedin, 'Saudi dissent more than just jihadis,' in Joshua Craze and Mark Huband, *The Kingdom: Saudi Arabia and the Challenge of the 21st Century* (London: Hurst and Co., 2009), p. 34.

97. Barry Buzan, 'Will the "global war on terrorism" be the new Cold War?', *International Affairs*, 82(6), 2006, pp. 1102–03.

98. Morten Kelstrup, 'Globalisation and Societal Insecurity: the Securitisation of Terrorism and Competing Strategies for Global Governance,' in Stefano

Guzzini and Dietrich Jung (eds), *Contemporary Security Analysis and Copenhagen Peace Research* (London: Routledge, 2004), p. 112.

99. 'Rice calls for Mid-East Democracy,' BBC News, 20 June 2005.
100. Personal interview, Dubai, October 2009.
101. Personal interview, Bahrain, December 2008.
102. Gerd Nonneman, 'Political Reform in the Gulf Monarchies: From Liberalization to Democratization? A Comparative Perspective,' in Ehteshami and Wright, *Middle East Oil Monarchies*, pp. 9–13.
103. Ehteshami and Wright, 'Political Change,' p. 915.
104. Marina Ottaway, *Evaluating Middle East Reform. How Do We Know When It Is Significant?* Carnegie Paper 56, Washington DC: Carnegie Endowment for International Peace, p. 6.
105. Khaldoun Al-Naqeeb, 'How Likely is Democracy in the Gulf?' in John Fox, Nada Mourtada-Sabbah and Mohammed al-Mutawa (eds), *Globalization and the Gulf* (London: Routledge, 2006), p. 134.
106. 'Boycott of 2010 Poll Likely, Says Bahraini Society,' *Bahrain Tribune*, 11 September 2008.
107. Lynn E. Davis, *Globalization's Security Implications*, Santa Monica, CA: RAND Issue Paper 2003, p. 1.
108. Mary Kaldor, Helmut Anheier & Marlies Glasius, 'Global Civil Society in an Era of Regressive Globalisation,' *Global Civil Society 2003* (Oxford: Oxford University Press, 2003), p. 7.
109. Marc Lynch, 'Globalization and Arab Security,' in Jonathan Kirshner (ed.), *Globalization and National Security* (New York: Routledge, 2006), pp. 191.
110. Thomas Hegghammer, 'Saudi Militants in Iraq: Backgrounds and Recruitment Patterns,' Norwegian Defence Research Establishment (FFI), February 2007, p. 9.
111. Paul Dresch, 'Societies, Identities and Global Issues,' in Paul Dresch and James Piscatori (eds), *Globalization and Identity in the Arab States of the Gulf* (London: I.B. Tauris, 2005), p. 11.
112. Personal interview, Kuwait, October 2009.
113. M.J. Williams, 'The Coming Revolution in Foreign Affairs: Rethinking American National Security,' *International Affairs*, 84(6), 2008, p. 1115.

2. SECURITY AS DISCOURSE: IRAQ, IRAN AND TRANS-NATIONAL EXTREMISM

1. Anoushiravan Ehteshami, 'Reform from Above: The Politics of Participation in the Oil Monarchies' *International Affairs*, 79(1) 2003, p. 55.
2. Joseph Kechichian, *Power and Succession in Arab Monarchies: A Reference Guide* (Boulder, CO: Lynne Rienner, 2008), p. 420.
3. Davidson, *The United Arab Emirates*, p. 66.

4. Toby Dodge, 'The Causes of US Failure in Iraq,' *Survival*, 49(1), 2007, p. 87.
5. Walter Pincus, 'Violence in Iraq Called Increasingly Complex,' *Washington Post*, 17 November 2006.
6. http://www.iraqbodycount.org/; Gilbert Burnham, Riyadh Lafta, Shannon Doacy and Les Roberts, 'Mortality after the 2003 invasion of Iraq: a cross-sectional cluster sample survey,' *The Lancet*, 11 October 2006.
7. Patricia Weiss Fagan, 'Iraqi Refugees: Seeking Stability in Syria and Jordan.' Center for International and Regional Studies, Georgetown University School of Foreign Service in Qatar, Occasional Paper 1, 2009, p. 2.
8. Kuwait became the logistical centre of the multi-national forces while Qatar hosted the headquarters of US Central Command and Bahrain hosted the headquarters of the US Fifth Fleet.
9. Furtig, 'Conflict and Cooperation', p. 638.
10. Personal interview, Bahrain, October 2009.
11. 'Saudi King Calls US Presence in Iraq 'Illegitimate', *New York Times*, 28 March 2007.
12. David Pollock, 'Kuwait: Keystone of US Gulf Policy.' The Washington Institute for Near East Policy: Washington D.C., 2007, p. 41.
13. Hegghammer, 'Saudi Militants in Iraq', p. 11.
14. Personal interview, Kuwait, December 2008; Anthony Cordesman and Khalid Al-Rodhan, 'The Gulf Military Forces in an Era of Asymmetric War: Kuwait.' Washington, D.C., Center for Strategic and International Studies, June 2006, p. 23.
15. Personal interview, London, August 2009; Christopher Davidson, 'Dubai: The Security Dimensions of the Region's Premier Free Port,' *Middle East Policy*, 15(2), 2008, pp. 156.
16. For example, see Rob Lowe and Claire Spencer, 'Iran, its Neighbours and the Regional Crises.' London: Chatham House Report, 2006; Mai Yamani, 'Arcs and Crescents,' *The World Today*, 62(12), 2006; Ted Galen Carpenter and Malou Innocent, 'The Iraq War and Iranian Power,' *Survival*, 49(4), 2007, Joseph Kechichian, 'Can Arab Monarchies Endure a Fourth War in the Persian Gulf?' *Middle East Journal*, 61(2), 2007.
17. Carpenter and Innocent, 'Iraq War and Iranian Power,' p. 67.
18. Quoted in Nawaf Obaidi, 'Stepping into Iraq: Saudi Arabia will Protect Sunnis if the US Leaves,' *Washington Post*, 29 November 2006.
19. Abdulaziz Sager, 'The GCC States and the Situation in Iraq.' Dubai: Gulf Research Centre, 10 July 2008.
20. Yamani, 'Arcs and Crescents', p. 8.
21. Furtig, 'Conflict and Cooperation', p. 635.
22. Chris Toensing, 'From the Editor,' *Middle East Report*, 242, 37(1), 2007, p. 47.
23. Louer, *Transnational Shia Politics*, p. 223.
24. Katherine Meyer, Helen Rizzo and Yousef Ali, 'Changed Political Attitudes: The Case of Kuwait,' *International Sociology*, 22(3), 2007, p. 300.

25. Reidar Visser, 'Basra, the Reluctant Seat of "Shiastan",' *Middle East Report* 242, 37(1), 2007, p. 23.

26. Fakhro, 'Uprising in Bahrain,' p. 183; Toby Craig Jones, 'Rebellion on the Saudi Periphery: Modernity, Marginalization and the Shi'a Uprising of 1979', *International Journal of Middle East Studies*, 38(2), 2006, p. 213.

27. Personal interview, Kuwait, December 2008.

28. Sager, GCC States.

29. 'US Wants Gulf States to Impose Curbs on Iran,' *Khaleej Times*, 14 December 2008.

30. Kenneth Katzman, 'Iran's Activities and Influence in Iraq.' Congressional Research Service Report for Congress, Washington, D.C., 16 June 2008, p. 6.

31. 'Britain Ends Combat Operations in Iraq,' *The Independent*, 30 April 2009.

32. Toby Dodge, 'Iraq and the Next American President,' *Survival*, 50(5), 2008, p. 47.

33. Eric V. Thompson, 'The Iraqi Military Re-Enters the Gulf Security Dynamic,' *Middle East Policy*, 16(3), 2009, p. 28.

34. 'US Arms to Iraq Worry Kuwait,' *Gulf Times*, 23 September 2008; personal interviews, Kuwait, December 2008 and March 2009.

35. Personal interviews, London, August and December 2009.

36. 'Clash Over Tribal Councils Intensifies in Iraq,' *New York Times*, 4 November 2008.

37. 'U.N. Preparing Iraq-Kuwait Reconciliation Plan,' Reuters, 16 November 2009.

38. United Nations Assistance Mission for Iraq [UNAMI], 'Humanitarian Crisis in Iraq: Facts and Figures,' United Nations, 2007.

39. International Narcotics Control Board [INCB], 'Report of the International Narcotics Control Board for 2007,' www.incb.org.

40. 'Iraq Emerging as Key Route in Global Drugs Trade,' Agence France-Presse, 5 July 2008.

41. Shahram Chubin, 'Iran's Power in Context,' *Survival*, 51(1), 2009, p. 165.

42. Furtig, 'Conflict and Cooperation', p. 629.

43. F. Gregory Gause, 'What Saudis Really Think About Iran,' *Foreign Policy*, 6 May 2010.

44. Winspeare Guicciardi, 'Good Offices Mission Bahrain,' 24 April 1970, T.N.A., FCO 8/1370.

45. 'The Iranian Policy in the Gulf is Indeed Puzzling, Because This Policy is Rife with Contraventions,' *Arab Times*, 21 July 2007; 'Iran Ignorant of International Laws,' *Gulf News*, 16 February 2009.

46. Nicole Stracke, 'Where is the UAE Islands Dispute Heading,' Dubai: Gulf Research Centre, 25 September 2008.

47. 'Saudi Shi'ites: New Light on an Old Divide. Interview by Mahan Abedin,' *Asia Times*, 26 October 2006.

48. Louer, *Transnational Shia Politics*, pp. 297–98.

49. Leo Kwarten, *Why the Saudi Shiites Won't Rise Up Easily*. Beirut: A Conflicts Forum Monograph, 2009, p. 7.

50. Gause, *Oil Monarchies*, p. 90.

51. Personal interview, Abu Dhabi, October 2009.

52. Toby Craig Jones, 'The Iraq Effect in Saudi Arabia,' *Middle East Report* 237, 35(4), 2005, p. 25.

53. Personal interview, Bahrain, December 2008.

54. See chapter one.

55. Halliday, *Middle East in International Relations*, p. 152.

56. 'Iran Criticises US Missile Deployments in Gulf,' Reuters, 2 February 2010.

57. Rathmell et al. (eds), *New Persian Gulf Security System*, p. 3.

58. Personal interviews, London, July 2008, Kuwait, Bahrain, Qatar and Dubai, December 2008, and Kuwait, March 2009.

59. Valbjorn and Bank, 'New Arab Cold War,' p. 6.

60. 'Senior Iran Official Predicts Imminent Demise of Gulf State Royals,' *World Tribune* (Nicosia), 15 August 2008.

61. 'Iran Dismisses Gulf Sleeper Cell "Lies",' *Gulf Times*, 17 September 2008.

62. 'Iran Boasts its Forces Can Control the Gulf,' *Agence France-Presse*, 17 September 2008.

63. 'Defector Accuses Iran of Running Sleeper Cells in Gulf,' Agence France-Presse, 16 September 2008.

64. 'Iran Dismisses Sleeper Cell "Lies",' *Gulf Times*, 17 September 2008.

65. 'Kuwait Busts Alleged Iran Spy Cell: Paper,' *Agence France-Presse*, 1 May 2010.

66. Dalia Dassa Kaye and Frederic M. Wehrey, 'A Nuclear Iran: The Reaction of Neighbours,' *Survival*, 49(2), 2007, p. 111.

67. 'Possibility of a Nuclear-Armed Iran Alarms Arabs,' *New York Times*, 1 October 2009.

68. 'UAE Diplomat Mulls Hit on Iran's Nukes, Prefers Strike to Armed Foe,' *Washington Times*, 6 July 2010.

69. 'Sanctions Slow Iran's Trade but Not Stop,' Associated Press, 18 August 2008.

70. 'Dubai's Downfall Expose the Political Ties that Bind as a Tangled Web,' *The Daily Telegraph*, 3 December 2009.

71. 'Oman and Iran will Complete Kish Gas Field Development by 2012,' *Gulf News*, 12 September 2008; 'Qatar, Iran, to Sign Key Agreements,' *Gulf News*, 2 February 2010.

72. Kristian Coates Ulrichsen, *Gulf Security: Challenges and Responses*. (London: Royal College of Defence Studies, 2008), p. 3.

73. 'Gates Says Iran Still a Threat,' Reuters, 8 December 2007.

74. Neil Partrick, *Dire Straits for U.S. Mid-East Policy: The Gulf Arab States and US-Iran Relations*. London: Royal United Services Institute, January 2008.

75. 'Kuwait Won't Allow Land to be Used for Attack on Iran,' *Kuwait Times*, 4 February 2010.

76. Buzan and Waever, Regions and Powers, pp. 3–4.

77. See chapter one.

78. Bruce Riedel and Bilal Saab, 'Al Qaeda's Third Front: Saudi Arabia,' *The Washington Quarterly*, 31(2), 2008, p. 34.

79. Personal interviews, London, July 2008, and Kuwait, December 2008.

80. Hegghammer, 'Islamist Violence', p. 712.

81. Christian Koch, 'Gulf States Plan for Day that Oil Runs Dry,' *Jane's Intelligence Review*, December 2006, p. 22.

82. Benjamin Schwarz, 'America's Struggle Against the Wahhabi/Neo-Salafi Movement,' *Orbis*, 51(1), 2007, p. 124.

83. Cordesman, 'The Gulf Military Forces in an Era of Asymmetric War: Qatar,' Washington DC: Center for Strategic and International Studies, June 2006, p. 14.

84. Personal interview, London, July 2008; Davidson, *Dubai*, p. 295.

85. Christopher Blanchard and Alfred Prados, 'Saudi Arabia: Terrorist Financing Issues. Congressional Research Service Report for Congress, Washington D.C., 14 September 2007, p. 2.

86. Maurice Greenberg, William Wechsler and Lee Wolowsky, 'Terrorist Financing. Report of an Independent Task Force Sponsored by the Council on Foreign Relations.' New York, October 2002, p. 1

87. 'US Actions Against Kuwaiti Society Doesn't Reflect Distinguished Ties: Al-Kharafi,' *Kuwait Times*, 16 June 2008.

88. 'Kuwaiti MPs Allege Conspiracy Against Democracy,' *Kuwait Times*, 18 June 2008.

89. 'UAE Takes New Measures Against Money Laundering,' *The Peninsula*, 15 May 2009; 'UAE Tightens Money-Laundering Rules on Foreigners,' *Reuters*, 13 August 2009.

90. 'UAE to Step Up Efforts Against Money Laundering,' *Khaleej Times*, 18 February 2010.

91. United States Government and Accountability Office, 'Combating Terrorism: U.S. Agencies Report Progress Countering Terrorism and its Financing in Saudi Arabia, but Continued Focus on Counter Terrorism Financing Efforts Needed.' Washington D.C., September 2009.

92. 'How the GCC Can Rediscover That Spirit of Unity,' *The National*, 13 December 2009.

93. Riedel and Saab, 'Al Qaeda's Third Front,' p. 37.

94. 'Imams Fail in their Desired Roles,' *Arab News*, 17 October 2008.

95. Christopher Boucek, 'Saudi Arabia's 'Soft' Counterterrorism Strategy: Prevention, Rehabilitation, and Aftercare.' Carnegie Paper 97. Carnegie Endowment for International Peace: Washington, D.C., September 2008, p. 3.

96. Paul Holtom, Mark Bromley, Pieter Wezeman and Siemon Wezeman, 'Trends in International Arms Transfers, 2009,' SIPRI Fact Sheet, 2010, pp. 5–6.

97. *The Military Balance 2010* (London: International Institute for Strategic Studies, 2009), pp. 235–82.

98. Anthony Cordesman, 'The Gulf Military Balance in 2010: An Overview,' Washington, D.C.: Center for Strategic and International Studies, p. 37.

99. Ibid. pp. 40–41.

100. Personal interview, London, July 2008.

101. Davidson, *Dubai*, p. 277.

102. Schwarz, America's Struggle, p. 125.

103. 'Former Guantanamo Detainee Tied to Attack,' *New York Times*, 8 May 2008.

104. Coates Ulrichsen, 'Challenges and Responses', p. 4.

105. 'Freed by the U.S., Saudi Becomes a Qaeda Chief,' *New York Times*, 22 January 2009.

106. Personal interviews, London, July 2008, Kuwait, December 2008, and Dubai, October 2009.

107. Ginny Hill, 'What is Happening in Yemen?' *Survival*, 52(2), 2010, pp. 108.

108. 'Yemen Expelled 16,000 Foreign Al-Qaeda Suspects: Vice President,' Qatar News Agency, 16 June 2008.

109. 'Saleh Informs Sultan of Al-Qaeda Plots Uncovered in Yemen,' *Arab News*, 14 August 2008.

110. 'Saudi Arabia to Try 1,200 More Terror Suspects,' Saudi Gazette, 26 October 2008.

111. 'Yemen Identifies US Embassy Attackers,' *Gulf Today*, 2 November 2008.

112. Jeremy Sharp, 'Yemen: Where is the Stability Tipping Point?' *Arab Reform Bulletin*, 6(6), July 2008.

113. '23 Al-Qaeda Suspects Escape from Political Security Prison,' *Yemen Times*, 4 February 2006.

114. Anthony Cordesman, 'Gulf Threats, Risks and Vulnerabilities.' Washington, D.C.: Center for Strategic and International Studies, August 2009.

115. This will be examined in detail in chapter seven.

116. 'Bomber Behind Yemen Attack Trained in Somalia,' Reuters, 18 March 2009.

117. 'Yemeni Rebels Sent Arms to Shabab: Somalia,' Reuters, 3 January 2010.

118. Roy Love, 'Economic Drivers of Conflict and Cooperation in the Horn of Africa: A Regional Perspective and Overview.' (London: Chatham House Africa Programme Briefing Paper, December 2009), p. 3.

119. See, for example, Al-Qaeda in the Arabian Peninsula's magazine, *Sada al-Malahim*, particularly issue 11 released on 29 October 2009. Also '113 Terror Suspects Arrested in Kingdom,' *Arab News*, 25 March 2010.

120. 'Al Qa'eda Spreads its Terror Web,' *The National*, 21 September 2009.

121. 'Yemeni Insurgents Hit Hard,' *Arab News*, 6 November 2009.

122. 'Saudis Struggle Against Yemeni Rebels,' *Khaleej Times*, 14 January 2010.

123. Personal interview, London, February 2010.

124. 'Bomber Behind Yemen Attack Trained in Somalia,' Reuters, 18 March 2009.

125. 'Detroit Terror Attack: Al-Qaeda Regional Group Claims Responsibility,' *Daily Telegraph*, 28 December 2009.

126. Fawaz Gerges, 'What Next for Yemen?' Presentation at the London School of Economics and Political Science, 9 February 2010.

127. 'Gulf States Key to Resolving Yemen's Ills,' Agence France-Presse, 29 January 2010.

128. Gregory Johnsen, 'Welcome to Qaedastan,' www.foreignpolicy.com, January/February 2010.

129. 'Yemen Opposition Slams Outcome of London Conference', *Earth Times*, 28 January 2010.

130. 'Act Locally: Why the GCC Needs to Help Save Yemen,' *The National*, 7 January 2010.

131. 'Yemen's Issues Responsibilities of its People—Attiyah,' Kuwait News Agency, 28 January 2010.

132. 'Gulf States Key to Resolving Yemen's Ills,' Agence France-Presse, 29 January 2010.

133. Personal interview, Qatar, January 2010.

134. Personal interview, Dubai, October 2009; 'Riyadh Awards $900m Border Fence Deal,' *Middle East Economic Digest*, 52(25), 20 June 2008.

135. Personal interviews, Kuwait, December 2008 and October 2009, Qatar and Dubai, October 2009.

136. Personal interviews, Kuwait and Dubai, October 2009.

137. 'Gulf States Key to Resolving Yemen's Ills,' Agence France-Presse, 29 January 2010.

138. Personal interview, London, November 2009.

3. CONTEXTUAL PARAMETERS AND FUTURE TRENDS

1. Personal interview, Kuwait, October 2009.

2. Michael Dillon, 'Global Security in the 21st Century: Circulation, Complexity and Contingency,' in Christopher Browning and Paul Cornish (eds), The Globalization of Security. ISP/NSC Briefing Paper 05/02, Chatham House, October 2005, p. 3.

3. Personal interviews, Bahrain, December 2008 and Kuwait, March 2010.

4. Personal interviews, Dubai, December 2008 and October 2009.

5. Mary Kaldor, *New and Old Wars: Organized Violence in a Global Era* (2nd ed., Cambridge: Polity Press, 2006), p. 4.

6. Adam Roberts and Dominik Zaum, Selective Security: War and the United Nations Security Council Since 1945. Adelphi Paper No. 395. London: International Institute for Strategic Studies, June 2008, p. 18.

7. Robyn Eckersley, 'Environmental Security, Climate Change, and Globalizing Terrorism,' in Damien Grenfell and Paul James (eds), *Rethinking Insecurity, War and Violence* (London: Routledge, 2009), p. 87.

8. Mary Kaldor, *Human Security: Reflections on Globalization and Intervention* (Cambridge: Polity Press, 2007), p. 182.

9. Our Global Neighbourhood: Report of the Commission on Global Governance. Oxford: Oxford University Press, 1996. Summary Analysis available at http://sovereignty.net/p/gov/gganalysis.htm.

10. Arab Human Development Report 2009: Challenges to Human Security in the Arab Countries. New York: UNDP, 2009, p. 1.

11. 'Sheikha Fatima's Efforts in Women's Cause Hailed,' *Gulf Times*, 13 November 2008.

12. Mary Kaldor, Helmut Anheier and Marlies Glasius, 'Global Civil Society in an Era of Regressive Globalization,' in Mary Kaldor (ed.), *Global Civil Society 2003* (Oxford: Oxford University Press), p. 5.

13. Ehteshami, 'Reform from Above,' p. 55.

14. Madawi Al-Rasheed, 'An Assessment of Saudi Political, Religious and Media Expansion,' in Madawi Al-Rasheed (ed.), *Kingdom Without Borders: Saudi Arabia's Political, Religious and Media Frontiers* (London: Hurst and Co., 2008, p. 23.

15. David Held and Anthony McGrew (eds), *The Global Transformations Reader: An Introduction to the Globalization Debate* (Cambridge: Polity Press, 2000), p. 11.

16. Jan-Aart Scholte, 'Civil Society and Democratically Accountable Global Governance,' in David Held and Mathias Koenig-Archibugi (eds), *Global Governance and Public Accountability* (Oxford: Blackwell and Wiley, 2005), p. 90.

17. Eckart Woertz, 'The Gulf Economies in 2008,' in Abdulaziz Sager (ed.), *Gulf Yearbook 2008–2009* (Dubai: Gulf Research Centre, 2009), p. 233.

18. 'Copenhagen Negotiators Bicker and Filibuster While the Biosphere Burns,' *The Guardian*, 18 December 2009; personal interview, Dubai, November 2009.

19. Emma Murphy, 'ICT and the Gulf Arab States: A Force for Democracy?' In Ehteshami and Wright, *Middle East Oil Monarchies*, p. 183.

20. Personal interview, Kuwait, December 2008.

21. 'Facebook Girl Beaten and Shot Dead by Her Father For Talking Online,' *Daily Mail*, 31 March 2008.

22. 'Asia's Importance Growing in Global Economy,' IMF Survey Online, 12 May 2010, http://www.imf.org/external/pubs/ft/survey/so/2010/CAR051210A.htm.

23. Kristian Coates Ulrichsen, 'Gulf States' Perspectives on Global Governance,' Global Policy, 2(1) (2011).

24. Rathmell, Karasik and Gompert, New Persian Gulf Security System, p. 6.

25. Personal interview, Kuwait, October 2009.

26. Lynch, 'Globalization and Arab Security' (Op. Cit), p. 191.
27. Al-Rasheed, 'An Assessment of Saudi Political, Religious and Media Expansion' (Op. Cit), p. 2.
28. Ibid., p. 171.
29. Christopher Davidson, 'Persian Gulf-Pacific Asia Linkages in the 21st Century: A Marriage of Convenience?' LSE Kuwait Research Paper No. 7, January 2010, pp. 7–8.
30. Justin Dargin, 'Qatar's Natural Gas: the Foreign Policy Driver,' *Middle East Policy*, 14(3), 2007, p. 142.
31. J.E. Peterson, 'Qatar and the World: Branding for a Micro-State,' *Middle East Journal*, 60(4), 2006, p. 746.
32. 'Barclays Secures Funds from Qatar and Abu Dhabi,' The Times, October 31, 2008; 'Qatar Takes Stake in VW-Porsche Group,' *Gulf Times*, 15 August 2009.
33. Qamar Agha, 'Indo-Gulf Ties: Post-Cold War Era,' in I.P. Khosla (ed.), India and the Gulf (Association of Indian Diplomats: New Delhi, 2009, p. 152.
34. 'Prime Minister Dr. Manmohan Sing's Speech at the Inauguration of the Centre for West Asian Studies, Jamia Millia Islamia University, New Delhi, 29 January 2005,' in Khosla, India and the Gulf, pp. 207–11.
35. 'Qatar and India Agree to Expand Security Ties,' *Gulf News*, 10 November 2008.
36. Personal interview, London, May 2010.
37. Ranjit Gupta, 'China as a Factor in India's Relations with the GCC Countries,' in Khosla, India and the Gulf, p. 80.
38. David Malone and Rohan Mukherjee, 'India and China: Conflict and Cooperation,' *Survival*, 52(1), 2010, p. 137.
39. Yetiv and Lu, 'China, Global Energy and the Middle East,' p. 199.
40. 'China's Pearl in Pakistan's Waters,' *Asia Times*, 4 March 2005.
41. 'Chinese Warships Make First Visit to Port Zayed,' *The National*, 24 March 2010.
42. Andrew Kennedy, 'China's New Energy-Security Debate,' *Survival*, 52(3), 2010, p. 142.
43. Personal interview, Amman, May 2010.
44. 'Putin 1st Russian Leader to Visit Saudis,' *Washington Post*, 11 February 2007.
45. Michael Smith, 'Russia and the Persian Gulf: The Deepening of Moscow's *Middle East Policy*.' Conflict of Studies and Research Centre Paper 07/25. UK Defence Academy, 2007, p. 5.
46. 'Riyadh Mulls Big Russian Missile Buy,' www.upi.com, 22 March 2010.
47. 'Qatar, Russia Agree on Yamal Gas Joint Project,' *The Peninsula*, 20 April 2010.
48. Tarik Oguzlu, 'The Changing Dynamics of Turkey-Israel Relations: A Structural Account,' Mediterranean Politics, 15(2), 2010, pp. 281–83.

49. 'Turk Telekom Signs Fibre Accord with Three Nations,' *Hurriyet*, 16 June 2010.
50. 'Davutoglu Calls on Iran Sceptics to Accept Nuclear Deal,' *Hurriyet*, 18 May 2010.
51. Shibley Telhami, '2010 Arab Public Opinion Poll,' conducted by the University of Maryland in conjunction with Zogby International, 5 August 2010, slides 66–67.
52. Personal interview, Cambridge, July 2010.
53. Ibid.
54. 'Pirates Hijack Saudi Tanker off African Coast: US,' Agence France-Presse, 18 November 2008.
55. 'EU NavFor EU Operation Atalanta,' Maritime Security Centre, http://www.mschoa.org/ForceInfo.aspx#EUNavfor.
56. James Kraska and Brian Wilson, 'The Co-Operative Strategy and the Pirates of the Gulf of Aden,' RUSI Journal, 154(2), 2009, p. 76.
57. Ben Simpfendorfer, *The New Silk Road: How a Rising Arab World is Turning Away From the West and Rediscovering China* (Basingstoke: Palgrave Macmillan, 2009), pp. 30–32.
58. 'China's Growth Shifts the Geopolitics of Oil,' *New York Times*, 19 March 2010.
59. Anthony Cordesman, 'Security Cooperation in the Middle East.' Washington, D.C., Center for Strategic and International Studies, 2007, p. 3.
60. Paul Aarts, Roos Meertens and Joris van Duijne, 'Kingdom with Borders: The Political Economy of Saudi-European Relations,' in Al-Rasheed (ed.), *Kingdom without Borders*, p. 140.
61. Daniel Yergin, 'It's Still the One,' *Foreign Policy*, September/October 2009.
62. Halliday, *International Relations of the Middle East*, p. 271.
63. Jim Krane, 'Energy Conservation Options for GCC Governments,' Dubai School of Government Policy Brief No. 18, February 2010, p. 1.
64. Anthony Cordesman and Khalid Al-Rodhan, 'The Gulf Military Forces in an Era of Asymmetric Wars: Bahrain.'.Center for Strategic and International Studies: Washington, D.C., 2006, p. 20.
65. Fakhro, 'Uprising in Bahrain,' p. 184.
66. Personal interview, Bahrain, October 2009.
67. Statement by Michele Cervone D'Urso (Head of the EU Delegation to Yemen) to the Yemen Forum roundtable meeting at Chatham House, London, 18 February 2010.
68. BP Statistical Review of World Energy, June 2009, p. 6. www.bp.com/statisticalreview
69. Gause, 'Persistence of Monarchy' (Op. Cit), p. 186.
70. Kristian Coates Ulrichsen, 'Gulf Security: Changing Internal and External Dynamics.' LSE Kuwait Programme Working Paper No. 2, May 2009, p. 32.
71. Kaldor, Karl and Said, *Oil Wars*, p. 28.

72. Personal interview, Bahrain, December 2008.
73. Statement by Jalal Omar Yaqoub (Deputy Finance Minister of Yemen) to the Yemen Forum roundtable meeting at Chatham House, London, 18 February 2010.
74. Personal interview, Kuwait, December 2008.
75. Mohamed Raouf, 'Water Issues in the Gulf: Time for Action.' Middle East Institute Policy Brief No. 22, January 2009, p. 8.
76. Andy Spiess, 'Developing Adaptive Capacity for Responding to Environmental Change in the Arab Gulf States: Uncertainties to Linking Ecosystem Conservation, Sustainable Development and Society in Authoritarian Rentier Economies,' Global and Planetary Change, 64, 2008, p. 245.
77. Personal interview, Kuwait, May 2008.
78. 'US-allied Arab States Back Abbas in Hamas Row,' *Khaleej Times*, 4 February 2009; 'Arab League Chief Kicks Off Tour to Mend Inter-Arab Rifts,' *Khaleej Times*, 8 February 2009.
79. 'Doha Emergency Summit Deepens Arab Differences Over Gaza Issue,' www.chinaview.cn, 17 January 2009.
80. 'Why Oman Pulled Out of the Single Currency,' *Gulf News*, 21 January 2007.
81. 'GCC Monetary Union: Progress to Date and Outstanding Issues.' Riyadh: SAMBA Financial Group, May 2009, p. 5.
82. 'UAE/Saudi Economy: Not So Neighbourly,' Economist Intelligence Unit, 24 August 2009.
83. 'GCC to Adopt Single Visa System—Al Awadhi,' Kuwait News Agency, 1 June 2009.
84. Cordesman and Al-Rodhan, Gulf Military Forces: Bahrain, p. 12; 'Naval Battle Between UAE and Saudi Arabia Raises Fears for Gulf Security,' *The Daily Telegraph*, 26 March 2010.
85. 'Bahraini Sailor Injured in Qatari Shooting,' *Gulf News*, 9 May 2010.
86. Abdullah Baabood and Geoffrey Edwards, 'Reinforcing Ambivalence: The Interaction of Gulf States and the European Union,' European Foreign Affairs Review, 12, 2007, p. 537.
87. Gerd Nonneman, 'EU-GCC Relations: Dynamics, Patterns and Perspectives.' Dubai: Gulf Research Centre, 2006, p. 24.
88. Baabood and Edwards, 'Reinforcing Ambivalence,' p. 547.
89. Personal interview, Qatar, January 2010.
90. John Fox, Nada Mourtada-Sabbah and Mohammed Al-Mutawa, 'The Arab Gulf Region: Traditionalism Globalized or Globalization Traditionalized?' in Fox, Mourtada-Sabbah and Al-Mutawa, *Globalization and the Gulf*, p. 23.
91. Personal interview, Qatar, January 2010.
92. Roberto Aliboni, 'Europe's Role in the Gulf: a Transatlantic Perspective.' Paper presented at the EU-Gulf Relations: Enhancing Political, Economic and Security Cooperation seminar, Rome, November 2005, p. 7.

4. DEMOGRAPHIC AND STRUCTURAL IMBALANCES IN GULF ECONOMIES

1. Personal interviews, Kuwait, March 2010.
2. Ibrahim Saif, 'The Oil Boom in the GCC Countries, 2002–2008: Old Challenges, Changing Dynamics.' Carnegie Middle East Paper No. 15, March 2009, p. 1.
3. Alasdair Drysdale, 'Population Dynamics and Birth Spacing in Oman,' *International Journal of Middle East Studies*, 42(1), 2010, p. 124.
4. Renee Richer, 'Conservation in Qatar: Impacts of Increasing Industrialization.' Center of International and Regional Studies: Georgetown School of Foreign Service in Qatar. Occasional Paper No. 2, 2006, p. 3; 'Bahrain Shia MPs Walk Out Over Population Row,' Reuters, 14 May 2008.
5. http://www.prb.org/Datafinder/Geography/MultiCompare.aspx?variables =115&regions=120%2c126%2c128%2c129%2c130%2c133%2c135% 2c
6. Anthony Cordesman, 'Security Challenges and Threats in the Gulf: A Net Assessment.' Washington, D.C.: Center for Strategic and International Studies, March 2008, p. 100.
7. http://www.prb.org/Datafinder/Geography/MultiCompare.aspx?variables =110&regions=120%2c126%2c128%2c129%2c130%2c133%2c184% 2c72%2c135%2c
8. Drysdale, Alasdair, 'Population Dynamics and Birth Spacing in Oman,' *International Journal of Middle East Studies*, 42(1), 2010. p. 124.
9. 'Farzaneh Roudi-Fahimi & Mary Mederios Kent, 'Challenges and Opportunities—The Population of the Middle East and North Africa,' *Population Bulletin* 62, 2007, p. 1.
10. Onn Winckler, 'Labor and Liberalization: The Decline of the GCC Rentier System,' in Joshua Teitelbaum (ed.), *Political Liberalization in the Persian Gulf* (London: Hurst and Co., 2009), p. 60.
11. Longva, 'Neither Autocracy nor Democracy but Ethnocracy' (Op. Cit), p. 134.
12. Dresch, 'Societies, Identities and Global Issues' (Op. Cit), p. 16.
13. Jones, 'Rebellion on the Saudi Periphery,' p. 219.
14. Ragut Assaad, Ghada Barsoum, Emily Cupito and Daniel Egel, 'Youth Exclusion in Yemen: Tackling the Twin Deficits of Human Development and Natural Resources.' Wolfensohn Center for Development: Dubai School of Government, Working Paper 9, November 2009, p. 10.
15. Personal interviews and observation, Bahrain, December 2008.
16. 'Sectarian Tension Takes Volatile Form in Bahrain,' *New York Times*, 27 March 2009.
17. Okruhlik, 'Rentier Wealth,' pp. 296–97; Fred Wehrey, 'Bahrain: Elections and Managing Sectarianism,' *Arab Reform Bulletin*, 4(10), December 2006.

18. Mohammed Zaher, 'GCC Common Market: Crucial Steps to Capture Gains from Integration,' National Bank of Kuwait GCC Research Note, 15 October 2008, p. 4.
19. Winckler, 'Labor and Liberalization' (Op. Cit), p. 69.
20. Sharon Shochat, 'The Gulf Cooperation Council Economies: Diversification and Reform,' LSE Kuwait Research Programme introductory paper, February 2008, p. 34, table 4.3.
21. Longva, 'Neither Autocracy nor Democracy but Ethnocracy,' p. 120.
22. Cited in Richer, 'Conservation in Qatar' (Op. Cit), p. 3.
23. See, for example, *Building Towers, Cheating Workers: Exploitation of Migrant Construction Workers in the United Arab Emirates* (11 November 2006) and *The Island of Happiness: Exploitation of Migrant Workers on Saadiyat Island, Abu Dhabi* (19 May 2009), both issued by Human Rights Watch.
24. 'Dealing with Human Rights Abuse in Kuwait,' *Kuwait Times*, 23 June 2009.
25. 'Former President Estrada Criticizes 'Appalling' Labor Conditions,' *Al Watan Daily*, 14 June 2009.
26. Roger Hardy, 'Migrants Demand Labour Rights in Gulf,' *BBC News*, 27 February 2008.
27. Telephone interview, Qatar, November 2008, personal interview, Kuwait, December 2008.
28. 'Gulf States Told to Give Arabs Job Preference,' *Gulf Times*, 16 November 2008.
29. 'Bahrain Labour Market Reforms Bridge Gap Between Nationals, Expats,' Kuwait News Agency, 30 August 2009.
30. Personal interview, Kuwait, May 2008.
31. Personal interviews, Dubai, Kuwait, Qatar and Bahrain, December 2008.
32. 'Emirati Job Demands Too High, Say Experts,' *The National*, 19 April 2010.
33. Kristian Coates Ulrichsen, 'Internal and External Security in the Arab Gulf States,' *Middle East Policy*, 16(2), 2009, p. 49.
34. Personal interview, Qatar, January 2010.
35. 'Absent Workers Have Not Reported in Years, Still Receive Full Benefits,' *Al-Watan* Daily, 14 November 2009.
36. 'Federal Employees Get 70% Rise in Basic Pay,' *The National*, 21 December 2009.
37. 'GCC Unemployment Rates Skyrocketing,' *Bahrain Tribune*, 24 November 2007.
38. Christopher Boucek, 'Yemen: Avoiding a Downward Spiral,' Carnegie Middle East Program Paper 102, September 2009, p. 11.
39. Neil Quilliam, 'Political Reform in Bahrain: The Turning Tide,' in Ehteshami and Wright, *Middle East Oil Monarchies*, p. 94.
40. Personal interview, Bahrain, October 2009.

41. 'Sheikh Salman bin Hamad al-Khalifa, Crown Prince of Bahrain, on Economic Reform,' Middle East Business Intelligence, 22 February 2008.
42. Steven Wright, 'Fixing the Kingdom: Political Evolution and Socio-Economic Challenges in Bahrain,' Center of International and Regional Studies: Georgetown School of Foreign Service in Qatar, Occasional Paper No. 3, 2008, p. 3.
43. J.E. Peterson, 'Bahrain: Reform—Promise and Reality,' in Teitelbaum (ed.), *Political Liberalization in the Persian Gulf*, p. 170.
44. Personal interview, Kuwait, March 2010.
45. Zvika Krieger, 'Reforms in Higher Education Raise Questions,' *Arab Reform Bulletin*, December 2007.
46. Ana Echague and Edward Burke, 'Strong Foundations? The Imperatives for Reform in Saudi Arabia.' Madrid: FRIDE Working Paper 84, 2009, p. 8.
47. 'Mohammed Upbeat on Economy,' *Khaleej Times*, 5 September 2009; 'Dubai's Downfall Exposes The Political Ties That Bind As a Tangled Web,' *Daily Telegraph*, 2 December 2009.
48. 'The Murky Gulf,' *Financial Times*, 16 February 2010.
49. Christopher Davidson, 'Dubai and Abu Dhabi: Implosion and Opportunity,' Open Democracy, 4 December 2009.
50. John Irish, 'Dubai's Opaque Bond Plan Leaves Investors Wary,' Reuters, 28 July 2009.
51. Vincent Romani, 'The Politics of Higher Education in the Middle East: Problems and Prospects.' Brandeis University Crown Center for Middle East Studies: Middle East Brief No. 36, May 2009, p. 1.
52. 'About NYU Abu Dhabi—The Vision,' http://nyuad.nyu.edu/about/index.html.
53. Gari Donn and Yahya Al-Manthri, *Globalisation and Higher Education in the Arab Gulf States* (Oxford: Symposium Books, 2010), pp. 160–61.
54. Kristian Coates Ulrichsen, 'Knowledge-based Economies in the GCC' presentation to the Political Economy of the Gulf working group, Georgetown School of Foreign Service in Qatar, 23 January 2010.
55. 'Saudi University to Break Several Barriers,' Agence France-Presse, 22 September 2009.
56. 'KAUST Will Serve as Bridge Between Cultures: Abdullah,' *Arab News*, 16 September 2009.
57. The university has an endowment of $10 billion, reportedly making it the sixth richest university in the world.
58. Donn and Al-Manthri, *Globalisation and Higher Education*, p. 15.
59. F. Gregory Gause, 'Saudi Arabia: The Second Sex and the Third Rail,' *Foreign Policy*, 19 April 2010.
60. Gawdat Bahgat, 'Education in the Gulf Monarchies: Retrospect and Prospect,' *International Review of Education*, 45(2), 1999 p. 127.
61. Mamoun Fandy, 'Enriched Islam: The Muslim Crisis of Education,' *Survival*, 49(3), 2007, p. 79.

62. David A. King, 'The Scientific Impact of Nations: What Different Countries Get For Their Research Spending,' *Nature*, 430, 15 July 2004, p. 314.
63. 'Reforms Will Help Business,' *Middle East Economic Digest*, 18 July 2008.
64. 'Qatar Implementing National Vision,' *Middle East Economic Digest*, 18 June 2009.
65. Personal interviews, Qatar, January 2010 and Kuwait, March 2010.
66. Davidson, *Abu Dhabi*, p. 150.
67. 'Our Vision: Economic Vision for Bahrain 2030,' Bahrain Economic Development Board, 2008, article 3.3.
68. Laura Guazzone, 'Islamism and Islamists in the Contemporary Arab World,' in Laura Guazzone (ed.), *The Islamist Dilemma: The Political Role of Islamist Movements in the Contemporary Arab World* (Reading: Ithaca Press, 1995), p. 3.
69. Michelle Dunne, 'Interview with Ali al-Rashed, National Assembly Member and Candidate,' *Arab Reform Bulletin*, May 2008; personal interviews, Kuwait, October 2009.
70. Krieger, 'Reforms in Higher Education.'
71. MENA Development Report, 'The Road Not Traveled: Education Reform in the Middle East and North Africa.' Washington, D.C.: The International Bank for Reconstruction and Development/The World Bank, 2007, p. 5.
72. Ibid. p. 8
73. 'Tunis Declaration on "Building Knowledge Economies",' Islamic Educational, Scientific and Cultural Organization, 3 December 2009.
74. Personal interview, Kuwait, March 2010.
75. Gabriella Gonzalez, Lynn Karoly, Louay Constant, Hanine Salem and Charles Goodman, 'Facing Human Capital Challenges of the 21st Century: Education and Labour Market Initiatives in Lebanon, Oman, Qatar, and the United Arab Emirates.' RAND-Qatar Policy Institute, 2008, p. xvii.
76. Personal interviews, Kuwait, March 2010.
77. Personal interviews, London and Kuwait, March 2010.
78. Personal interviews, Kuwait, March 2010.
79. 'George Mason Uni to Close RAK Branch,' *The National*, 26 February 2009; 'University Branches in Dubai Are Struggling,' *New York Times*, 27 December 2009.
80. Talat Diab and Ahmad Bishara, 'Higher Planning Council State of Kuwait: Seminar on the Introduction of High Technology in Kuwait.' Kuwait, 1999, p. 5.
81. Joseph Kostiner (ed.), *Middle East Monarchies: The Challenge of Modernity* (London: Lynne Rienner, 2000), p. 9.
82. Personal interviews, Qatar, January 2010.
83. Koch, 'Gulf States Plan,' pp. 23–24.
84. Valeri, *Oman*, p. 202.

85. Anthony Cordesman and Khalid Al-Rodhan, 'The Gulf Military Forces in an Age of Asymmetric Warfare—Oman.' Center for International and Strategic Studies: Washington, D.C., 2006, p. 25.
86. Valeri, *Oman*, p. 206.
87. 'Qatar National Vision 2030,' http://www1.gsdp. gov.qa/portal/page/portal/GSDP_Vision_Root/GSDP_EN/What%20We%20Do/QNV_2030
88. 'Ras Laffan Industrial City Investment Reaches $70bn,' *The Peninsula*, 23 September 2009.
89. Ibid.
90. 'Nakilat Building a World-Class Shipping Fleet,' *Middle East Economic Digest*, 21 January 2010.
91. Dargin, 'Qatar's Natural Gas,' p. 140.
92. Personal interview, Qatar, December 2008; Wright, 'Fixing the Kingdom,' pp. 12–13.
93. http://www.kingabdullahcity.com/en/Home/index.html
94. Rodney Wilson, 'Economic Governance and Reform in Saudi Arabia,' in Ehteshami and Wright, *Middle East Oil Monarchies*, p. 137 & p. 144.
95. Saif, 'The Oil Boom in the GCC,' p. 14.
96. Steffen Hertog, *Princes, Brokers, and Bureaucrats: Oil and the State in Saudi Arabia* (Ithaca: Cornell University Press, 2010), pp. 28–29.
97. 'Politics, Succession and Risk in Saudi Arabia,' *Gulf States Newsletter*, special report, 2010, p. 4.
98. 'King Abdullah University Allows Genders to Mix,' *Al-Arabiya.net*, 23 September 2009.
99. 'Saudi SR172.5bn Investment Projects Drive ME Petrochem Output Capacity,' *Saudi Gazette*, 25 August 2009.
100. 'Saudi Arabia to Generate 10.8m Job Opportunities by 2014,' *Saudi Gazette*, 10 August 2009.
101. 'The Gulf as a Global Financial Centre: Growing Opportunities and International Influence.' London: Chatham House Report, 2008, p. 48.
102. Andrew England, 'Family Groups in Gulf Must Embrace Corporate Governance,' *The Peninsula*, 23 June 2009.
103. 'Scrutiny Turns to Family Firms,' *Emirates Business 24/7*, 17 July 2009.
104. Martin Hvidt, 'The Dubai Model: An Outline of Key Development-Process Elements in Dubai,' *International Journal of Middle East Studies*, 41(3), 2009, pp. 401–2.
105. 'Oil Share Dips in Dubai GDP,' *AMEinfo.com*, 9 June 2007.
106. Davidson, *Dubai* and *Abu Dhabi*.
107. 'Dubai's Downfall Expose the Political Ties That Bind as a Tangled Web,' *Daily Telegraph*, 2 December 2009.
108. Davidson, *Dubai* and *Abu Dhabi*.
109. 'Dubai Opens a Tower to Beat All,' *New York Times*, 4 January 2010.
110. Personal interview, Kuwait, October 2009.
111. Diab and Bishara, Higher Planning Council, pp. 3–5.

112. Personal interviews, Kuwait, March 2010.

113. Michael Herb, 'Kuwait: The Obstacle of Parliamentary Politics,' in Teitelbaum, Political Liberalization, p. 154.

114. Kristian Coates Ulrichsen, 'Kuwaiti Development: A Valuable Example,' *The Gulf Business News and Analysis*, 24–30 October 2009, p. 29.

115. 'Kuwait Loses KD 9 Billion in Downturn,' *Kuwait Times*, 11 February 2009.

116. Personal interviews, Kuwait, March 2010.

117. Mahfouz Tadros, 'Foreign Direct Investment in GCC Countries: The Case of Kuwait,' unpublished article, p. 1.

118. Personal interview, Kuwait, March 2010.

119. Peterson 2007, 30.

120. Nonneman, 'Political Reform' (Op. Cit), p. 19.

121. Steffen Hertog, 'Gulf Countries: The Current Crisis and Lessons of the 1980s,' *Arab Reform Bulletin*, July 2009; 'The Report: Kuwait 2010.' Oxford: Oxford Business Group, pp. 72 and 74.

122. Personal interview, London, March 2010.

5. THE POLITICAL ECONOMY OF RESOURCE INSECURITY

1. See, for example, Terry Lynn Karl, *The Paradox of Plenty: Oil Booms and Petro-States* (Berkeley: University of California Press, 1997); Philippe Le Billon (ed.), *Geopolitics of Resource Wars: Resource Dependence, Governance and Violence* (London: Routledge, 2005); Mary Kaldor, Terry Lynn Karl and Yahia Said, *Oil Wars* (London: Pluto Press, 2007).

2. Ginny Hill, 'Yemen: Fear of Failure.' Chatham House Briefing Paper, January 2010, p. 9.

3. Marie Lillo, 'Ensuring Food Security: For the GCC, the Solution Lies in Africa.' Dubai: Gulf Research Centre, 1 July 2008.

4. Halvor Mehlum, Kalle Moene and Ragnar Torvik, 'Social Policies and the Phasing In of Oil in the Norwegian Economy,' Gulf Research Unit, University of Oslo, 2 March 2010.

5. 'GCC Inflation to Rise by 3%: Expert,' *Arab News*, 13 May 2008; 'Food Crisis in Yemen,' Reuters, 5 May 2010.

6. 'New Signs Show Inflation in Gulf Set to Rise Further,' Reuters, 20 June 2008.

7. 'UAE Detains 3000 Indian Workers Over Camp Riot,' *Arab News*, 9 July 2008; 'Kuwait Police Break Up Demo by Asian Workers,' Agence France-Presse, 29 July 2008.

8. Eckart Woertz, Samir Pradhan, Nermina Biberovic and Christian Koch, 'Food Inflation in the GCC Countries.' Dubai: Gulf Research Centre Report, May 2008, p. 16.

9. Eckart Woertz, 'The Gulf Economies in 2008,' in Sager, *Gulf Yearbook 2008–2009*, p. 238.

10. Raouf, 'Water Issues in the Gulf,' p. 22.
11. Spiess, 'Developing Adaptive Capacity,' p. 245.
12. 'Dairy Kingdom,' Center for Strategic and International Studies Middle East Program newsletter, April 2010, p. 1.
13. Andrew England and Javier Blas, 'Water Concerns Prompt Saudis to Cease Grain Production,' *Financial Times*, 27 February 2008.
14. Boucek, 'Yemen: Avoiding a Downward Spiral,' p. 6.
15. 'IDB and UNSGAB Team Up to Support Water Sector in Arab Countries.' Press release, 23 November 2008, available at www.isdb.org.
16. Raouf, 'Water Issues in the Gulf,' p. 3.
17. Ilan Berman & Paul Michael Wihbey, 'The New Water Politics of the Middle East,' *Strategic Review*, 1999, http://www.iasps.org/strategic/water.htm.
18. Raouf, 'Water Issues in the Gulf,' p. 3.
19. 'In Yemen, a Race for Profit is Hastening a Water Crisis,' *Los Angeles Times*, 3 August 2008.
20. Boucek, 'Yemen: Avoiding a Downward Spiral,' pp. 6–7.
21. Eckart Woertz, Samir Pradhan, Nermina Biberovic and Chan Jingzhong, 'Potential for GCC Agro-Investments in Africa and Asia.' Dubai: Gulf Research Centre Report, September 2008, pp. 6–7.
22. 'Saudis Setting Up Fund to Buy Agricultural Land Abroad,' *Gulf Times*, 26 August 2008.
23. 'Saudi Agri Firms Eye Investment Abroad,' Reuters, 20 March 2009.
24. 'Saudis in Talks to Lease Pakistani Farmland,' Reuters, 2 September 2009.
25. 'Qatar, Sudan in Farming Tie-up,' *Gulf Times*, 22 July 2008.
26. 'Qatar, Thailand Keen on Forging New Agreements,' *Gulf Times*, 6 July 2009.
27. 'Pakistan Offers Farmland to Saudi Arabia, UAE,' *Saudi Gazette*, 4 September 2008.
28. Personal interview, Dubai, October 2009.
29. 'GCC Food Imports Cost $10bn Last Year: Study,' *The Peninsula*, 21 July 2008.
30. 'Gulf States and ASEAN Eye New Trade Block Based on Food, Oil,' *The Peninsula*, 1 July 2009.
31. Personal interview, Dubai, October 2009.
32. 'Seized! The 2008 Land Grab for Food and Financial Security.' *Grain Briefing*, October 2008, p. 3.
33. Personal interview, Dubai, October 2009.
34. Ibid.
35. 'Qatar Investigating Food Supplies,' www.arabianbusiness.com, 3 January 2008; 'Inflation in Kuwait Soars to 9.5%,' *The Peninsula*, 25 April 2008.
36. Personal interview, Dubai, December 2008.
37. Paul Rogers, 'Abqaiq's Warning,' *Open Democracy*, 2 March 2006.
38. Raouf, 'Water Issues in the Gulf,' p. 2.
39. Personal interviews, Kuwait and Bahrain, December 2008.

40. 'Bahrain's Energy Consumption Doubles in Two Years,' *Bahrain Tribune*, 4 June 2008.

41. Steffen Hertog and Giacomo Luciani, 'Energy and Sustainability Policies in the GCC.' LSE Kuwait Research Programme Working Paper No. 6, November 2009, pp. 5–6.

42. 'GCC States to Sign Power Swap Deal,' *Emirates Business 24/7*, 4 July 2009.

43. 'GCC States Sign Power Grid Pact,' *Gulf Times*, 8 July 2009.

44. Justin Dargin, 'The Ties That Bind: The Dolphin Project and Intra-GCC Relations.' The Dubai Initiative Policy Brief, Belfer Center for Science and *International Affairs*: Harvard University, 2009, p. 5.

45. Krane, 'Energy Conservation Options,' p. 1.

46. Ibid., pp. 2–3.

47. 'Kuwait Plans to Quadruple Gas Output by 2030,' Reuters, 28 April 2010.

48. 'Abu Dhabi Home For World Energy Body,' *The Peninsula*, 30 June 2009.

49. Personal interview, Cambridge, September 2009.

50. 'Abu Dhabi Sets 7% Renewable Energy Target,' *The National*, 19 January 2009.

51. Ian Jackson, 'Nuclear Energy and Proliferation Risks: Myths and Realities in the Persian Gulf,' *International Affairs*, 85(6), 2009, p. 1159.

52. 'UAE Keen on Peaceful Use of Nuclear Energy,' *Khaleej Times*, 28 September 2009.

53. 'US-UAE Nuclear Deal to Take Effect Soon—State Dept,' Reuters, 22 October 2009.

54. 'UAE-US Nuclear Pact Comes to Fruition,' *Khaleej Times*, 18 December 2009.

55. 'UAE Deal Boosts KEPCO's Expansion Plan,' *Korea Herald*, 29 March 2010; 'Nuclear Power Plant Security Unveiled,' *The National*, 30 May 2010.

56. 'Nuclear Programmes in the Middle East: In the Shadow of Iran.' London: International Institute of Strategic Studies Dossier, May 2008, p. 35.

57. 'Kuwait Calls For Clearing Mideast of WMD,' Kuwait News Agency, 16 September 2009; 'Oman's Peaceful Nuclear Energy Plans Seek Economic Prosperity,' *Oman Daily Observer*, 16 September 2009.

58. 'Saudi Looks to Nuclear Future,' *The National*, 18 April 2010.

59. Kaye and Wehrey, 'Nuclear Iran,' pp. 111–12.

60. Brendan Taylor, 'Sanctions as Grand Strategy.' Adelphi Paper No. 411. London: International Institute of Strategic Studies, 2010, pp. 59–60.

61. Krane, 'Energy Conservation Options,' p. 2.

62. Raouf, 'Water Issues in the Gulf,' p. 8.

63. Personal interviews, Kuwait, March 2010.

64. Personal interview, Bahrain, December 2008.

65. Personal interviews, Dubai, October 2009 and Kuwait, December 2008 and March 2010.

66. Saif, 'Oil Boom in GCC,' p. 1.
67. Thomas Homer-Dixon, 'Environmental Scarcities and Violent Conflict: Evidence from Cases,' in Michael Brown, Owen Cote, Sean Lynn-Jones and Steven Miller (eds), New Global Dangers: Changing Dimensions of International Security (Cambridge, Mass: MIT Press, 2004), pp. 265–66.
68. Ibid. p. 269.
69. Jones, 'Rebellion on the Saudi Periphery,' p. 213.
70. Louer, *Transnational Shia Politics*, pp. 151–52.
71. Jones, 'Rebellion on the Saudi Periphery,' p. 219.
72. John Peterson, 'Bahrain: The 1994–1999 Uprising.' Arabian Peninsula Background Note, No. APBN-002. Published on www.JEPeterson.net, January 2004, p. 1.
73. Fakhro, 'Uprising in Bahrain,' p. 177.
74. Ibid., p. 187.
75. Personal interview, Bahrain, October 2009.
76. Quilliam, 'Political Reform in Bahrain,' p. 84.
77. Author's personal experience while working at the Gulf Centre for Strategic Studies in London at the time.
78. Edward Burke, 'Bahrain: Reaching a Threshold.' Madrid: FRIDE Working Paper No. 22, June 2008, p. 4.
79. Ibid.
80. Abd al-Nabi al-Ekry, 'Al-Wefaq and the Challenges of Participation,' *Arab Reform Bulletin*, May 2007.
81. 'Bahrain Shia MPs Walk Out Over Population Row,' Reuters, 14 May 2008.
82. Wright, 'Fixing the Kingdom,' p. 9.
83. Personal interview, Bahrain, December 2008.
84. Jane Kinninmont, 'Assessing al-Wefaq's Parliamentary Experiment,' *Arab Reform Bulletin*, October 2007.
85. 'Boycott of 2010 Poll Likely, Says Bahraini Society,' *Bahrain Tribune*, 11 September 2008.
86. Stephen Day, 'Updating Yemeni National Unity: Could Lingering Regional Divisions Bring Down the Regime?,' *Middle East Journal*, 62(3), 2008, pp. 422–24.
87. Boucek, 'Yemen: Avoiding a Downward Spiral,' p. 4.
88. Day, Stephen, 'Updating Yemeni National Unity: Could Lingering Regional Divisions Bring Down the Regime?,' *Middle East Journal*, 62(3), 2008.

6. CLIMATE SECURITY AND ENVIRONMENTAL CHALLENGES

1. Paul Smith, 'Climate Change, Mass Migration and the Military Response,' Orbis, 51(4), 2007, p. 624.
2. Personal interview, Dubai, November 2009.
3. Thomas Homer-Dixon, 'Environmental Scarcities and Violent Conflict: Evidence from Cases,' in Michael Brown, Owen Cote, Sean Lynn-Jones and

Steven Miller (eds), *New Global Dangers: Changing Dimensions of International Security* (Cambridge, Mass: MIT Press, 2004), p. 629.

4. Paul Aarts and Dennis Janssen, 'Shades of Opinion: The Oil Exporting Countries and International Climate Politics,' in Gerd Nonneman (ed.), *Analyzing Middle East Foreign Policies and the Relationship with Europe* (London: Routledge, 2005, p. 223.

5. Mari Luomi, 'Oil or Climate Politics?: Avoiding a Destabilizing Resource Split in the Arab Middle East.' Finnish Institute of *International Affairs*, Briefing Paper No. 58, 2010, p. 2.

6. Mohamed Raouf, 'Climate Change Threats, Opportunities, and the GCC Countries.' Middle East Institute Policy Brief No. 12, 2008, p. 5.

7. Mari Luomi, 'Abu Dhabi's Alternative-Energy Initiatives: Seizing Climate-Change Opportunities,' *Middle East Policy*, 16(4), 2009, p. 104.

8. Michael Clarke, 'Rethinking Security and Power,' in David Held and David Mepham (eds), *Progressive Foreign Policy: New Directions for the UK* (Cambridge: Polity Press, 2007), p. 18.

9. Jeffrey Mazo, 'Climate Conflict: How Global Warming Threatens Security and What to Do About It.' London: International Institute for Strategic Studies/Routledge, 2010, p. 15.

10. Spiess, 'Developing Adaptive Capacity,' p. 244.

11. David Held and Anthony McGrew, Introduction, in David Held and Anthony McGrew (eds), *Governing Globalization: Power, Autonomy and Global Governance* (Cambridge: Polity Press, 2000), p. 5.

12. Michael Dillon, 'Security in the 21st Century: Circulation, Complexity and Contingency,' in Chatham House Briefing Paper 05/02, 'The Globalisation of Security,' October 2005 p. 3.

13. Kaldor, *Human Security*, p. 12.

14. Richard Russell, 'The Persian Gulf's Collective-Security Mirage,' *Middle East Policy*, 12(4), 2005, p. 77.

15. Robyn Eckersley, 'Environmental Security, Climate Change and Globalizing Terrorism,' in Damian Grenfell and Paul James (eds), *Rethinking Insecurity, War and Violence* (London: Routledge, 2009) p. 87.

16. Ibid. p. 88.

17. 'A More Secure World: Our Shared Responsibility. Report of the High-Level Panel on Threats, Challenges and Change,' December 2004, http://www.un.org/secureworld

18. Mazo, 'Climate Conflict,' p. 33.

19. Eckersley, 'Environmental Security,' p. 88.

20. Nick Mabey, 'Delivering Climate Security: International Security Responses to a Climate Changed World.' London: Royal United Services Institute Whitehall Paper Series 69, 2008, pp. 5–7.

21. Mazo, 'Climate Conflict,' p. 84.

22. Smith, 'Climate Change,' p. 632.

23. Oli Brown and Alec Crawford, 'Rising Temperatures, Rising Tensions: Climate Change and the Risk of Violent Conflict in the Middle East.' International Institute for Sustainable Development, 2009, pp. 2–3.

24. cf. Spiess, Developing Adaptive Capacity and Joanna Depledge, 'Striving for No: Saudi Arabia in the Climate Change Regime. Global Environmental Politics, 8(4), 2008.

25. Raouf, 'Climate Change Threats,' pp. 12–13.

26. 'Terrorism, Nuke Arms Spread, Climate Change Key Challenges in Gulf Region,' Kuwait News Agency, 14 December 2008.

27. M.J. Williams, 'The Coming Revolution in Foreign Affairs: Rethinking American National Security,' *International Affairs*, 84(6), 2008, p. 1115.

28. Mabey, 'Delivering Climate Security,' p. 3.

29. Benito Muller, 'Copenhagen 2009: Failure or Final Wake-Up Call For Our Leaders?' (Oxford: Oxford Institute for Energy Studies, EV 49, February 2010), pp. 23–25.

30. David Held, 'Multilateralism and Global Governance: Accountability and Effectiveness,' in Held and Mepham, *Progressive Foreign Policy*, p. 199.

31. Raouf, 'Climate Change Threats,' p. 5.

32. Luomi, 'Abu Dhabi's Alternative-Energy Initiatives,' p. 115.

33. Spiess, 'Developing Adaptive Capacity,' p. 244.

34. Raouf, 'Climate Change Threats,' p. 15.

35. Personal interview, Dubai, November 2009.

36. Depledge, Striving for No, p. 20.

37. 'Climate Action Plan to Harm Gulf Economies: Saudi Official,' *Saudi Gazette*, 20 March 2009.

38. 'Saudis say trust in climate science "shaken",' *The National*, 8 December 2009.

39. Mari Luomi, 'Bargaining in the Saudi Bazaar: Common Ground For a Post-2012 Climate Agreement?,' Finnish Institute of International Affairs Briefing Paper No. 48, December 2009, p. 2.

40. 'Abu Dhabi Home For World Energy Body,' *The Peninsula*, 30 June 2009.

41. Telephone interview, Dubai, September 2009.

42. http://www.kaust.edu.sa/

43. Raouf, 'Climate Change Threats,' p. 7.

44. Luomi, 'Saudi Bazaar,' pp. 4–5.

45. 'Climate Change Middle East.' Met Office Hadley Centre, March 2009, pp. 2–4.

46. Renee Richer, 'Conservation in Qatar: Impacts of Increasing Industrialization.' Center for Regional and International Studies, Georgetown School of Foreign Service in Qatar: Occasional Paper No. 1, 2008, p. 7.

47. 'In Yemen, a Race for Profit is Hastening a Water Crisis,' *Los Angeles Times*, 3 August 2008.

48. Frederic Launay, 'Environmental Situational Awareness for the GCC Countries.' Dubai: Gulf Research Centre, 2006, p. 43.

49. Spiess, 'Developing Adaptive Capacity,' p. 246.

50. Ibid.

51. See chapter seven.

52. 'Climate Change Alert for Bahrain,' *Gulf Daily News*, 17 February 2009.

53. 'Working Group I Fourth Assessment Report "The Physical Science Basis." Intergovernmental Panel on Climate Change, 2007, chapter five, pp. 408–09.

54. 'Working Group II Fourth Assessment Report "Impacts, Adaptation and Vulnerability." Intergovernmental Panel on Climate Change, 2007, chapter six, p. 317.

55. Personal interview, Dubai, November 2009.

56. Personal interview, Bahrain, December 2008.

57. Personal interview, Dubai, November 2009.

58. Personal interview, Cambridge, September 2009.

59. David Pollock, 'Kuwait: Keystone of U.S. Gulf Policy.' Washington, D.C.: Washington Institute for Near East Policy, Policy Focus 76, 2007, p. 31.

60. Personal interviews, Kuwait, December 2008.

61. Raouf, 'Water Issues in the Gulf,' p. 2.

62. Personal interviews, Kuwait, December 2008 and Dubai, November 2009.

63. Mohammed Raouf, 'Green Gulf Report.' Dubai: Gulf Research Centre, 2009, p. 6.

64. Patrick Dowling, 'The Meteorological Effects of the Kuwait Oil Fires.' College of William and Mary, PhD Dissertation, 1996; personal interviews, Kuwait, March 2010.

65. 'The Economic and Environmental Impact of the Gulf War on Kuwait and the Persian Gulf.' Washington, D.C., American University, January 2000. http://www1.american.edu/TED/kuwait.htm

66. 'Peace in Middle East is Joint Responsibility of World Community: Oman,' *Khaleej Times*, 30 September 2008.

67. 'The Report: Abu Dhabi 2007.' Oxford: Oxford Business Group;' online abstract.

68. 'Living Planet Report 2008.' World Wildlife Federation, p. 34. http://assets.panda.org/downloads/living_planet_report_2008.pdf

69. Personal interview, Dubai, November 2009.

70. Spiess, 'Developing Adaptive Capacity,' p. 249.

71. Kristian Coates Ulrichsen, 'Gulf Security: Changing Internal and External Dynamics.' London: LSE Kuwait Research Programme Working Paper No. 3, May 2009, p. 29.

72. Masood Ahmed, 'GCC: Crisis Highlights Policy Challenges,' Carnegie Middle East Centre: International Economic Bulletin, March 2010.

73. 'Government Revenues Decline in Oman,' Oman Daily Observer, 15 August 2009; Ginny Hill, 'What is Happening in Yemen?,' *Survival*, 52(2), 2010, p. 108.

74. Personal interview, Kuwait, March 2010.

75. Luomi, 'Abu Dhabi's Alternative-Energy Initiatives,' p. 115.

76. Aarts and Janssen, 'Shades of Opinion,' p. 226.

7. YEMEN'S CONTESTED TRANSITION

1. CIA World Factbook: Yemen, updated 21 April 2010. https://www.cia.gov/library/publications/the-world-factbook/geos/ym.html
2. Day, Updating Yemeni National Unity, p. 431.
3. 'Yemen LNG Launches Second Production Train,' *Yemen Observer*, 8 April 2010.
4. Boucek, 'Yemen: Avoiding a Downward Spiral,' p. 1.
5. Gavin Hales, 'Fault Lines: Tracking Armed Violence in Yemen.' Yemen Armed Violence Assessment Issue Brief No. 1, 2010, p. 1.
6. Peter Salisbury, 'Yemen: The Region's Failing State,' *Middle East Economic Digest*, 23 July 2009.
7. Gregory Johnsen, 'Yemen: Empty Economic Reforms Slow Bid to Join the GCC,' *Arab Reform Bulletin*, February 2007.
8. 'Subsidies Biggest Danger to the Yemeni Economy,' *Kuwait Times*, 27 May 2010.
9. 'Gulf States Key to Resolving Yemen's Ills,' Agence France-Presse, 29 January 2010.
10. Stephen Day, The Political Challenge of Yemen's Southern Movement. Carnegie Endowment for International Peace: Middle East Program paper 108, March 2010, p. 4.
11. Hill, 'Yemen: Fear of Failure,' p. 3.
12. Intissar Fakir, 'Yemen: Economic and Regional Challenges,' *Arab Reform Bulletin*, July 2008.
13. Jalal Omar Yaqoub, 'Reform Priorities for Yemen and the 10-Point Agenda,' Yemen Forum roundtable meeting, Chatham House, London, 18 February 2010.
14. Hill, 'What is Happening in Yemen,' p. 106.
15. 'Yemeni MPs Approve Election Delay,' *Arab News*, 27 February 2010.
16. 'Yemen Says Opposition Allied with Armed Foes of State,' Reuters, 25 April 2010.
17. 'Yemeni President's Unity Pitch Rejected,' *The National*, 23 May 2010.
18. Sarah Phillips, 'Evaluating Political Reform in Yemen,' Carnegie Papers: Democracy and Rule of Law Program, No. 80, February 2007, p. 4.
19. Day, 'Yemen's Southern Movement,' p. 2.
20. Ibid. p. 7.
21. Sharp, 'Stability Tipping Point.'
22. Day, 'Yemen's Southern Movement,' p. 9.
23. 'Warning of Humanitarian Crisis in Yemen,' *The National*, 23 September 2009.
24. 'Qatar Brokers Yemen Peace Deal,' Al-Jazeera.net, 1 February 2008.
25. 'Yemen Vows to Crush Shia Rebellion,' *The Peninsula*, 20 August 2009.
26. Hill, 'What is Happening in Yemen?,' p. 109.
27. See chapter two. Also, 'Yemen: Why It's a Bigger Problem for Saudi Than the U.S.' *Christian Science Monitor*, 21 January 2010.

28. Neil Partrick, 'Riyadh's Yemen Policy Muddle,' *Middle East International*, 2(12), 2010, p. 29.

29. Christopher Boucek, 'War in Saada: From Local Insurrection to National Challenge.' Carnegie Middle East Paper No. 110, 2010, pp. 12–13.

30. 'In an Unexpected Development, Al-Qaeda's Leader on the Arabian Peninsula Announces His Group's Support for the Southern Movement,' Mareb Press online, www.marebpress.net, 13 May 2009.

31. Angel Rabasa, 'New World Disorder: Different Types of Ungoverned Territories Warrant Different Responses,' RAND Review, Fall 2007.

32. Hill, 'Fear of Failure,' p. 2.

33. 'Yemen Points to Iranian Backing For Rebels,' *Khaleej Times*, 19 August 2009.

34. 'US Offers Yemen Help in 'Fight Against Terrorism,' Agence France-Presse, 8 September 2009.

35. 'Top U.S. Military Commander Meets with Yemeni President,' CNN, 3 January 2010; 'Petraeus: More Security Funds Heading to Yemen, But Not Troops,' CNN, 10 January 2010, www.cnn.com

36. Sheila Carapico, 'Special Operations in Yemen,' *Foreign Policy*, 13 May 2010.

37. Hill, 'What is Happening in Yemen?,' p. 106.

38. 'Yemen: Why It's a Bigger Problem for Saudi Than the U.S.' *Christian Science Monitor*, 21 January 2010.

39. Partrick, 'Riyadh's Yemen Policy Muddle,' p. 29.

40. Ibid.

41. Saeed Shehabi, 'The Role of Religious Ideology in the Expansionist Policies of Saudi Arabia, in Al-Rasheed, Kingdom Without Borders, p. 191.

42. Boucek, War in Saada, p. 2.

43. 'Yemen Rebel Leader Denies Seeking Shia State in North,' *The Peninsula*, 30 September 2009.

44. Yemen Forum Roundtable Meeting, London, Chatham House, 18 February 2010.

45. Personal interview, London, May 2010.

46. 'U.S. Has Few Resources to Face Threats in Yemen,' *New York Times*, 8 January 2010.

47. Rabasa, 'New World Disorder.'

48. John Peterson, 'The Nature of Succession in the Gulf,' *Middle East Journal*, 55(4), 2001, p. 580.

49. 'Leaders Meet to Plan Yemen Aid Allocation,' *The National*, 28 February 2010.

50. 'Social Cohesion Consultation Report,' West Asia North Africa Forum, October 2009, p. 5.

51. 'Yemen Needs Aid and Tough Love From Its Friends,' *The National*, 1 March 2010.

52. Hill, 'What is Happening in Yemen?,' p. 106.

53. Prince Hassan bin Talal, 'Policy Options for Modernising the Middle East's Industrial Base,' Europe's World, 2009.

8. CONCLUSION: A NEW APPROACH TO SECURITY

1. 'Human Development Report 1994: New Dimensions of Human Security,' (New York: UNDP, 1994), pp. 3–4.
2. Kaldor, *Human Security*, p. 182.
3. Mary Kaldor, Mary Martin and Sabine Selchow, 'Human Security: A New Strategic Narrative for Europe,' *International Affairs*, 83(2), 2007, p. 281.
4. Janne Haaland Matlary, 'Much Ado About Little? Human Security and the EU,' *International Affairs*, 84(1), 2008, p. 142.
5. 'Sheikha Fatima's Efforts in Women's Cause Hailed,' *Gulf Times*, 13 November 2008.
6. 'First Ladies Call For Dialogue With UN Panel on Human Security,' *Khaleej Times*, 12 November 2008.
7. Arab Human Development Report 2002: Creating Opportunities for Future Generations; Arab Human Development Report 2003: Building a Knowledge Society; Arab Human Development Report 2004: Towards Freedom in the Arab World, and Arab Human Development Report 2005: Towards the Rise of Women in the Arab World.
8. 'Arab Human Development Report 2009: Challenges to Human Security in the Arab Countries.' UNDP: New York, 2009, pp. 17–18.
9. www.wanaforum.org
10. Jim Krane, *Dubai: The Story of the World's Largest City* (London: Atlantic Books, 2009), p. 211.
11. Shamlan Yousef al-Issa, 'Dealing with Human Rights Abuse in Kuwait,' *Al-Watan Daily*, 23 June 2009.
12. I am grateful to Professor Emma Murphy of Durham University for this observation.
13. For an example of Sheikha Mozah's activism, see 'Protect Education from Crises: Sheikha Mozah,' *The Peninsula*, 2 November 2008.
14. Jeremy Jones and Nicholas Ridout, 'Democratic Development in Oman,' *Middle East Journal*, 59(3), 2005, p. 390.
15. 'Pioneer Bahraini Women,' Bahrain Brief, Gulf Centre for Strategic Studies, July 2006, p. 1
16. Personal interviews, Kuwait, March 2010.
17. 'UAE Calls For Women's Participation in the Protection of Peace and Security,' Emirates News Agency, 1 November 2008.
18. Coates Ulrichsen, 'Gulf Security,' p. 33.
19. Personal interview, Kuwait, March 2010.
20. Peter Jones, 'Maritime Confidence-building in the Gulf,' Security and Terrorism Research Bulletin, Gulf Research Centre, Dubai, May 2008, p. 21.

POSTSCRIPT

1. 'Bahrain Returns to the Bad Old Days,' *The Guardian*, 13 Sep. 2010.
2. Christopher Davidson & Kristian Coates Ulrichsen, 'Bahrain on the Edge,' Open Democracy, 19 Oct. 2010.
3. 'Kuwait Cuts Working Hours to Save Power,' *The National*, 20 Jun. 2010.
4. 'Amnesty Urges Kuwait to Free Writer Jassem,' *Kuwait Times*, 28 Nov. 2010.
5. 'Kuwait Frees Professor Who Attended Political Rally,' *The National*, 11 Feb. 2011.
6. Christopher Davidson, 'Violence and Opposition in Kuwait,' Current Intelligence, 20 Dec.2010; 'Kuwaiti Interior Minister Resigns Over Custody Death,' BBC News, 7 Feb. 2011.
7. 'Politics, Succession and Risk in Saudi Arabia,' Gulf States Newsletter Special Report, January 2010, pp. 17–18.
8. 'Bahrain Police Disperse Demonstrators Ahead of Major Rally,' Associated Press, 15 Feb. 2011.
9. 'Bloodshed in Bahrain: A Gulf State That Is An Odd Man Out,' *The Economist*, 17 Feb. 2011.
10. In both instances, the handouts were dressed up as acts of royal benevolence, in Kuwait's case in commemoration of the fiftieth anniversary of independence and the twentieth anniversary of liberation, and in the case of Bahrain the tenth anniversary of the National Action Charter.
11. 'FNC Election Rules Revised: UAE,' *Khaleej Times*, 16 Feb. 2011.
12. Christopher Davidson, 'Lords of the Realm,' *Foreign Policy*, 21 Feb. 2011.
13. 'Saudi Prince Calls for Reform Amid Regional Unrest,' *The Telegraph*, 17 Feb. 2011.
14. Kristian Coates Ulrichsen, David Held & Alia Brahimi, 'The Arab 1989?' Open Democracy, 11 Feb. 2011.
15. Kristin Smith Diwan, 'Reform or Flood in the Gulf,' *Foreign Policy*, 20 Feb. 2011.

SELECT BIBLIOGRAPHY

Aarts, Paul and Gerd Nonneman (eds), *Saudi Arabia in the Balance: Political Economy, Society, Foreign Affairs* (London: Hurst and Co., 2005).

Adib-Moghaddam, Arshin, *The International Politics of the Persian Gulf* (New York: Routledge, 2006).

Agha, Qamar, 'Indo-Gulf Ties: Post-Cold War Era,' in I.P. Khosla (ed.), *India and the Gulf* (New Delhi: Association of Indian Diplomats, 2009).

Al-Ekry, Abd al-Nabi, 'Al-Wefaq and the Challenges of Participation,' *Arab Reform Bulletin*, May 2007.

Al-Rasheed, Madawi (ed.), *Kingdom Without Borders: Saudi Arabia's Political, Religious and Media Frontiers* (London: Hurst and Co., 2008).

Al-Sayegh, Fatma, 'Merchants' Role in a Changing Society: The Case of Dubai, 1900–90,' *Middle Eastern Studies*, 34(1), 1998.

Al-Shayeji, Abdullah, 'Dangerous Perceptions: Gulf Views of the U.S. Role in the Region,' *Middle East Policy*, 5(1997).

Ansari, Ali, *Modern Iran: the Pahlavis and After* (Harlow: Pearson Longman, 2007).

Anscombe, Frederick, *The Ottoman Gulf: The Creation of Kuwait, Saudi Arabia and Qatar* (New York: Columbia University Press, 1997).

Anthony, John Duke, Jean-Francois Seznec, Taynar Ari and Wayne White, 'War with Iran: Regional Reactions and Requirements,' *Middle East Policy*, 15(3), 2008.

Arab Human Development Report 2009: Challenges to Human Security in the Arab Countries. New York: UNDP, 2009.

Assaad, Ragut, Ghada Barsoum, Emily Cupito and Daniel Egel, 'Youth Exclusion in Yemen: Tackling the Twin Deficits of Human Development and Natural Resources.' Wolfensohn Center for Development: Dubai School of Government, Working Paper 9, November 2009.

Baaboud, Abdulla and Geoffrey Edwards, 'Reinforcing Ambivalence: The Interaction of Gulf States and the European Union,' *European Foreign Affairs Review*, 12, 2007.

Blanchard, Christopher and Alfred Prados, 'Saudi Arabia: Terrorist-Financing Issues'. Congressional Research Service Report for Congress, Washington D.C, 2007.

Boucek, Christopher, 'Saudi Arabia's "Soft" Counterterrorism Strategy: Prevention, Rehabilitation, and Aftercare.' Carnegie Paper 97. Carnegie Endowment for International Peace: Washington, D.C., September 2008.

———, 'Yemen: Avoiding a Downward Spiral,' Carnegie Middle East Program Paper 102, September 2009.

———, 'War in Saada: From Local Insurrection to National Challenge.' Carnegie Middle East Paper No. 110, 2010.

Brown, Oli and Alec Crawford, 'Rising Temperatures, Rising Tensions: Climate Change and the Risk of Violent Conflict in the Middle East.' International Institute for Sustainable Development, 2009.

Burke, Edward, 'Bahrain: Reaching a Threshold.' Madrid: FRIDE Working Paper No. 22, June 2008.

Buzan, Barry, 'Will the "global war on terrorism" be the new Cold War?,' International Affairs, 82(6), 2006.

Buzan, Barry and Ole Wæver, Regions and Powers: The Structure of International Security (Cambridge: Cambridge University Press, 2003).

Buzan, Barry, Ole Wæver and Jaap de Wilde, Security: A New Framework for Analysis (Boulder, CO: Lynne Rienner, 1998).

Carpenter, Ted Galen and Malou Innocent, 'The Iraq War and Iranian Power,' Survival, 49(4), 2007.

Chubin, Shahram, 'Iran's Power in Context,' Survival, 51(1), 2009.

Clarke, Michael, 'Rethinking Security and Power,' in David Held and David Mepham (eds), Progressive Foreign Policy: New Directions for the UK (Cambridge: Polity Press, 2007).

Coates Ulrichsen, Kristian, Gulf Security: Challenges and Responses. London: Royal College of Defence Studies, 2008.

——— 'Gulf Security: Changing Internal and External Dynamics.' LSE Kuwait Programme Working Paper No. 2, May 2009.

——— 'Internal and External Security in the Arab Gulf States,' Middle East Policy, 16(2), 2009.

Cordesman, Anthony, 'Security Cooperation in the Middle East.' Washington, D:C., Center for Strategic and International Studies, 2007.

———, 'Security Challenges and Threats in the Gulf: A Net Assessment.' Washington, D.C.: Center for Strategic and International Studies, March 2008.

———, 'Gulf Threats, Risks and Vulnerabilities.' Washington, D.C.: Center for Strategic and International Studies, August 2009.

Cordesman, Anthony, and Khalid Al-Rodhan, 'The Gulf Military Forces in an Era of Asymmetric War: Bahrain,' Washington DC: Center for Strategic and International Studies, June 2006.

———, 'The Gulf Military Forces in an Era of Asymmetric War: Kuwait,' Washington DC: Center for Strategic and International Studies, June 2006.

———, 'The Gulf Military Forces in an Era of Asymmetric War: Qatar,' Washington DC: Center for Strategic and International Studies, June 2006.

———, 'The Gulf Military Forces in an Era of Asymmetric War: Oman,' Washington DC: Center for Strategic and International Studies, June 2006.

Craze, Joshua and Mark Huband (eds), *The Kingdom: Saudi Arabia and the Challenge of the 21st Century* (London: Hurst and Co., 2009).

Crystal, Jill, *Oil and Politics in the Gulf: Rulers and Merchants in Kuwait and Qatar* (Cambridge: Cambridge University Press, 1990).

Dargin, Justin, 'Qatar's Natural Gas: the Foreign Policy Driver,' *Middle East Policy*, 14(3), 2007.

———, 'The Ties That Bind: The Dolphin Project and Intra-GCC Relations.' The Dubai Initiative Policy Brief, Belfer Center for Science and *International Affairs*: Harvard University, 2009.

Davidson, Christopher, *The United Arab Emirates: A Study in Survival* (London: Lynne Rienner, 2006).

———, *Dubai: The Vulnerability of Success* (London: Hurst and Co., 2008).

———, 'Dubai: The Security Dimensions of the Region's Premier Free Port,' *Middle East Policy*, 15(2), 2008.

———, *Abu Dhabi: Oil and Beyond* (London: Hurst and Co. 2009).

———, 'Persian Gulf-Pacific Asia Linkages in the 21st Century: A Marriage of Convenience?' LSE Kuwait Research Paper No. 7, January 2010.

Davis, Lynn E., 'Globalization's Security Implications'. Santa Monica, CA: RAND Issue Paper 2003.

Day, Stephen, 'Updating Yemeni National Unity: Could Lingering Regional Divisions Bring Down the Regime?' *Middle East Journal*, 62(3), 2008.

———, 'The Political Challenge of Yemen's Southern Movement.' Carnegie Endowment for International Peace: Middle East Program paper 108, March 2010.

Depledge, Joanna, 'Striving for No: Saudi Arabia in the Climate Change Regime.' *Global Environmental Politics*, 8(4), 2008.

Dillon, Michael, 'Global Security in the 21st Century: Circulation, Complexity and Contingency,' in Christopher Browning and Paul Cornish (eds), *The Globalization of Security*. ISP/NSC Briefing Paper 05/02, Chatham House, October 2005.

Dodge, Toby, 'The Causes of US Failure in Iraq,' *Survival*, 49(1), 2007.

Donn, Gari and Yahya Al-Manthri, *Globalisation and Higher Education in the Arab Gulf States* (Oxford: Symposium Books, 2010).

Drysdale, Alasdair, 'Population Dynamics and Birth Spacing in Oman,' *International Journal of Middle East Studies*, 42(1), 2010.

Echague, Ana and Edward Burke, 'Strong Foundations? The Imperatives for Reform in Saudi Arabia.' Madrid: FRIDE Working Paper 84, 2009.

Eckersley, Robyn, 'Environmental Security, Climate Change, and Globalizing Terrorism,' in Damien Grenfell and Paul James (eds), *Rethinking Insecurity, War and Violence* (London: Routledge, 2009).

Ehteshami, Anoushiravan, 'Reform from Above: The Politics of Participation in the Oil Monarchies' *International Affairs*, 79(1) 2003.

——, *Globalization and Geopolitics in the Middle East: Old Games, New Rules* (London: Routledge, 2007).

——, and Steven Wright, *Reform in the Middle East Oil Monarchies* (Reading: Ithaca Press, 2008).

——, 'Political Change in the Arab Oil Monarchies: From Liberalization to Enfranchisement,' *International Affairs*, 83(5), 2007.

Fakir, Intissar, 'Yemen: Economic and Regional Challenges,' *Arab Reform Bulletin*, July 2008.

Fakhro, Munira, 'The Uprising in Bahrain: An Assessment' in Gary Sick and Lawrence Potter (eds) *The Persian Gulf at the Millennium: Essays in Politics, Economy, Security and Religion* (London: Macmillan, 1997).

Fox, John, Nada Mourtada-Sabbah and Mohammed al-Mutawa (eds), *Globalization and the Gulf* (London: Routledge, 2006).

Furtig, Henner, 'Conflict and Cooperation in the Persian Gulf: The Interregional Order and US Policy,' *Middle East Journal*, 61(4), 2007.

Gause, F. Gregory, *Oil Monarchies: Domestic and Security Challenges in the Arab Gulf States* (New York: Council on Foreign Relations Press, 1994.

——, *The International Relations of the Persian Gulf* (Cambridge: Cambridge University Press, 2010).

Gonzalez, Gabriella, Lynn Karoly, Louay Constant, Hanine Salem and Charles Goodman, 'Facing Human Capital Challenges of the 21st Century: Education and Labour Market Initiatives in Lebanon, Oman, Qatar, and the United Arab Emirates.' RAND-Qatar Policy Institute, 2008.

Greenberg, Maurice, William Wechsler and Lee Wolowsky, 'Terrorist Financing. Report of an Independent Task Force Sponsored by the Council on Foreign Relations.' New York, 2002.

Gupta, Ranjit, 'China as a Factor in India's Relations with the GCC Countries,' in I.P. Khosla (ed.), *India and the Gulf* (New Delhi: Association of Indian Diplomats, 2009).

Guzzini, Stefano and Dietrich Jung (eds), *Contemporary Security Analysis and Copenhagen Peace Research* (London: Routledge, 2004).

Hales, Gavin, 'Fault Lines: Tracking Armed Violence in Yemen.' Yemen Armed Violence Assessment Issue Brief No. 1, 2010.

Halliday, Fred, *Arabia without Sultans* (London: Saqi Books, 2nd ed. 2002).

——, *The Middle East in International Relations: Power, Politics and Ideology* (Cambridge: Cambridge University Press, 2005).

Hegghammer, Thomas, 'Islamist Violence and Regime Stability in Saudi Arabia,' *International Affairs*, 84(4), 2008.

——, 'Saudi Militants in Iraq: Backgrounds and Recruitment Patterns,' Norwegian Defence Research Establishment (FFI), February 2007.

Hertog, Steffen, 'Gulf Countries: The Current Crisis and Lessons of the 1980s,' *Arab Reform Bulletin*, July 2009.

Hertog, Steffen and Giacomo Luciani, 'Energy and Sustainability Policies in the GCC.' LSE Kuwait Research Programme Working Paper No. 6, November 2009.

Hertog, Steffen, *Princes, Brokers, and Bureaucrats: Oil and the State in Saudi Arabia* (Ithaca: Cornell University Press, 2010).

Hill, Ginny, 'Yemen: Fear of Failure.' Chatham House Briefing Paper, January 2010.

———, 'What is Happening in Yemen?' *Survival*, 52(2), 2010.

Holtom, Paul, Mark Bromley, Pieter Wezeman and Siemon Wezeman, 'Trends in International Arms Transfers, 2009,' Stockholm: SIPRI Fact Sheet, March 2010.

Homer-Dixon, Thomas, 'Environmental Scarcities and Violent Conflict: Evidence from Cases,' in Michael Brown, Owen Cote, Sean Lynn-Jones and Steven Miller (eds), *New Global Dangers: Changing Dimensions of International Security* (Cambridge, Mass: MIT Press, 2004).

Hudson, Michael (ed.), *Middle East Dilemma: The Politics and Economics of Arab Integration* (New York: Columbia University Press, 1999).

'Human Development Report 1994: New Dimensions of Human Security,' (New York: UNDP, 1994).

Hvidt, Martin, 'The Dubai Model: An Outline of Key Development-Process Elements in Dubai,' *International Journal of Middle East Studies*, 41(3), 2009.

Jackson, Ian, 'Nuclear Energy and Proliferation Risks: Myths and Realities in the Persian Gulf,' *International Affairs*, 85(6), 2009.

Johnsen, Gregory, 'Yemen: Empty Economic Reforms Slow Bid to Join the GCC,' *Arab Reform Bulletin*, February 2007.

Jones, Jeremy and Nicholas Ridout, 'Democratic Development in Oman,' *Middle East Journal*, 59(3), 2005.

Jones, Peter, 'Maritime Confidence-building in the Gulf,' Security and Terrorism Research Bulletin, Gulf Research Centre, Dubai, May 2008.

Jones, Toby Craig, 'The Iraq Effect in Saudi Arabia,' *Middle East Report* 237, 35(4), 2005

———, 'Rebellion on the Saudi Periphery: Modernity, Marginalization and the Shi'a Uprising of 1979,' *International Journal of Middle East Studies*, 38(2), 2006.

Kaldor, Mary, *New and Old Wars: Organized Violence in a Global Era* (2nd ed., Cambridge: Polity Press, 2006).

———, Terry Lynn Karl and Yahya Said, *Oil Wars* (London: Pluto Press, 2007).

———, *Human Security: Reflections on Globalization and Intervention* (Cambridge: Polity Press, 2007).

Karl, Terry Lynn, *The Paradox of Plenty: Oil Booms and Petro-States* (Berkeley: University of California Press, 1997).

Katzman, Kenneth, 'Iran's Activities and Influence in Iraq.' Congressional Research Service Report for Congress, Washington, D.C, 2008.

Kaye, Dalia Dassa and Frederic M. Wehrey, 'A Nuclear Iran: The Reaction of Neighbours,' *Survival*, 49(2), 2007.

Kechichian, Joseph, 'Can Arab Monarchies Endure a Fourth War in the Persian Gulf?' *Middle East Journal*, 61(2), 2007.

———, *Power and Succession in Arab Monarchies: A Reference Guide* (Boulder, CO: Lynne Rienner, 2008).

Kennedy, Andrew, 'China's New Energy-Security Debate,' *Survival*, 52(3), 2010.

Khosla, I.P. (ed.), *India and the Gulf* (Association of Indian Diplomats: New Delhi, 2009).

Kinninmont, Jane, 'Assessing al-Wefaq's Parliamentary Experiment,' *Arab Reform Bulletin*, October 2007.

Kirshner, Jonathan (ed.), *Globalization and National Security* (New York: Routledge, 2006).

Koch, Christian, 'Gulf States Plan for Day that Oil Runs Dry,' *Jane's Intelligence Review*, December 2006.

Kostiner, Joseph (ed.), *Middle East Monarchies: The Challenge of Modernity* (London: Lynne Rienner, 2000).

Krane, Jim, *Dubai: The Story of the World's Largest City* (London: Atlantic Books, 2009.

———, 'Energy Conservation Options for GCC Governments,' Dubai School of Government Policy Brief No. 18, February 2010.

Kraska, James and Brian Wilson, 'The Co-Operative Strategy and the Pirates of the Gulf of Aden,' *RUSI Journal*, 154(2), 2009.

Krause, Keith, 'Insecurity and State Formation in the Global Military Order: The Middle Eastern Case,' *European Journal of International Relations*, 2(3), 1996.

———, 'Theorizing Security, State Formation and the 'Third World' in the Post-Cold War World,' *Review of International Studies*, 24(1), 1998.

Krieger, Zvika, 'Reforms in Higher Education Raise Questions,' *Arab Reform Bulletin*, December 2007.

Launay, Frederic, 'Environmental Situational Awareness for the GCC Countries.' Dubai: Gulf Research Centre, 2006.

Le Billon, Philippe, (ed.), *Geopolitics of Resource Wars: Resource Dependence, Governance and Violence* (London: Routledge, 2005).

Louer, Laurence, *Transnational Shia Politics: Religious and Political Networks in the Gulf* (London: Hurst and Co., 2008).

Louis, Wm Roger, 'The British Withdrawal from the Gulf, 1967–71,' *Journal of Imperial and Commonwealth History*, 31(1), 2003.

Love, Roy, 'Economic Drivers of Conflict and Cooperation in the Horn of Africa: A Regional Perspective and Overview.' London: Chatham House Africa Programme Briefing Paper, December 2009.

Lowe, Rob and Claire Spencer, 'Iran, its Neighbours and the Regional Crises.' London: Chatham House Report, 2006.

Luomi, Mari, 'Abu Dhabi's Alternative-Energy Initiatives: Seizing Climate-Change Opportunities,' *Middle East Policy*, 16(4), 2009.

———, 'Bargaining in the Saudi Bazaar: Common Ground For a Post-2012 Climate Agreement?' Finnish Institute of *International Affairs* Briefing Paper No. 48, December 2009.

———, 'Oil or Climate Politics?: Avoiding a Destabilizing Resource Split in the Arab Middle East.' Finnish Institute of *International Affairs*, Briefing Paper No. 58, 2010.

Mabey, Nick, 'Delivering Climate Security: International Security Responses to a Climate Changed World.' London: Royal United Services Institute Whitehall Paper Series 69, 2008.

Maloney, David and Rohan Mukherjee, 'India and China: Conflict and Cooperation,' *Survival*, 52(1), 2010.

Mazo, Jeffrey, *Climate Conflict: How Global Warming Threatens Security and What to Do About It.* (London: International Institute for Strategic Studies/Routledge, 2010).

McKnight, Sean, Neil Partrick & Francis Toase (eds), *Gulf Security: Opportunities and Challenges for the New Generation* (RUSI Whitehall Paper Series 51, 2000).

Meyer, Katherine, Helen Rizzo and Yousef Ali, 'Changed Political Attitudes: The Case of Kuwait,' *International Sociology*, 22(3), 2007.

Nonneman, Gerd, (ed.), *Analyzing Middle Eastern Foreign Policies* (London: Routledge, 2005).

———, 'EU-GCC Relations: Dynamics, Patterns and Perspectives.' Dubai: Gulf Research Centre, 2006.

Oguzlu, Tarik, 'The Changing Dynamics of Turkey-Israel Relations: A Structural Realist Account,' *Mediterranean Politics*, 15(2), 2010.

Okruhlik, Gwenn, 'Rentier Wealth, Unruly Law, and the Rise of Opposition: the Political Economy of Oil States,' *Comparative Politics*, 31(3), 1999.

Onley, James, and Suleyman Khalaf, 'Shaikly Authority in the Pre-oil Gulf: An Historical-Anthropological Study,' *History and Anthropology*, 17(3), 2006.

———, *The Arabian Frontier of the British Raj: Merchants, Rulers and the British in the Nineteenth-Century Gulf* (Oxford: Oxford University Press, 2007).

Ottaway, Marina, *Evaluating Middle East Reform. How Do We Know When It Is Significant.* Carnegie Paper 56. Washington DC: Carnegie Endowment for International Peace.

Partrick, Neil, *Dire Straits for U.S. Mid-East Policy: The Gulf Arab States and US-Iran Relations.* London: Royal United Services Institute, January 2008.

———, 'Riyadh's Yemen Policy Muddle,' *Middle East International*, 2(12), 2010.

Petersen, Tore and Richard Nixon, *Great Britain and the Anglo-American Alignment in the Persian Gulf and Arabian Peninsula: Making Allies Out of Clients* (Brighton: Sussex Academic Press, 2009).

Peterson, J.E., 'The Nature of Succession in the Gulf,' *Middle East Journal*, 55(4), 2001.

———, 'Bahrain: The 1994–1999 Uprising.' Arabian Peninsula Background Note, No. APBN-002. Published on www.JEPeterson.net, January 2004.

———, 'The Emergence of Post-Traditional Oman,' Sir William Luce Fellowship Paper No. 5. University of Durham, 2004.

———, 'Qatar and the World: Branding for a Micro-State,' *Middle East Journal*, 60(4), 2006.

Phillips, Sarah,'Evaluating Political Reform in Yemen,' Carnegie Papers: Democracy and Rule of Law Program, No. 80, February 2007.

Pollock, David, 'Kuwait: Keystone of US Gulf Policy.' The Washington Institute for Near East Policy: Washington D.C., 2007.

Potter, Lawrence (ed.), *The Persian Gulf in History* (New York: Palgrave Macmillan, 2009).

Rabasa, Angel, 'New World Disorder: Different Types of Ungoverned Territories Warrant Different Responses,' RAND Review, Fall 2007.

Raouf, Mohamed, 'Climate Change Threats, Opportunities, and the GCC Countries.' Middle East Institute Policy Brief No. 12, 2008.

'Water Issues in the Gulf: Time for Action.' Middle East Institute Policy Brief No. 22, January 2009.

Rathmell, Andrew, Theodore Karasik and David Gompert, 'A New Persian Gulf Security System,' RAND Issue Paper (2003).

Richer, Renee, 'Conservation in Qatar: Impacts of Increasing Industrialization.' Center of International and Regional Studies: Georgetown School of Foreign Service in Qatar. Occasional Paper No. 2, 2006.

Riedel, Bruce and Bilal Saab, 'Al Qaeda's Third Front: Saudi Arabia,' *The Washington Quarterly*, 31(2), 2008.

Roberts, Adam and Dominik Zaum, *Selective Security: War and the United Nations Security Council Since 1945*. Adelphi Paper No. 395. London: International Institute for Strategic Studies, June 2008.

Romani, Vincent, 'The Politics of Higher Education in the Middle East: Problems and Prospects.' Brandeis University Crown Center for Middle East Studies: Middle East Brief No. 36, May 2009.

Russell, Richard, 'The Persian Gulf's Collective-Security Mirage,' *Middle East Policy*, 12(4), 2005.

Sager, Abdulaziz, 'The GCC States and the Situation in Iraq.' Dubai: Gulf Research Centre, 10 July 2008.

——— (ed.), *Gulf Yearbook 2008–2009* (Dubai: Gulf Research Centre, 2009).

Said Zahlan, Rosemary, *The Making of the Modern Gulf States* (Reading: Ithaca Press, 2nd ed. 1998).

Saif, Ibrahim, 'The Oil Boom in the GCC Countries, 2002–2008: Old Challenges, Changing Dynamics.' Carnegie Middle East Paper No. 15, March 2009.

Schwarz, Benjamin, 'America's Struggle Against the Wahhabi/Neo-Salafi Movement,' Orbis, 51(1), 2007.

Sharp, Jeremy, 'Yemen: Where is the Stability Tipping Point?' *Arab Reform Bulletin*, 6(6), July 2008.

Simpfendorfer, Ben, *The New Silk Road: How a Rising Arab World is Turning Away From the West and Rediscovering China* (Basingstoke: Palgrave Macmillan, 2009).

Slot, Benjamin, *Mubarak Al-Sabah: Founder of Modern Kuwait 1896–1915* (London: Arabian Publishing, 2005).

Smith, Michael, 'Russia and the Persian Gulf: The Deepening of Moscow's *Middle East Policy*.' Conflict of Studies and Research Centre Paper 07/25. UK Defence Academy, 2007.

Smith, Paul, 'Climate Change, Mass Migration and the Military Response,' Orbis, 51(4), 2007.

Smith, Simon, *Kuwait, 1950–1965: Britain, the al-Sabah, and Oil* (Oxford: Oxford University Press, 1999).

Spiess, Andy, 'Developing Adaptive Capacity for Responding to Environmental Change in the Arab Gulf States: Uncertainties to Linking Ecosystem Conservation, Sustainable Development and Society in Authoritarian Rentier Economies,' *Global and Planetary Change*, 64, 2008.

Taylor, Brendan, 'Sanctions as Grand Strategy.' Adelphi Paper No. 411. London: International Institute of Strategic Studies, 2010.

Teitelbaum, Joshua (ed.), *Political Liberalization in the Persian Gulf* (London: Hurst and Co., 2009).

Thompson, Eric V., 'The Iraqi Military Re-Enters the Gulf Security Dynamic,' *Middle East Policy*, 16(3), 2009.

Tripp, Charles, *A History of Iraq* (Cambridge: Cambridge University Press, 2000).

Valbjorn, Morten and Andre Bank, 'Signs of a New Arab Cold War: The 2006 Lebanon War and the Sunni-Shi'i Divide,' *Middle East Report* 242, 37(1), 2007.

Valeri, Marc, *Oman: Politics and Society in the Qaboos State* (London: Hurst and Co., 2009).

Visser, Reidar, *Basra: The Failed Gulf State: Separatism and Nationalism in Southern Iraq* (Munster: Lit Verlag, 2005).

Wehrey, Fred, 'Bahrain: Elections and Managing Sectarianism,' *Arab Reform Bulletin*, 4(10), December 2006.

Weiss Fagan, Patricia, 'Iraqi Refugees: Seeking Stability in Syria and Jordan.' Center for International and Regional Studies, Georgetown University School of Foreign Service in Qatar, Occasional Paper 1, 2009.

Woertz, Eckart, Samir Pradhan, Nermina Biberovic and Christian Koch, 'Food Inflation in the GCC Countries.' Dubai: Gulf Research Centre Report, May 2008.

Woertz, Eckart, Samir Pradhan, Nermina Biberovic and Chan Jingzhong, 'Potential for GCC Agro-Investments in Africa and Asia.' Dubai: Gulf Research Centre Report, September 2008.

Wright, Steven, 'Fixing the Kingdom: Political Evolution and Socio-Economic Challenges in Bahrain,' Center of International and Regional Studies: Georgetown School of Foreign Service in Qatar, Occasional Paper No. 3, 2008.

Yetiv, Steve and Chunglong Lu, 'China, Global Energy and the Middle East,' *Middle East Journal*, 61(2), 2007.

Zoubir, Yahia and Louisa Dris-Ait-Hamadouche, 'US-Saudi Relationship and the Iraq War: The Dialects of a Dependent Alliance,' *Journal of Third World Studies*, 24(1), 2007.

INDEX